Unlike political or economic institutions, social movements have an elusive power, but one that is no less real. From the French and American Revolutions through the democratic and workers' movements of the nineteenth century, to the social and political movements of today, movements exercise a fleeting but powerful influence on politics and society. This study surveys the history of the social movement, puts forward a theory of collective action to explain its surges and declines, and offers an interpretation of the power of movement that focuses on its effects on personal lives, policy reforms, and political culture. While emphasizing the cultural, organizational and personal sources of the power in movement, the book interprets the rise and fall of social movements as part of political struggle and as the outcome of changes in political opportunity structure.

Power in movement

This series publishes comparative research that seeks to explain important, cross-national domestic political phenomena. Based on a broad conception of comparative politics, it hopes to promote critical dialogue among different approaches. While encouraging contributions from diverse theoretical perspectives, the series will particularly emphasize work on domestic institutions and work that examines the relative roles of historical structures and constraints, of individual or organizational choice, and of strategic interaction in explaining political actions and outcomes. This focus includes an interest in the mechanisms through which historical factors impinge on contemporary political choices and outcomes.

Works on all parts of the world are welcomed, and priority will be given to studies that cross traditional area boundaries and that treat the United States in comparative perspective. Many of the books in the series are expected to be comparative, drawing on material from more than one national case; but studies devoted to single countries will also be considered, especially those that pose their problem and analysis in such a way that they make a direct contribution to comparative analysis and theory.

OTHER BOOKS IN THE SERIES

Allan Kornberg and Harold D. Clarke, *Citizens and Community: Political Support in a Representative Democracy*

David D. Laitin, *Language Repertories and State Construction in Africa*

Ellen Immergut, *Health Politics: Interests and Institutions in Western Europe*

Sven Steinmo, Kathleen Thelan, and Frank Longstreth, eds., *Structuring Politics: Historical Institutionalism in Comparative Analysis*

Thomas Janoski and Alexander M. Hicks, eds., *The Comparative Political Economy of the Welfare State*

Paul Pierson, *Dismantling the Welfare State: Reagan, Thatcher and the Politics of Welfare Retrenchment*

Herbert Kitschelt, *The Transformation of European Social Democracy*

Power in movement
Social movements, collective action and politics

SIDNEY TARROW

Cornell University

CAMBRIDGE
UNIVERSITY PRESS

Published by the Press Syndicate of the University of Cambridge
The Pitt Building, Trumpington Street, Cambridge CB2 1RP
40 West 20th Street, New York, NY 10011-4211, USA
10 Stamford Road, Oakleigh, Melbourne 3166, Australia

© Cambridge University Press 1994

First published 1994
Reprinted 1995 (twice)

Printed in the United States of America

Library of Congress Cataloging-in-Publication Data is available.

A catalogue record for this book is available from the British Library.

ISBN 0-521-41079-7 hardback
ISBN 0-521-42271-X paperback

For Chris

Contents

Tables and Figures

Preface and Acknowledgments

Like a social movement, a book is a collective action. Beneath the visible road markers of author and title, there lies a long and collective history of scholarship and collaboration. This book has had a particularly long and collective itinerary, and many debts, institutional and personal, lie just beneath its surface.

My curiosity about social movements began at the University of California at Berkeley. Berkeley in the 1960s was not only an incubator for social movement activity, it also provided a fertile and contentious environment for intellectual work. The study that resulted, *Peasant Communism in Southern Italy,* owed an intellectual debt to four of the teachers who I met there – David Apter, Reinhard Bendix, Ernst Haas and Joseph LaPalombara.

Anyone interested in the history of social movements sooner or later comes to France. The colleagues who welcomed me in 1969 at the Centre d'Etudes sur la Vie Politique Française became willing friends and unwitting accomplices in shaping the thinking that appears in this book. I am particularly grateful to the late Annick Percheron, to Guy Michelat and to René Mouriaux, who helped me organize a fruitful semester as a CNRS fellow in Paris in 1990, where some of the work in this book was done.

Many of the ideas that went into the book came out of my research on the movements of the late 1960s and early 1970s in Italy. The study that resulted, *Democracy and Disorder,* was the result of a productive year spent at the Center for Advanced Study in the Behavioral Sciences at Stanford in 1980–1, and of two subsequent research grants from the National Science Foundation. A grant from the German Marshall Fund of the United States in 1990 helped me examine the links between international politics and national movements.

Moving from systematic data analysis to interpretive narrative wasn't easy for this author, and I am grateful to the National Endowment for the Humanities for the fellowship that helped me do so. The NEH also sponsored three summer seminars for college teachers that I led between 1985 and 1992 on histories of collective action, providing a venue in which many of the ideas in the study developed. I wish to thank the thirty-five participants in those seminars for reading early versions of many of the chapters in this book.

Busy colleagues who take time to read other people's unformed work are owed a special debt. For detailed and thoughtful comments on drafts of all or most of the chapters in the book, I am grateful to Donatella della Porta, Bill Gamson, Eva Lotta Hedman, Mary and Peter Katzenstein, Bert Klandermans, Hanspeter Kriesi, Doug McAdam, David Meyer, Frances Piven, Dieter Rucht, Susan Tarrow and Richard Vallely. Individual chapters were read and commented upon by: Glenn Altschuler, Ron Aminzade, Ben Anderson, David Blatt, Stuart Blumin, Valerie Bunce, Ken Bush, Richard Cloward, Maria Cook, Seymour Drescher, Miriam Golden, Jeremy Hein, Lynn Hunt, David Kertzer, David Laitin, John Markoff, Diarmuid Maguire, Pauline Maier, Jerry Marwell, George Mosse, Victor Nee, Pam Oliver, Chris Rootes, Bill Sewell, Anne-Marie Szymanski, Sarah Tarrow, Marc Traugott, George Tsebelis and Xueguang Zhou. Reading Ben Anderson's work was the origin of the concept of "modularity." To these friends and colleagues I offer my thanks and apologies if I was not able to assimilate all the wisdom they offered.

A number of Cornell associates contributed their skills to the project and added substantially to what value it may have. Anita Lee, Tomoko Owazawa and Sung Woo ran down ornery references, checked the spelling and built the bibliographies for various chapters. Sarah Soule was able to shift from the role of student to that of collaborator, critic and editor with grace and sensitivity. Eva Lotta Hedman convinced me that the relevance of the work was not limited to a corner of Europe and North America. The patience and good humor of Lynette Harvey, Carolyn Lynn and Karel Sedlacek are also gratefully acknowledged.

I owe special thanks to three people for the role they played in this book's conception and completion: In three decades of scholarly work, Charles Tilly has fashioned an approach to collective action and social movements that shows that social research can both be theory driven and within history; Peter Lange went beyond his role as general editor of the Cambridge Comparative Politics Series to encourage, cajole, poke, prod and kibbitz the author with a unique combination of theoretical rigor and political acumen; Mary Katzenstein was a source of thoughtful and encouraging advice without intruding herself into the book's formation.

For more years than she may care to remember, Susan Tarrow has awakened to the sound of computer keys clacking in the next room, a racket that followed her from Ithaca to places as widespread as Elba, Florence, Oxford, Paris and Sydney. The computer is indifferent to her suffering, but I will be eternally grateful for her forbearance and her love.

Power in movement

Introduction

Power and movement: two words that seldom appear together in learned or popular discourse. Yet all through history, ordinary people have erupted into the streets and exerted considerable power – if only briefly. In the last thirty years, alone, the American Civil Rights movement, the peace, environmental and feminist movements, and revolts against authoritarianism all over the world have brought masses of people into the streets demanding change. They often succeeded; but even when they failed, their movements had profound effects, and set in motion important political and international changes.

Power in movement grows when ordinary people join forces in contentious confrontation with elites, authorities and opponents. Mounting, coordinating and sustaining this interaction is the peculiar contribution of the social movement. Movements are created when political opportunities open up for social actors who usually lack them. They draw people into collective action through known repertoires of contention and by creating innovations around their margins. At their base are the social networks and cultural symbols through which social relations are organized. The denser the former and the more familiar the latter, the more likely movements are to spread and be sustained.

Triggered by the incentives created by political opportunities, combining conventional and challenging forms of action and building on social networks and cultural frames is how movements overcome the obstacles to collective action and sustain their interactions with opponents and with the state. How they do so, and the dynamics and outcomes of the protest cycles they produce, are the main subjects of this book.

There are three major puzzles in the relations between power and movement. First, although ordinary people possess the resources for collective action during many periods of history, they mainly accept their fate or rise up timidly, only to be repressed. Under what conditions does the power in movement arise?

A second question relates to the dynamics of movement. Popular power arises quickly, reaches a peak and soon evaporates or gives way to repression and routine. Is there a common dynamic in the careers of social movements, linking their enthusiastic births to peaks of contention to their disillusioned ends?

The third question relates to movement outcomes. Do movements have an impact beyond the short-lived mobilizations that fill the evening news? The deterrents are considerable: Participants tire and defect; early protests that succeed create opportunities for others and for countermovements; elites control dissidence through reform or repression, while counterelites lead discontent off in new directions. If the impact of movements is so mediated and short lived, is the power in movement real?

THE APPROACH OF THE STUDY

These are the questions that I will address in this study. I will not attempt to present a history of the social movement. Nor will I press a particular theoretical perspective on the reader or attack others – a practice that has added more heat than light to this area of study. Instead, I will offer a broad framework for understanding the social movements, protest cycles and revolutions that began in the West and spread around the world over the past two centuries.

Too often scholars have focused on particular theories or aspects of movement to the detriment of others. An example is how the subject of revolution has been treated. As Charles Tilly observes in a recent book, "great" revolutions are usually studied as *sui generis* phenomena (1993b), which makes it impossible to say how they differ from less great ones or from rebellions, social turmoil, riots and routine contention. The systematic study of "violence," which began in the wake of the American riots of the 1960s, has been segmented from that of peaceful protest. Movement organizations have frequently been detached by scholars from the mass phenomena that are thought to produce them and from the institutional politics that surround them. Strikes and industrial conflict have produced their own academic specialty, with little attention paid to the intersections between labor insurgency and the political struggle.

The irreducible act that lies at the base of all social movements and revolutions is *contentious collective action*. Collective action takes many forms – brief or sustained, institutionalized or disruptive, humdrum or dramatic. Most of it occurs within institutions on the part of constituted groups who act in the name of goals that would hardly raise an eyebrow. It becomes contentious when it is used by people who lack regular access to institutions, act in the name of new or unaccepted claims and behave in ways that fundamentally challenge others. It produces social movements when social actors concert their actions around common claims in sustained sequences of interaction with opponents or authorities.

Contentious collective action is the basis of social movements; not because movements are always violent or extreme, but because it is the main, and often the only recourse that most people possess against better-equipped opponents.

Although the forms of collective action differ as much as the forms of repression and social control used to combat them, contentious collective action is the common denominator among the movements that we will examine in this book. Organizers know this and use it to exploit political opportunities, create collective identities, bring people together in organizations and mobilize them against more powerful opponents.

The theory of collective action is, therefore, where we must begin. But a word of caution: Collective action is not an abstract category that can stand outside of history and apart from politics for every kind of collective endeavor – from market relations, to interest associations, to protest movements, to peasant rebellions and revolutions.[1] The contentious forms of collective action that are associated with the social movement are historically and sociologically distinct. They have power because they challenge opponents, bring out solidarities and have meaning within particular population groups, situations and political cultures.

This means that, although we begin with the theory of collective action, we will not get very far before we must relate collective action to people's social networks, to their ideological discourses and to their political struggles. To the general formulations of collective action theory, we will need to add the concrete record of history and the insights of sociology and political science. In particular, bringing people together in coordinated collective action at strategic moments of history against powerful targets requires a *social* solution – what I will call the need to solve the social transaction costs of collective action. This involves mounting collective challenges, drawing on common purposes, building solidarity and sustaining collective action – the basic properties of social movements.

THE BASIC PROPERTIES OF MOVEMENTS

With the emergence of the national social movement in the eighteenth century, early theorists focused on the three facets of movement they feared the most: extremism, deprivation and violence. Nineteenth-century industrialism and the horrors of the interwar period gave new force to this persuasion. Many of the movements of the latter period – fascism, Nazism, Stalinism – fit the image of violence and extremism formed at the start of the French and Industrial Revolutions. With the exacerbation of ethnic and nationalist tensions since the fall of Communism, a revival of this approach is already visible.

But these characteristics are the polar expressions of more fundamental characteristics of movement. Extremism is an exaggerated form of the frames of meaning that are found in all social movements; deprivation is one particular source of the common purposes that all movements reflect; and violence is an exacerbation of collective challenges – seldom sustained without official sanction. Movements, I will argue, arc better defined as *collective challenges by people with common purposes and solidarity in sustained interaction with elites, opponents and authorities.*[2] This definition has four empirical properties: collective challenge, common purpose, solidarity and sustained interaction. Let us examine each of them briefly.

Collective challenge

There are many forms of collective action – from voting and interest group affiliation to bingo tournaments and football matches. But these are not the forms of action that are most characteristic of social movements. Movements mount challenges through disruptive direct action against elites, authorities, other groups or cultural codes. Most often public in nature, this disruption can also take the form of coordinated personal resistance or the collective affirmation of new values.

Collective challenges are most often marked by interrupting, obstructing, or rendering uncertain the activities of others. But particularly in repressive systems, it is sometimes signified by slogans, by forms of dress or music or by renaming familiar objects with new or different symbols. Even in liberal states, people may identify with movements by words, forms of address and private behavior that signify – and are reinforced by – their collective purpose. Such movements have been characterized as "discursive communities."[3]

Collective challenge is not the only kind of action we see in social movements. Movements – especially organized ones – engage in a variety of actions. These range from providing "selective incentives" to members, to building consensus among current or prospective supporters, to lobbying and negotiating with authorities and to challenging cultural codes through new religious or personal practices. But the most characteristic actions of social movements are collective challenges. This is not because movement leaders are psychologically prone to violence, but because, in seeking to appeal to new constituencies and assert their claims, they lack the stable resources – money, organization, access to the state – that interest groups and political parties control. Without such resources, and representing new or unrepresented constituencies, movements use collective challenge to become the focal point of supporters and gain the attention of opponents and third parties.

Common purpose

Many reasons have been proposed for why people affiliate with social movements, ranging from the juvenile desire to flaunt authority all the way to the vicious instincts of the mob. While it is true that some movements are marked by a spirit of play and carnival while others reveal the grim frenzy of the mob, there is a much more common – if more prosaic – reason why people band together in movements: to mount common claims against opponents, authorities or elites. This does not require us to assume that all such conflicts arise out of class interest, or that leadership has no autonomy; but only that common or overlapping interests and values are at the basis of their common actions.

Both the theory of "fun and games" and that of mob frenzy ignore the considerable risks and costs involved in acting collectively against well-armed authorities. The rebel slaves who challenged the Roman Empire risked certain death when they were defeated; the dissenters who launched the Reformation against the Catholic Church took similar risks. Nor could the black college students who sat-in at segregated lunch counters in the American South expect much fun at the hands of the thugs who awaited them with bats and verbal abuse. People do not risk their skins or sacrifice their time to social movement activities unless they think they have good reason to do so. Common purpose is that reason.

Solidarity

The most common denominator of social movements is thus interest; but interest is no more than an objective category imposed by the observer. It is participants' *recognition* of their common interests that translates the potential for movement into collective action. By mobilizing consensus, movement entrepreneurs play an important role in stimulating such consensus. But leaders can only create a social movement when they tap more deep-rooted feelings of solidarity or identity. This is almost certainly why nationalism and ethnicity – based on real or "imagined" ties – or religion – based on common devotion – have been more reliable bases of movement organization in the past than social class.[4]

Is a riot or a mob a social movement? Usually not, because their participants typically lack more than temporary solidarity. But sometimes even riots reveal a common purpose or solidarity. The ghetto riots all over America in the 1960s or in Los Angeles in 1992 were not movements in themselves, but the fact that they were triggered by police abuse indicates that they arose out of a widespread sense of injustice. Rioters' attacks on others – Catholics in eighteenth-century England, Jews in 1930s Germany, Asian-Americans in Los Angeles in 1992 – show that crowds acquire an identity through attacks on an "other." Mobs, riots and spontaneous assemblies are more an indication that a movement is in the process of formation than movements themselves.

Sustaining collective action

Long before there were organized movements, there were riots, rebellions and general turbulence. It is only by sustaining collective action against antagonists that a contentious episode becomes a social movement. Common purposes, collective identities and an identifiable challenge help movements to do this. But unless they can sustain this challenge against opponents, they will either evaporate into the kind of individualistic resentment that James Scott calls "resistance,"[5] harden into intellectual opposition or retreat into isolation. The social movements that have left the deepest mark on history have done so because they sustained collective action against better-equipped opponents.

Yet movements are seldom under the control of a single leader or organization; how then can they sustain collective challenges in the face of personal egotism, social disorganization and state repression? This is the dilemma that has animated collective action theorists and social movement scholars over the past few decades. It will be the first problem to be addressed in the theoretical chapter that follows. The basic argument is that changes in the political opportunity structure create incentives for collective actions. The magnitude and duration of these collective actions depend on mobilizing people through social networks and around identifiable symbols that are drawn from cultural frames of meaning.

AN OUTLINE OF THE BOOK

In the past twenty years, heavily influenced by economic thought, political scientists and sociologists have focused their analyses of social movements on what seems like a puzzle: that collective action occurs even though it is so difficult to bring about. Yet, that puzzle is a puzzle – and not a sociological law – because, in many situations and against many odds, collective action *does* occur; often on the part of people with few resources and little permanent power.

Examining the parameters of the collective action problem, and proposing how social movements "solve" it is the first task of Chapter 1. But the chapter approaches two other theoretical issues that are equally important: first, the dynamics of social movements once they have begun; and, second, the reasons why their outcomes are so varied. Although Chapter 1 outlines these theories in a general way, the evidence for them will be found in specific movements analyzed throughout the remainder of the book.

In Part I, I will show how and where the national social movement developed in the eighteenth-century West, when the resources for turning collective action into social movements could be brought together. The focus is first on what I will call, with Charles Tilly, the modern "repertoire" of collective action (1978); and then, on the changes in state and society that supported that transformation. It was when flexible, adaptable and indirect forms of collective action – what I will call the *modular* repertoire – were diffused through print, association and state building that national social movements developed. They brought together broad coalitions of supporters around general claims, using the political opportunities created by the expansion of the national state to do so. The state, I will argue, served not only as a *target* of collective claims, but increasingly as a *fulcrum* of claims against others.

Even deep-seated claims remain inert unless they are activated. In Chapter 5, I argue that the major activating factor consists of the changes in political opportunities that give rise to new waves of movements and shape their unfolding. Although particular actors interact regularly with opponents in stable cleavage structures, the rise and fall of social movements is too irregular to be explained by such stable cleavages. Political opportunities are both seized and expanded by social movements, turned into collective action and sustained by mobilizing structures and cultural frames.

These are not random processes. Repeated confrontations link particular social actors with antagonists through forms of collective action that become recurring routines: the strike between workers and their employers; the demonstration between protesters and opponents; the insurrection between insurgents and the state. The national social movement developed as a sustained collective challenge to elites, authorities or opponents by people with collective purposes and solidarity, or by those who claimed to represent them. The main forms of collective challenge that empower people in movement all over the world today will be analyzed in Chapter 6.

In Chapters 7 and 8, I will examine the two kinds of resources of social movements which make it possible for them to solve their coordination problem: the use of cultural and ideological frames to mobilize consensus and their structures of mobilization. In the literature on social movements, these – in the form of "ideology" versus "organization" – have often been seen as competing paradigms. Here they will be viewed as complementary solutions to the problem that movements need to solve; that is, how to mount, coordinate and sustain collective action among participants who lack more conventional resources and explicit programmatic goals.

In the final section of the book, I will turn from these analytical aspects of movements to their dynamics and outcomes. From the late eighteenth century on, once the resources for sustained collective action became available to ordinary people and to those who claimed to represent them, movements spread to entire societies, producing the periods of turbulence and re-alignment that I call "cycles of protest." As I show in Chapter 9, the importance of this change is that, once a cycle begins, the costs of collective action are lowered for other actors; new movements that arise in such contexts do not need to depend as much on internal resources as on the generalized opportunities of cycles of protest.

The theoretical importance of this change is that, in cycles, all kinds of movements develop and the causal connection between broad macro–social trends and movement emergence is much weaker than most scholars have supposed. In the presence of such general periods of turbulence, even the poor and disorganized can draw upon opportunities created by the "early risers" who trigger the cycle, and on the influential allies who step forward to take their lead. But because structures of opportunity change so rapidly, these successes are usually brief and their outcomes sometimes tragic. This is the argument of Chapter 10.

Such periods of movement have repercussions that sometimes result in immediate repression, sometimes in reform, often in both. But in political/institutional and in personal/cultural terms, the effects of protest cycles go well beyond a movement's visible actions, both in the changes that governments initiate, and in the periods of demobilization that follow. They leave behind permanent expansions in participation, popular culture and ideology, as I will argue in Chapter 10.

This takes us to the social movements of the current period and to those of the future. In the last few decades, a wave of democratization has spread across the globe, culminating in the dramatic changes in Central and Eastern Europe in 1989. In the 1990s, a new wave of ugly movements, rooted in ethnic and nationalist claims, broke out, bringing the world to a peak of turbulence and violence that it has not known for many years. The central question raised by these waves of movement is: Will they eventually be absorbed and institutionalized into ordinary politics just as the strike and the demonstration were in the nineteenth century? Or have collective action and popular politics burst through the boundaries of convention and provided the bases for a *movement society* – one in which disruptive, even catastrophic, conflicts will become a regular part of life for much of the world's population?

In the concluding chapter, I will argue for a synthesis of these alternatives. Disruptive conflicts have surely broken out in the 1990s, as they always do at the ends of wars and during the collapse of empires. But just as the election campaign and the strike were absorbed into institutional politics during the nineteenth century – changing their nature irrevocably – the new forms of participation that have arisen since the 1960s may be domesticated by the end of the twentieth. The shape of the future will depend not on how violent or widespread collective action becomes, but on how it is absorbed into – and transforms – the national state. But since the latter may, itself, be dissolving into broader transnational and supranational bodies, the social movement may follow suit. In our time, the world may be experiencing a new and far-reaching power in movement.

1

Collective action and social movements

The theory of collective action has been preoccupied with how individuals become convinced to act on behalf of collective goods. But this is less problematic than many collective action theorists have thought, for collective action occurs all the time. Movements *do* have a collective action problem, but it is *social:* coordinating unorganized, autonomous and dispersed populations into common and sustained action. They solve this problem by responding to political opportunities through the use of known, modular forms of collective action, by mobilizing people within social networks and through shared cultural understandings. An example drawn from recent American politics will introduce these variables.

MARCHING ON WASHINGTON

On the morning of April 25th, 1993, a march began in Washington, D.C.[1] Marching on Washington has become a routine form of protest in the America of the 1990s. By bus, train and private car, marchers arrive in the nation's capital, converge on the Mall and are led by an army of well-drilled parade marshals to the steps of the Lincoln Memorial. There, leaders inspire them, lead them in song and assure them that their collective presence will bear fruit. Representatives of the media take up favored positions, endorsements from absent dignitaries are read out, and members of Congress assure those present that their cause is just.

Elements of drama alternate with moments of farce and outbursts of spontaneity. Parties precede the demonstration and ritual visits to congressmen's offices follow, allowing the demonstrators to remind their representatives that their votes have weight. At day's end, warmed by the sunshine and fellowship, the marchers repair to their vehicles, assured that they have struck a blow for justice, for freedom and especially for rights.

But this march is unusual for several reasons. First, it advances a cause – the rights of gay and lesbian Americans – that a few decades ago would have brought few people into the streets. Now it brings what are by some estimates almost a million supporters of that cause to the nation's capital.[2] Second, it focuses on a particular right – that of gay men and lesbians to serve in the military – that angers conservatives and makes liberals uneasy.[3] Third, in their dress, their manner and their comportment, the marchers show Americans an image of their diversity: from men and women in uniform, to well-dressed yuppies, to college students, housewives and ministers of the gospel.[4] According to an article in the *Washington Post,* 26 April 1993, only the occasional drag queen in full regalia reminds Americans that this group is somehow "different."

Aware of that difference, the march's organizers face a dilemma: how to put forward a set of unsettling demands for unconventional people in ways that will not make enemies of potential allies. They do so by playing down their difference before the media and the country while celebrating it in private.[5] Like most of those who have demonstrated on this ground in the past, gay and lesbian Americans say they want no more than the rights that other Americans enjoy. Their speeches echo a pattern that is familiar since the 1960s; their songs follow the refrains of the civil rights marches of the past, and "straight" and consensual slogans flank the assertion of their right to serve in the military. No differently than most who have marched here in the past, they solve the dilemma of difference by adapting familiar routines to a radical purpose.

The march on Washington helps us to pose three basic questions of social movement theory: first, *why* people act collectively in face of the many reasons why they "shouldn't"; second, why they do so *when* they do; and, third, what are the *outcomes* of collective action? In this chapter I will first review how collective action theorists have posed these questions, beginning from three major marxist theorists – Marx, Lenin and Gramsci – and turning from them to the more recent choice–theoretic tradition. I will then propose a theoretical framework that begins from the social nature of collective action, and proceeds from there to the dynamics and the outcomes of movements. I will argue that movements depend on their external environments (and especially on political opportunities) to coordinate and sustain collective action. As a result, to apply usefully to social movements, the theory of collective action must be extended from individual to collective decision making: from simple microeconomic models to socially and historically embedded choices; and from single movements to the dynamics of the political struggle. This is why we will begin with structural theorists like Marx, Lenin and Gramsci who provide a firmer grasp of the collective context of movements.

MARX, LENIN AND GRAMSCI

It would not have occurred to the earliest theorists of social movements, Marx and Engels, to ask what makes individuals engage in collective action:[6] or rather, they would have posed the question as a problem of society's structural development rather than one of individual choice. But although they paid little attention to the link between social structure and individuals, Marx and Engels were surprisingly modern in understanding the problem of collective action as one that is rooted in social structure. And Lenin and Gramsci had a clear understanding of the role of political opportunities, organization and culture in producing collective action.

Karl Marx answered the question of how individuals get involved in collective action in class terms: People will engage in collective action, he thought, when their social class is in fully developed contradiction with its antagonists. In the case of the Western proletariat, this meant when capitalism had forced it into large-scale factories where it lost the ownership of its tools but developed the resources to act collectively. Among these resources were class consciousness and unions. It was the rhythm of socialized production in the factory that would pound the proletariat into a class for itself and the unions that would give it form.[7]

Marx dealt summarily with a problem that has worried movement activists ever since: Why members of a group who "should" revolt often fail to do so. Like modern theorists, he was concerned with the problem that the workers' movement could not succeed unless a significant proportion of its members cooperated in collective action. But in explaining why this so often failed to happen, Marx used an unsatisfactory theory of "false" consciousness – unsatisfactory because no one could say whose consciousness was false and whose was real. He thought that class conflict, and the solidarity that would come from years of toiling side by side with other workers, would eventually solve this dilemma.

We now know that as capitalism developed, it produced divisions among the workers and institutional mechanisms that integrated them into capitalist democracy. Through nationalism and protectionism, workers often even allied with capitalists, suggesting that more than class conflict would be necessary to produce collective action on their behalf. A form of consciousness had to be created that would transcend the narrow trade union consciousness of the workers and transform it into revolutionary collective action. But without a clear-cut concept of organization and of working class culture, Marx left this problem to be solved by his successors as he lost himself in the intricacies of capitalist economics.

The organizational problem was Lenin's major preoccupation. Learning from the Western experience that workers on their own will act only on behalf of "trade union interests," Lenin proposed the solution of an elite of professional revolutionaries (1929: 52 ff.). Substituting itself for Marx's proletariat, this vanguard would act as the self-appointed guardian of the workers' "real" interests. When it succeeded in gaining power, as in Russia in 1917, it transposed the equation, substituting its own party interest for that of the working class. But in 1902 this was far in the future; to Lenin, organization seemed the solution to the collective action problem.

Lenin's organizational amendments to Marx's class theory were a response to the political opportunity structure of Czarist Russia. In superimposing an intellectual vanguard on an unsophisticated working class, he was adapting the theory to the political context of a repressive state and to the backward society it ruled – both of which he saw retarding class consciousness and inhibiting collective action.[8] The theory of the vanguard was an organizational response to a historical situation in which the working class was unable to produce a revolution on its own. But it solidified the tendency already found in European social democracy to think of the masses as needing direction, and of leaders as the source of the "consciousness" to provide it.

When Lenin's revolution failed to spread to the West, Marxists like Antonio Gramsci realized that at least in Western societies, organization was not sufficient to raise a revolution and that it would be necessary to develop the workers' own consciousness. Gramsci accepted Lenin's injunction that the revolutionary party had to be a vanguard (just as he thought Italy shared many of Russia's social conditions), but he added to Lenin's solution two theorems: first, a fundamental task of the party was to create a historic bloc of forces around the working class (1971: 168); second, this could only occur if a cadre of "organic intellectuals" developed from within the working class to complement the "traditional" intellectuals in the party (pp. 6–23).

Both innovations turned out to hinge on a strong belief in the power of culture. For Gramsci, the movement became not only an organizational weapon – as it was for Lenin – but a "collective intellectual" whose message would be transmitted to the masses through a cadre of intermediate leaders.[9] This would produce consensus among the workers, create the capacity for autonomous initiatives and build bridges to other classes. The process would be a long and a slow one, requiring the party to operate within the "trenches and fortifications" of bourgeois society, proselytize among nonproletarian groups and learn to deal with cultural institutions like the church.

But Gramsci's solution – as embodied in the fate of the Italian Communist party after World War II – posed a new dilemma. If the party as collective intellectual engaged a long-term dialogue between the working class and bourgeois society, what would prevent the cultural power of the latter – what Gramsci called "the common sense of capitalist society" – from dominating the party, rather than vice versa?[10] Collective action there would be; but it might well be on behalf of the collective interest of the bourgeoisie.

All this was in the future. For the moment, Gramsci's contribution was not only to show that the Western working class was locked in a structure of long-term strategic interaction with other classes and with the state, but that the relations between leaders and followers could not follow Lenin's bimodal model of an intellectual vanguard imposing its consciousness on the base. To Lenin's insistence on organization, Gramsci added an appreciation of the need for consensus; and, instead of his assumption that a vanguard of leaders would come from the intelligentsia, Gramsci saw the need for multiple levels of leadership and initiative.

Each of these three theorists emphasized a different element of the structural foundations of collective action: Marx wrote of the fundamental cleavages of capitalist society that created a mobilization potential; Lenin of the movement organizations that were necessary to structure it and prevent its dispersion into narrow corporate claims; and Gramsci of the cultural foundation necessary to build broad consensus around the party's goals.

The modern theory of social movements is based on all three of these elements and on one other as well: Although Marx underestimated the independent impact of politics, Lenin and Gramsci anticipated modern social movement theory in their appreciation of politics as an *interactive* process among workers, capitalists and the state. They saw that it was not primarily in the factory, but in interaction with the state that the fate of the working class movement would be decided. This was evident in both Lenin's success, which took advantage of the wartime collapse of the Czarist regime, and in Gramsci's failure, which was the result of the collapse of political opportunities in the West after the 1914–18 war.

These features of collective action – the translation of a movement's mobilization potential into action through organization, consensus mobilization and political opportunity structure – form the skeleton of contemporary social movement theory. But in place of Lenin's centralized party, we now recognize the importance of looser mobilizing structures; instead of Gramsci's collective intellectual, we focus on broader, and less controllable cultural frames; and for the tactical political opportunism that both theorists favored, we work from a more structural theory of political opportunities. But first, a newer strand of collective action theory must be introduced and assimilated.

INDIVIDUAL AND COLLECTIVE CHOICE

The decade of the 1960s revitalized social movements – and social movement theory – in both Europe and the United States. A generation of scholars, many of them coming out of the movements of that decade, made the field of social movements and political protest central to the study of modern history, political science and sociology. But the theory of movements has also been affected by intellectual trends in the academy, shifting attention from the marxists' emphasis on social class to political economists' focus on individuals seeking marginal improvement in their lives. For many scholars, the problem came to be seen as not how classes struggle and states rule, but how collective action on behalf of collective goods is even *possible* among individuals who are guided by narrow self-interest – especially when others appear ready to defend these interests for them.[11]

The most influential student of this dilemma was the American economist Mancur Olson (1965). Although Olson acknowledged the importance of nonmaterial incentives, his theory started and finished with the individual. For Olson, the problem of collective action was aggregative: How to involve as high a proportion of a group as possible on behalf of its collective good. Only in this way could the group convince its opponents of its own strength.

In his book, *The Logic of Collective Action,* Olson posited that only a large group's important members have sufficient interest in its collective good to take on its leadership – not quite Lenin's "vanguard," but not far from it. The only exception to this rule is in very small groups in which individual and collective goods are closely associated (pp. 43ff.).[12] The larger the group, the more people prefer to "free ride" on the efforts of the individuals whose interest in the collective good is strong enough to pursue it.[13]

To overcome this problem, would-be leaders must either impose constraints on their members or provide them with "selective incentives" to convince them that their participation is worthwhile (p. 51). Thus, the collective good of unions is to provide their members with joint goods that all the workers in a plant will enjoy whether they participate or not. And if this is so, why would anyone join the union? Only by offering the workers selective incentives like pension plans or recreational opportunities – or by constraining them with automatic dues deductions – will the union gain their participation. For Olson, as for Lenin, the collective action problem had an organizational solution.

Students of social movements were quick to object that Olson disposed of collective action too hastily during a period of history – the 1960s – that was bursting with participation.[14] They argued that people participate in movements not only as the result of self-interest, but because of deeply held beliefs, the desire to socialize with others and because they too understand the Olsonian dilemma.[15] Collective action *does* take place, in large groups and small, under conditions of both high and low risk. A more fundamental question was whether social movements actually fit Olson's theory. I will argue that they do not, and that the real problem for social movements is social.

Two American sociologists, John McCarthy and Mayer Zald, thought that Olson's theory did apply to movements but saw a new solution to the collective action problem in professional movement organizations.[16] Observing in the 1960s the rise of many such organizations (1973), they thought that the greater affluence and widespread organizational skills available in modern society provide organizers with resources with which to mobilize people. These organizers are not simply those who have a large stake in a collective good, as Olson had theorized, but professional "movement entrepreneurs" with the skills and opportunities to draw existing reservoirs of grievances into social movement organizations – what McCarthy and Zald called SMOs (1977).[17]

McCarthy and Zald seem not to have been worried about the fact that Olson was not primarily concerned with social movements, but with interest groups.[18] In fact, Olson had generalized from an even narrower category – economic associations. In this realm, his version of the collective action problem clearly applied, and for three reasons. First, in economic associations, the measure of success is marginal utility, clearly defined and generally understood. Second, for such organizations, the proportion of the group that engages in collective action is crucial – for if significant portions of the members do not support their leaders, opponents will have little reason to take them seriously. Finally, such associations are formally and transparently organized; they consist of identifiable leaders attempting to mobilize formally associated members into collective action around a finite set of goals.

But none of these criteria applies theoretically to social movements.[19] First, the reason for an individual's affiliation with a movement is not necessarily marginal utility – not even when that concept is broadened beyond its economic meaning.[20] Research has shown that people associate with movements for a wide spectrum of reasons: from the desire for personal advantage, to group solidarity, to principled commitment to a cause, to the desire to be part of a group. This heterogeneity of motivations makes the problem of coordination much more difficult for a social movement than for an interest group, but it also makes it possible for movements to draw on resources other than pecuniary ones to involve people in collective action.[21]

Second, while the proportion of the members who participate in collective action is a critical measure of the strength of an economic association, movements have no certain size or clear membership and are often *in formation* at the time of their public appearance. This makes Olson's criterion of proportional participation meaningless for social movements. While "bringing out" a large number of people can be an important measure of a movement's power, *how many* people need to participate depends on the "structure of the struggle" they are involved in (Fireman and Gamson 1979: 17). Indeed, for some forms of collective action, numbers are even inversely proportional to the movement's power.[22]

Third, the transparent, bimodal relationship between leaders and followers that Olson saw in economic associations is absent from movements, many of which do not even have formal structures. To the extent that movements are organized, they are made up of a far more mediated and informal set of relationships among organizations, coalitions of organizations, intermediate groups, members, sympathizers and crowds. "It is misleading to equate a social movement with any kind of single collective decision-making entity," writes sociologist Pam Oliver, "no matter how loosely structured" (1989: 4).[23]

The gay march on Washington in April 1993 illustrates all three of these differences. First, although some of those who attended the march had a personal interest in gaining access to the military, most did not. They participated for a variety of reasons, mostly connected with their solidarity with the gay community. Second, though organizers made a major effort to bring large numbers of people to the capital, the proportion of the gay community that turned out was irrelevant to their success or failure – indeed, no one knows how many gay and lesbian Americans there are. Third, the gay movement is not an organization. Although we can identify a national leadership that mounted the march, like most major demonstrations in America, it was run by a coalition of disparate groups, each with its own network of affiliates, members, friends and allies and hangers-on. And as the occasional expressions of exotic behavior at the march showed, the organizers had little control over their supporters.[24]

On the other hand, the organizers of the gay rights march *did* face a collective action problem: that of bringing together a coalition of groups, organizations and individuals they didn't control in a coordinated campaign of collective action. They had to bring them to a given place at a given time, direct their energies against an identifiable set of targets, and sustain their claims afterwards through different forms of collective action. To do all this, they needed to bring supporters to Washington from all over the country on the same day and convince them – and, through them, a larger public – that proceeding down the Mall to the Lincoln Memorial was a meaningful act. They also had to convince the country that their action had a particular meaning, coordinating the efforts of scores of autonomous organizations, persuading allies, opinion groups and the media that the demonstration was important and preventing outbursts of excessive zeal. Finally, they had to follow up by lobbying members of Congress after the march was over. Their problem was not one of overcoming individual "free riders," as Olson's theory predicts; it was "social" – coordinating, sustaining and giving meaning to collective action.

THE SOCIAL IN SOCIAL MOVEMENTS

An analogy from the theory of industrial organization will help us to highlight the difference between Olson's theory and our own. In Oliver Williamson's theory of the firm, companies depend on external suppliers and producers of components, but reduce this dependency by internalizing their assets. Williamson argues that when companies become concerned over opportunistic advantage-taking on the part of controllers of key assets, they absorb the processes – the supply of components and information – and decrease the transaction costs of production and distribution.[25] Some transaction costs – like the costs of regulation – can never be absorbed, but the internalization of contracts minimizes the costs of exchange. The result is to produce large-scale industrial units whose size and structure are determined by the technical criteria of control over assets.

But not all firms can, or even wish to internalize their assets, and there are alternatives to solving the transaction cost problem in this way. For example, as firms grow, they become unwieldy and insensitive to their environments and lose internal control. An alternative to internalization is for small-scale firms that are loosely linked in producer associations to cooperate in acquiring supplies and information and distributing their products. Building on existing cultural understandings and social networks, they and their competitor/colleagues make what Hardin would call "contracts by convention" (1982: ch. 11). In some cases, as in the vertical fragmentation of Japanese firms studied by Ronald Dore (1986), and in the small-scale sector of the "Third Italy" (Trigilia 1986), they gain in efficiency over large consolidated units by depending on the local trust and social networks that large-scale industrial monoliths lack. As Trigilia writes of the Italian small-scale sector:

local institutional resources have influenced entrepreneurial capacity and cooperation among the actors, making it possible to reduce the transaction costs both between firms and between managers and workers. (1986: 142)

Social movements – not being groups and lacking compulsory coordination – are seldom in a position to solve their collective action problem through internalization. (In Chapter 8, I will even argue that when this has been tried, it has had *negative* consequences for the movements which tried it.) Like the small-scale producers studied by Trigilia, they draw upon external resources – opportunities, conventions, understandings and social networks – to coordinate and sustain collective action. When they succeed, even resource-poor actors can mount and sustain collective action against powerful opponents.

The most important opportunities are changes in the structure of political opportunity. The most important conventions relate to the forms of collective action that movements employ. Their major external resources are the social networks in which collective action occurs and the cultural and ideological symbols that frame it. Together, opportunities, repertoires, networks and frames are the materials for the construction of movement. Let us begin with the structure of political opportunity.

Political opportunity structure

The main argument of this study is that people join in social movements in response to political opportunities and then, through collective action, create new ones. As a result, the "when" of social movement mobilization – when political opportunities are opening up – goes a long way towards explaining its "why." It also helps us to understand why movements do not appear only in direct response to the level of supporters' grievances. For if it is political opportunities that translate the potential for movement into mobilization, then even groups with mild grievances and few internal resources may appear in movement, while those with deep grievances and dense resources – but lacking opportunities – may not. The concept of political opportunity structure will also help us to explain how movements are diffused; how collective action is communicated and new networks are formed from one social group to another as opportunities are seized and created.

By political opportunity structure, I refer to consistent – but not necessarily formal, permanent or national – dimensions of the political environment which either encourage or discourage people from using collective action. The concept of political opportunity emphasizes resources *external* to the group – unlike money or power – that can be taken advantage of even by weak or disorganized challengers. Social movements form when ordinary citizens, sometimes encouraged by leaders, respond to changes in opportunities that lower the costs of collective action, reveal potential allies and show where elites and authorities are vulnerable.

The most salient changes in opportunity structure result from the opening up of access to power, from shifts in ruling alignments, from the availability of influential allies and from cleavages within and among elites as I will argue in Chapters 4 and 5. State structures create stable opportunities, but it is changing opportunities within states that provide the openings that resource-poor actors can use to create new movements.

How these aspects of political opportunity structure affect the mobilization of a movement could be seen in the march on Washington in April 1993. An electoral realignment had just occurred: from a Republican government favoring the religious right and the muscular military to a new Democratic president. The latter in an early campaign promise had promised to end the ban on gay men and lesbians in the military. There was an evident split within the political elite on the broad issue of "family values" which gave the National Gay and Lesbian Task Force the opportunity to gain policy advantage. And it found influential allies in the women's movement, among civil rights groups and even in Congress. Politics opened the gates of opportunity.

Contention by convention

Anthropologist David Kertzer writes that general knowledge of particular routines in a society's history helps movements to overcome their deficits in resources and communication (1988: 104 ff.). No less than in the case of religious rituals or civic celebrations, notes Kertzer, collective action is not born out of organizers' heads but is culturally inscribed and communicated. The learned conventions of collective action are part of a society's public culture.[26]

Particular groups have a particular history – and memory – of collective action. Workers know how to strike because generations of workers have struck before them; Parisians build barricades because barricades are inscribed in the history of Parisian contention; peasants seize the land carrying the symbols that their fathers and grandfathers used in the past. Political scientists Stuart Hill and Donald Rothchild put it this way:

Based on past periods of conflict with a particular group(s) or the government, individuals construct a prototype of a protest or riot that describes what to do in particular circumstances as well as explaining a rationale for this action. (1992: 192)

There are more general conventions of collective action that I will call, with Charles Tilly, the "repertoire of contention."[27] Tilly observes that people cannot employ routines of collective action of which they are ignorant; each society has a stock of familiar forms of action that are known by both potential challengers and their opponents – and which become habitual aspects of their interaction. If we accept the assumption that individuals have available knowledge of the history and previous outcomes of the forms of collective action in their societies, then we can see that leaders propose – and followers respond to – more than the abstraction of "collective action." They are drawn as well to a known repertoire of particular *forms* of collective action.

In the past, most forms of collective action were closely linked to particular groups and situations of conflict: the grain seizure, the ritual shaming or *charivari*, the anti-seignorial riot. But sometime in the late eighteenth century, a sea change occurred. Assisted by the widening diffusion of information through the print media and the knowledge generated by movement networks and associations, the same collective action routines began to be employed across wide territories, broad social sectors and for different kinds of issues – what I will call the *modular* repertoire. As I will show in Chapter 2, the petition, the strike, the demonstration, the barricade and the urban insurrection became learned responses applied in a variety of settings, providing conventions that assisted movements to bring together even very large and disparate groups.

Because movements seldom possess either selective incentives or constraints over followers, leadership has a creative function in collective action that more institutionalized groups lack. Leaders invent, adapt and combine various forms of collective action to stimulate support from people who might otherwise stay home. Albert Hirschman had something like this in mind when he complained that Olson regarded collective action *only* as a cost – when to many it is a benefit (1982: 82–91). For people whose lives are mired in drudgery and desperation, the offer of an exciting, risky and possibly beneficial campaign of collective action may be a gain. Leaders offer forms of collective action that are inherited or rare, habitual or unfamiliar, solitary or part of concerted campaigns. They link them to themes that are either inscribed in the culture or invented on the spot, or – more commonly – blend elements of convention with new frames of meaning. Protest is a resource, according to political scientist Michael Lipsky

(1968), and the forms of collective action that movements choose are a collective incentive to mobilization.

But there is a dilemma in the dependence of movements on collective action to communicate their claims and to link leaders and followers: On the one hand, the demonstration of numerical strength and solidarity can convince participants that they are stronger than they really are; on the other hand, dependence on the conventional repertoire creates certainty and even boredom about the results of a demonstration.

The result of the first problem is that – in exaggerating their strength – movement activists may force confrontations with authorities that they are almost sure to lose and that alienate possible supporters. The result of the second is that – in a demonstration-sated society – no one will listen to a movement because half-a-million people march down a boulevard. One result of this lack of impact is that some militants turn towards more routine forms of political activities, while others are tempted by more extreme forms of collective action, violence and symbolism to draw attention to themselves and radicalize confrontations with authorities. The result is to bring about the factional splits that are endemic to movements and to speed their decline.

The organizers of the gay rights march knew about the conventions of collective action when they marched on Washington. Had they invited the gay community to no more than a pleasant walk down a green sward towards a pile of marble, they would have walked alone. But marches on Washington, like Parisian barricades, British petitions and Chinese political theater, have a long and symbol-rich history. For a generation of Americans, they are associated with the stirring days of the Civil Rights movement, with Martin Luther King's "I have a Dream" speech, and with their own youth. Using the conventions of collective action in America helped the organizers to solve the coordination problem of collective action.

But these organizers also suffered from the dilemma of collective action. On the one hand, they were unable to control the minority of their supporters whose strategy was to physically demonstrate their "difference" – in some cases by marching seminude, in others by cross-dressing – thereby providing the movement's opponents with rare footage to support their anti-gay and lesbian ideologies. On the other hand, the ability to bring out almost one million people led the militants in the movement to exaggerate their power. For once the marchers went home, the processes of ordinary politics took over.

These aftereffects of collective action tell us that single campaigns are not social movements. Unless a movement sustains its interaction with opponents, allies and authorities, it is quickly discounted and easily repressed. As we shall see in the next chapter, for centuries, collective action arose among peasants, Protestants, taxpayers, householders and consumers without producing sustained interaction with authorities or elites. Today as well, violent, passionate collective action often erupts, only to be followed by dispersion and disillusionment.

Why is this the case? If movements were interest groups, with selective incentives to distribute and constraints to apply, we would have our answer: Movements succeed when they are well organized. But movements are not interest groups and – as we have seen – they often appear in the absence of well-defined organizations or leaders. The question thus becomes: Once opportunities appear, how is collective action diffused, coordinated and sustained?

Mobilizing structures

The answer begins with the social: Although it is individuals who decide whether or not to take up collective action, it is in their face-to-face groups, their social networks and their institutions that collective action is most often activated and sustained. This has been made clear through recent research both in the laboratory and in the real world of movement mobilization. Olson had focused on individuals, but by the early 1980s, scholars were finding that group processes transform the potential for collective action into movement participation. For example, sociologist Doug McAdam's work on the Freedom Summer campaign showed that – far more than their social background or ideologies – the social networks in which Freedom Summer applicants were embedded played a key role in determining who would participate and who would not (1986; 1988). At the same time, European scholars like Hanspeter Kriesi (1988) were finding that movement subcultures were the reservoirs in which collective action took shape. This dovetailed with what sociologist Alberto Melucci (1989) was learning about the role of movement networks in defining the collective identity of the movements he studied in Italy. Similarly, historians like Maurice Agulhon and Ted Margadant were finding that the sociability of traditional communities could serve as an incubator for movement mobilization.[28]

Experimental researchers were also learning about the importance of social incentives to cooperation. In an ingenious piece of research, William Gamson and his collaborators showed that a supportive group environment was essential to triggering individuals' willingness to speak out against unjust authority – authority that they might well tolerate if they faced it on their own (Gamson, Fireman, and Rytina 1982). Similarly, when Robyn Dawes and his associates carried out a series of experiments on collective choice, they found that neither egoistic motives nor internalized norms were as powerful in producing collective action as "the parochial one of contributing to one's group of fellow humans" (Dawes, Van de Kragt, and Orbell 1988: 96).[29]

Institutions are particularly economical "host" settings in which movements can germinate. This was particularly true in estate societies like prerevolutionary France, where the provincial *parlements* provided institutional space where liberal ideas could be aired (Egret 1977). But it is also true today. In America, sociologist Aldon Morris showed that the origins of the Civil Rights movement were bound up with the role of the black churches (1984). In Italy and Latin America, the Catholic Church was an unwitting accomplice in the formation of networks of "base" communities (Levine 1990; Tarrow 1988).

The role of social networks and institutions in stimulating movement participation challenges Olson's pessimistic conclusion that large groups will not support collective action for collective goods. For when we look at the morphology of movements, it becomes clear that they are only "large" in a nominal sense. They are really much more like an interlocking network of small groups, social networks and the connections between them.[30] Collective action may arise only among the best endowed or most courageous of these groups, but the connections between them affects the likelihood that one actor's action will incite another. As Gerald Marwell and Pam Oliver put it, "Olson's 'large group' problem is often resolved by a 'small group' solution" (1993: 54).[31] And since a movement is really a congeries of social networks loosely linked to one another, it may survive when an arithmetical "large group" would not.

The importance of this finding becomes clear when we study the morphology of demonstrations like the gay march on Washington. As in most major demonstrations today, few people came to Washington alone. They participated as members of friendship networks, interest groups, local branches of movement organizations and groups of professional colleagues.[32] The mobilization of preexisting social networks lowers the social transaction costs of mounting demonstrations, and holds participants together even after the enthusiasm of the peak of confrontation is over. In human terms, this is what makes possible the transformation of episodic collective action into social movements.

Consensus mobilization

But as Trigilia discovered in the small-firm sector of Central Italy, coordination depends not only on structural features of society like social networks and institutions, but on the trust and cooperation that are generated among participants by shared understandings; or, to use a broader category, on the collective action *frames* that justify, dignify and animate collective action. Ideology, as David Apter wrote in his classic essay, *Ideology and Discontent,* dignifies discontent, identifies a target for grievances and forms an umbrella over the discrete grievances of overlapping groups (ch. 1).

In recent years, students of movements have begun to use technical terms like cognitive frames, ideological packages and cultural discourses to describe the shared meanings that inspire people to collective action.[33] Whatever the terminology, rather than regarding ideology as either a superimposed intellectual category or as the automatic result of grievances, these scholars agree in seeing that movements shape grievances into broader claims in a process of purposive "framing work" (Snow and Benford 1988).

But while movement organizers actively engage in framing work, not all framing takes place under their auspices. In addition to building on inherited cultural understandings, they must compete with the framing that goes on all the time through the media which transmit messages that movements must attempt to shape and influence. As sociologist Todd Gitlin found, much of the communication that helped the American New Left to develop passed through the medium of the media and took the place of what would have had to be organizational efforts in earlier periods of history (1980). Just as movements build on existing social networks, they use the external resources of the media to try to mobilize a following. But against the inherent power of the media to shape perceptions, movements possess little cultural power.

The organizers of the April 1993 march on Washington paid the price for this weakness. Despite the organizers' efforts to project a conventional image, according to the *Washington Post,* 26 April 1993, some of the media went out of its way to photograph men dressed up in women's clothes and lesbians marching bare breasted. As Gramsci knew, consensus mobilization comes up against the cultural power of capitalist society – especially of the kind that requires no conscious manipulation but results from the ordinary business of the media and the state.

To summarize what will have to be shown in detail in later chapters: The collective action problem is social, not individual. Movements are produced when political opportunities broaden, when they demonstrate the existence of allies and when they reveal the vulnerability of opponents. By mounting collective actions, organizers become focal points that transform external opportunities, conventions and resources into movements. Repertoires of contention, social networks and cultural frames lower the costs of bringing people together in collective action, creating a broader and more widely diffused dynamic of movement.

THE DYNAMICS OF MOVEMENT

The power to trigger sequences of collective action is not the same as the power to control or sustain them. This dilemma has both an internal and an external dimension. Internally, a good part of the power of movements comes from the fact that they activate people over whom they have no control. This power is a virtue because it allows movements to mount collective actions without possessing the resources that would be necessary to internalize a support base. But the autonomy of their supporters also disperses the movement's power, encourages factionalism and leaves it open to defection, competition and repression.

Externally, movements are affected by the fact that the same political opportunities that have created them, and which diffuse their influence, also produce others – either complementary, competing or hostile. Particularly if collective action succeeds, these opportunities produce broader movement *cycles* which spread from movement activists to ordinary interest groups and citizens and, inevitably, bring in the state. As a result of this dynamic of movement diffusion and creation, movements succeed or fail as the result of forces outside their control. This takes us to the concept of the protest cycle.

Cycles of protest

As opportunities widen and information spreads about the susceptibility of a political system to challenge, not only activists, but ordinary people test the limits of social control. Clashes between early challengers and authorities reveal the weak points of the latter and the strengths of the former, enabling even timid social actors to align themselves on one side or another. Once triggered by a situation of generally widening political opportunities, information cascades outward and political learning accelerates. As Hill and Rothchild write,

As protests and riots erupt among groups that have long histories of conflict, they stimulate other citizens in similar circumstances to reflect more often on their own background of grievance and mass action. (p. 193)

During such periods, the opportunities created by early risers provide incentives for new movement organizations to form. Even conventional interest groups are tempted by unconventional collective action. Alliances are made – often across the boundary between challengers and members of the polity (Tilly 1978: ch. 2). New forms of collective action are experimented with and diffused. A dense and interactive "social movement sector" appears in which organizations compete and cooperate (Garner and Zald 1985). Movement organizations fight for the support of what may, at some point, turn out to be a declining base of support. The results of this competition are radicalization and outbidding, leading to violence, defection and increased repression.

The process of diffusion in protest cycles is not merely one of "contagion" – although a good deal of such contagion occurs. It also results when groups make gains that invite others to seek similar outcomes: when someone else's ox is gored by demands made by insurgent groups; and when the predominance of an organization or institution is threatened and it responds by adopting contentious collective action. For example, after its decline under the Bush administration in Washington, the fundamentalist Christian Right in America was given a second chance by the controversy about gay men and lesbians in the military.

As the cycle widens, movements create opportunities for elites and opposition groups, too. Alliances form between participants and challengers and oppositional elites make demands for changes that would have seemed foolhardy earlier. Governmental forces respond either with reform, repression or a combination of the two. The widening logic of collective action leads to outcomes in the sphere of politics, where the movements that began the cycle can have less and less influence over its outcomes.

At the extreme end of the spectrum, cycles of protest give rise to revolutions. Revolutions are not a single form of collective action; nor are they wholly made up of popular collective action. As in the movement cycles to which they are related, collective action in revolutions forces other groups and institutions to take part, providing the bases and cognitive frameworks for new social movements, unhinging old institutions and the networks that surround them and creating new ones out of the forms of collective action with which insurgent groups begin the process.

The difference between movement cycles and revolutions is that, in the latter, multiple centers of sovereignty are created, turning the conflict between challengers and members of the policy into a struggle for power (Tilly 1933b). This difference – which is substantial – has led to an entire industry of research on "great" revolutions, which are usually compared only to one another. This specialization has squandered the possibility of comparing revolutions to lesser conflagrations, making it impossible to isolate which factors in the dynamic of a protest cycle lead it down the path to revolution and which ones lead it to collapse.

Outcomes of movement

These arguments suggest that it will not be fruitful to examine the outcomes of social movements in a direct way. Decisions to take collective action usually occur in social networks in response to political opportunities, creating incentives and opportunities for others. Both challenge and response are nested in a complex social and policy system in which the interests and actions of other participants come into play, and traditions and experiences of contention and conflict become the resources of both challengers and their opponents. Particularly in general cycles of protest, policy elites respond, not to the claims of any individual group or movement, but to the degree of turbulence and to demands made by elites and opinion groups that may not correspond to the demands of those they claim to represent.

From the point of view of the outcomes of social movements, the important point is that, although movements almost always conceive of themselves as outside of and opposed to institutions, collective action inserts them into complex policy networks, and, thus, within the reach of the state. If nothing else, movements enunciate demands in terms of frames of meaning that are comprehensible to a wider society; they use forms of collective action drawn from an existing repertoire; and, they develop types of organization which often mimic the organizations they oppose.

Thus, we can begin to study collective action as a result of individual decisions made in an organizational framework, but we quickly arrive at the more complex and less tractable networks of politics. It is through the political opportunities seized and created by protesters, movements and allies that major cycles of protest and revolution begin. They, in turn, create opportunities for elites and counterelites, and action that has begun in the streets is resolved in the halls of government or by the bayonets of the army. Movements – and particularly the waves of movement that are the main catalysts of social change – are part of national struggles for power.[34]

This interpenetration of movements, institutions and political processes could be seen in the outcomes of the April 1993 march on Washington. After a month of detailed wrangling among lobbyists, congressmen and the military, Massachusetts Congressman Barney Frank called a press conference to propose a compromise. Gay men and lesbians should be able to serve freely in any branch of the military, he argued, provided they suppress their sexual preferences while on duty. According to the *New York Times,* 19 May 1993, when Frank was attacked by gay activists for caving in on so central an issue as lifting the ban completely, he answered: "We don't have the votes for that in Congress."

Dismayed gay activists condemned Frank for being a part of the system they abhorred. But it was the *movement* that had entered the system's logic by organizing a campaign that employed a standard repertoire of collective action, repressed its difference, built a coalition based on a network of organizations and on broadly accepted cultural understandings and linked its claims to an ongoing debate in Congress and in the country. In fact, as Congressman Frank pointed out, the march did not fail because its leaders played by the rules of Washington politics, but because they played the game badly. For when it came to the crucial but boring work of using their electoral muscle, too few demonstrators showed up in their representatives' offices.

The theoretical message of this story is that, because movements solve their transaction cost problem through external resources, it is far easier for them to mount collective action than to sustain it – especially when the terrain of the contest shifts from the streets to the halls of politics. As Frank observed, bringing almost a million demonstrators to Washington was easier to accomplish than convincing them to stay in town and petition their representatives when the march was over.

The outcome of the gay march also illustrates how easily movements create political opportunities for others. For despite their discipline and restraint, the movement's organizers could not counter the negative images with which the media and some political commentators chose to frame it. In the wake of the demonstration, right wing and veterans' groups mobilized to lobby Congress against gay access to the military. Under these pressures, even President Clinton, his own draft history a source of sensitivity, defected from the full support he had offered during the 1992 campaign and worked out a compromise with the military. And the religious Right had a field day claiming that a gay assault on America's religious values was underway.

The import of this story – as of this entire chapter – is that we can begin our study of social movements with the determinants of individual collective action. But because the collective action problem is not that of free riders, but of the coordination of collective action necessary to solve movements' transaction cost problem, we must turn to the opportunity structures that create incentives for movements to form; to the repertoire of collective action they use, to the social networks on which they are based and to the cultural frames around which their supporters are mobilized. These factors make the study of social movements specific, complex and historically rooted.

Both the complexity and the historical specificity of movements will best be understood if we first turn to the development of the national social movement. In the next three chapters, basing the account on information mainly drawn from Britain, France and the United States, I will trace the development of movements at the intersection between three broad sociopolitical processes: the development of modular forms of collective action; the growth of social networks and national communications media; and the consolidation of the political opportunity structure of the modern state.

PART I

The birth of the national social movement

2

Modular collective action[1]

In 1986, capping more than twenty years of work on collective action,[2] Charles Tilly published his massive work, *The Contentious French*. In it, Tilly wrote of the "repertoire of contention," defining it as "the whole set of means [a group] has for making claims of different kinds on different individuals or groups" (p. 2).[3] In a 1992 paper, Tilly returns to the theme, writing that in routinely operating polities with relatively stable governments

contenders experiment constantly with new forms in the search for tactical advantage, but do so in small ways, at the edge of well-established actions. Few innovations endure beyond a single cluster of events; they endure chiefly when associated with a substantial new advantage for one or more actors. (p. 7)

The repertoire is at once a structural and a cultural concept. Tilly's "well-established actions" are not only what people *do* when they are engaged in conflict with others; it is what they *know how to do* and what others *expect* them to do. Had sit-ins been used by challengers in eighteenth-century France, their targets would not have known how to respond to them, any more than the victim of a *charivari* on a college campus today would know what it meant. As Arthur Stinchcombe writes in his astute review of *The Contentious French*, "The elements of the repertoire are . . . simultaneously the skills of the population members and the cultural forms of the population" (1987: 1,248).

The repertoire changes over time, writes Tilly, but only glacially. Fundamental changes in the forms of collective action depend on major fluctuations in interests, opportunity and organization. These, in turn, are correlated with changes in states and capitalism. Major shifts in the repertoire resulted from the national state's penetration of society to make war and extract taxes, and from capitalism's concentration of large numbers of people in cities with the grievances and the resources to act collectively. Such structural changes lay behind the dramatic changes in the repertoire at the beginnings of the modern capitalist state.

What differences separate the new repertoire that developed out of those beginnings from the forms of behavior that dominated collective action over previous centuries? ''If we push back into the strange terrain of Western Europe and North America before the middle of the nineteenth century,'' writes Tilly, ''we soon discover another world'' of collective action (1983: 463). The older repertoire, in his view, was *local* and *patronized*. Relying heavily on the patronage of immediately available power holders, it often exploded at public celebrations using rich, irreverent symbolism drawn from religious rituals and popular culture. Participants often converged on the residences of wrongdoers and the sites of wrongdoing, commonly appearing as members or representatives of constituted corporate groups and communities (p. 464).

The new repertoire did not appear full-blown everywhere at once (pp. 464–5). Nor did the old forms ever completely disappear. The most visible triumphs of the new forms came in the period of the first Reform Act in England and in the 1848 revolutions on the continent. This new repertoire was *national* and *autonomous*.[4] Rather than appealing to patrons, collective action was organized in public places where challengers could aim at the seats of power, displaying programs, slogans and signs of common membership. And for the constituted bodies and communities of the past were substituted special interests and named associations (1983: 465). In his 1983 article,Tilly summarizes the differences between the old and the new repertoire like this:

Figure 2.1 *''Old'' and ''New'' Repertoires in Western Europe and North America.*

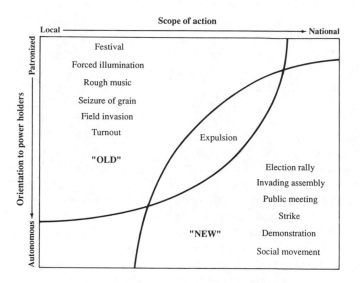

Source: Charles Tilly, ''Speaking Your Mind Without Elections, Surveys, or Social Movements,'' *Public Opinion Quarterly* 47. Published by the University of Chicago Press. Copyright 1983 by the Trustees of Columbia University.

Like all sweeping historical schemes, Tilly's concept of the repertoire can be criticized for overly privileging "anonymous sociological processes," and for underestimating the importance of great events – such as the French Revolution (Sewell 1990: 548). He can also be charged with insensitivity to the meanings of collective action for those who use it – another of Sewell's criticisms (pp. 540–5). But the most interesting issue in Tilly's concept of the repertoire is its relationship to the rise of the national social movement.

<h2 style="text-align:center">REPERTOIRES AND MOVEMENTS</h2>

For most writers – including this one – movements are sustained interactions between aggrieved social actors and allies, and opponents and public authorities. Tilly, himself, has given us a definition very close to this one (1984: 303–8).[5] Collective action is the most active term in this interaction, used by collective actors locked in conflict with opponents or elites. The problem with Tilly's schema is that the social movement appears in it as a *form* of collective action, along with the seizure of grain, the forced illumination, the strike, the election rally, the demonstration and other forms of action. In a sense, a movement *is* a form of action – though an aggregate one – but it is many other things as well. Designating the social movement as a form of collective action makes it difficult to pose the really interesting question that emerges from Tilly's historical sociology: *What was the relationship between changes in the repertoire of collective action and the birth of the national social movement?*

Was it simply, as Tilly argued in 1983, that the earlier forms of action were local and patronized, while the newer ones are national and autonomous? This contrast is important, but it ignores the question of what allowed the earlier local forms to evolve into national and autonomous ones. A more fundamental difference between the old and the new repertoires will provide a clue to the relationship between the new one and the rise of national social movements – the difference between the attachment of the old forms to particular claims and targets and the *modularity* of the new repertoire.

By modularity, I mean the capacity of a form of collective action to be utilized by a variety of social actors, against a variety of targets, either alone, or in combination with other forms. Employing the concept in 1993, Tilly argues that the new forms were modular "in that the same forms served many different localities, actors, and issues." (1993a: 272). In this chapter, I will outline and illustrate this concept and its implications for the creation and power of social movement.

<h3 style="text-align:center">Old and new repertoires</h3>

Implicit in the concept of a repertoire is that it is more or less general.[6] But the old and the new repertoires are not *equally* general. The forms of action used in attacks on millers and grain merchants, *charivaris* and religious conflicts from the sixteenth to the eighteenth centuries were not as widely used against others as the strikes, demonstrations and insurrections of the next two centuries. Herein lies a key to the nature of the modern repertoire. For it was precisely the *lack* of generality in the older forms of collective action that impeded the rise of the national social movement; and it was the general nature of the new ones that gave movements a common cultural and behavioral foundation. Two incidents from the history of French contention will illustrate these differences.

In the mid-1780s, as the foundations of France's Old Regime were crumbling, a series of scandal trials began to appear.[7] In one of the most notorious of these, the Cleraux affair, a servant who had resisted the advances of her master – a certain Thibault – was accused of robbing him and was hauled into court. Not only was the case decided in her favor (*pace* Dickens), but a wave of popular outrage against the courts and the lewd master surged across Paris. In a routine that had become familiar by the late eighteenth century, Thibault's house was sacked, his goods were thrown into the street and he was barely saved from the hands of the crowd. A contemporary observer described the *émotion* in this way:

What violences! What tumults! A furious multitude filled the streets, straining to tear down the Thibault house with an ax, then threatening to burn it; covering the family with curses and outrages; almost sacrificing them to their hatred.[8]

The affair contributed to the atmosphere of chaos and corruption surrounding the Old Regime, but its forms and its rhetoric were familiar from the European past.

Sixty years later, in February 1848, Alexis de Tocqueville left his house for Parliament amidst the tumult of Paris in revolt. Along his route, men were systematically putting up barricades as citizens quietly watched. "These barricades," he observed,

were skillfully constructed by a small number of men who worked industriously – not like criminals fearful of being caught *in flagrante delicto,* but like good workmen who wanted to do their job expeditiously and well. Nowhere did I see the seething unrest I had witnessed in 1830, when the whole city reminded me of one vast, boiling cauldron."[9]

Of "seething unrest" and "boiling cauldrons" Europe would see a great deal in the months following February 1848. But by midcentury, Frenchmen were calmly building barricades, knew where to put them up, and had learned to use them.[10] That regularity marked a fundamental change in the structure of popular politics since the attack on Master Thibault's house sixty years earlier. The contrast was more than one of scale. The tearing down of houses was a routine that had long been used against tax gatherers, brothel keepers and grain merchants.[11] But these were focused on the sites of wrongdoing and limited to direct attacks on suspected perpetrators. The barricade, in contrast, could be mounted on a variety of sites. Once its strategic advantages were known, it could be used for a variety of purposes; to attack opponents, unify people with different aims, or be diffused for use in a variety of types of confrontations with state authorities.[12]

In the 1780s, people knew how to seize shipments of grain, attack tax gatherers, burn tax registers and take revenge on wrongdoers, Jews and Protestants. But they were not yet familiar with the mass demonstration, the strike or the urban insurrection on behalf of common political goals. By the eve of the French Revolution of 1848, the petition, the public meeting, the demonstration and the barricade were well-known routines of collective action, and were employed for a variety of purposes and by combinations of social actors. Before examining these forms of the modular repertoire and their relation to the birth of the national social movement, let us first return to the "traditional" repertoire as it developed in early modern Europe to see how limited and segmented it was.

THE TRADITIONAL REPERTOIRE

For the great French historian Marc Bloch, there was a strong linkage between social structure and collective action. In writing of peasant revolts in feudal society, Bloch argued that "agrarian revolt seems as inseparable from the seignorial regime as the strike from the great capitalist enterprise" (1931: 175). Particular structures give rise to characteristic forms of collective action; Bloch saw a general identity between the forms of collective action that people used, and the substance of their claims which resulted from the structure of their conflicts with others.

When we look at the particular forms of contention Bloch studied, his axiom has two main correlates: First, that the relationship between challenger and challenged was direct; and, second, that the forms of collective action used were attached to the formers' grievances and the nature of their antagonism to their enemies. But the same logic leads to constraints on who acted alongside whom. The agrarian revolt was aimed at the landlord; it follows that peasants would associate through informal village networks with those who shared similar grievances against him. Not only were the forms of collective action directed at challengers relatively inflexible; they were rooted in the corporate structure of the feudal community.

There is a good deal of evidence that all three points were true of the estate societies that Bloch studied. In societies divided into orders, isolated by poor communication and lack of literacy and organized into corporate and communal groups, it was rare to find forms of collective action that were distinct from the conflicts that gave rise to them. When Protestants built a church in a Catholic district, the Catholic community would tear it down or burn it with the parishioners locked inside it (Davis 1973). When millers sold their grain outside a district during a time of dearth, it would be seized and sold at a just price (Tilly 1975). When authorities were responsible for the violent death of a local citizen, the funeral could turn into a riot or the guilty officials hung in effigy (Tamason 1980). The traditional repertoire was segmented; it aimed directly at its targets, and grew out of the corporate structure of an estate society.

Only when they were led by people who possessed organizational or institutional resources – for example, in the church – or when they coincided with opportunities presented by wars or conflicts over dynastic succession – like the English Reformation – did these episodes become part of broader confrontations. Then they could give rise to national – or even international cycles of movement. More often, they flared up like scattered sparks that were rapidly exhausted or snuffed out. For the most part, as Tilly has recently argued, "local people and local issues, rather than nationally organized programs and parties, entered repeatedly into the day's collective confrontations" (1993a: 257).

Inflexibility, direct action and corporate-based organization combined in four common types of popular revolt that dominate the historical record until well into the eighteenth century. In conflicts over bread, belief, land and death, ordinary people tried to correct immediate abuses or get even with those they hated, using routines of collective action that were both direct and inspired by their grievances. Except when overlaid with religious beliefs for which there was an overarching conflict structure, these actions could not bring together broad coalitions of actors on behalf of general claims or create a general repertoire of collective action.

Bread

Probably the most common source of disruptive collective action in the course of history are the periodic food riots and grain seizures that accompanied famines and price increases.[13] Though the result of natural causes, famines almost always brought higher prices, hoarding and speculation, providing protesters with concrete targets for their rage and desperation: merchants and middlemen, Jews and Protestants – more rarely, nobles and princes. As a result, providing the population with a steady and affordable source of grain became a major problem for the centralizing state.[14]

For several centuries, even as national and international markets replaced local grain sales, the forms of collective action surrounding dearth remained largely local, particularistic and unorganized. As E. P. Thompson wrote; "The records of the poor show . . . it is this miller, this dealer, those farmers hoarding grain, who provoke indignation and action" (1971: 98). Even in the French Revolution, the forms of food seizures remained traditional, although they were sometimes exploited by ambitious politicians.

The most ancient form of food protest was what Tilly calls the "retributive action," in which a crowd attacked a person or the property of a person accused of withholding food or profiteering (1975: 386). Preventing a food shipment from leaving a locality was a second variant, which "acted out the belief that the locals should be fed, at a proper price, before any surplus left town" (p. 387). A third form, the price riot, was more characteristic of urban areas, and became widespread only with the rapid growth of cities in the eighteenth century.

Grain seizures followed a well-known routine and might be metaphorically described as "collective bargaining by riot." They developed not so much where people were hungry "as where they believed others were unjustly depriving them of food to which they had a moral and political right" (p. 389). But they seldom demonstrated the common purpose or solidarity needed to mount a sustained campaign. Their limitations were the limitations of the societies in which they arose. As Tilly writes, "Small in scale, leaderless, and carried on by unarmed men, women and children, the food riot rarely consolidated into a larger rebellion" (p. 443).

Only when they were combined with other, broader claims that crossed local lines did conflicts over food produce a national social movement. The various "famine plot" agitations of the eighteenth century (Kaplan 1982) were a premonition of things to come – the revolution of 1789, when "ordinary complaints about the incompetence and/or immorality of the local authorities and merchants . . . took on a political cast" (Tilly 1975: 448). As the Jacobins learned to use the demand for cheap bread to defeat their political opponents, inter-elite conflict merged with and utilized contention on the streets (Schama: 756–7).

Belief

Men and women in early modern Europe did not protest for bread alone. For most of known time, it has been religion and religious conflict that produced collective action. In the centuries following the first millennium after Christ, waves of heretical sects developed within and against the Catholic Church. Some were local and were based on the charisma of a single leader and were easily suppressed. Others, like the Cathars, preached a dissident version of the Trinity and became briefly dominant in areas of Southern France, where it took a brutal Crusade to uproot them. Later ones, like the Camisards, already resemble the social movement (Tilly 1986: 174–8). Existing church organizations provided both the targets and the models for the rebellions of these heretical sects.

Collective actions mounted in the name of religion usually took their shape from the beliefs of the protesters, their actions a savage parody of their opponents' practices. In assaulting Catholics, French Protestants attacked and mimicked Catholic ritual and Catholics responded in kind.[15] The violence and cruelty of these religious conflicts certainly exceeded those of modern class conflict. But with hatred assuaged by blood, and offending practices suppressed, it was only when religious fervor joined with tax revolts, dynastic ambition or interstate conflict that rebels against religion gained access to the tools of the modern social movement.

With the appearance of the modern saint – the first social movement organizer – modern religious movements were born. As Michael Walzer has shown (ch. 1), the Calvinist saint was the forerunner of the modern movement militant. He not only believed deeply in his cause; he turned the mission of converting souls into a profession. The first "corresponding societies" were religious brotherhoods linked by couriers, secret codes and rituals. The first militants to regard themselves as the vanguard of a revolution were these missionary saints. But until then, religious movements ranged from physical attacks against Jews, Protestants, Catholics and heretics to the sporadic guerilla resistance of the Camisards.

Land

Almost as common as food riots and religious conflicts were peasant revolts. Traditional peasants depended on customary rights to land, water or forage to survive, and were most easily goaded into revolt when these rights were curtailed or abused. Rights were often claimed in the name of the peasant community whose members would accuse landlords of breaking ancient conventions and usurping signed contracts. Even modern "struggles for the land" frequently hearkened back to usurpations more than a century old.[16]

The forms of land revolt often followed a ritual that took shape around the demands of the landless or the land poor. Peasants brandishing pitchforks and scythes, or carrying the cross or a statue of the Virgin, would assemble in the town square and march to usurped land and "occupy" it. Such outbursts could spread from village to village without common agents or organizations. But once the occupation was over, local groups seldom found a way to organize around broader themes and almost never made common cause with the urban poor.[17] These revolts were, thus, as easy to isolate and snuff out as they had been to spark.

Death

It may be surprising to think of death as a source of collective action. But it is the reaction of the *living* – especially to violent death – that is the source of protest, rather than death itself. Death has the power to trigger violent emotions and bring together people who have little in common but their grief. It provides legitimate ceremonial sites for public gatherings, and is one of the few occasions on which officials will hesitate to charge into a crowd or ban public assemblies.

Death has always been connected to an institutionalized form of collective action – the funeral – that brings people together in ceremony and solidarity. In repressive systems that ban lawful assembly, funeral processions are often the only occasions during which protest can begin. When the death of a friend or relative is seen as an outrage, funeral gatherings can become sites for disruption. When a public figure offends the mores of the community, he can be symbolically killed with a mock funeral.

But the same reasoning tells us why death is seldom the source of a sustained social movement. For death's moment is brief, and the ritual occasion offered by a funeral is soon over. It was only in the nineteenth century, in the context of movements formed for other purposes, that funerals began to be the occasion for sustained mobilization against authorities (Tamason: 15–31). The funeral protest was a major form of mobilization in South Africa in the 1980s. Each time the police would shoot demonstrators, a major funeral demonstration followed.

Bread, belief, land and death: In all four areas of contention, the forms of collective action were violent and direct, brief, specific and linked to the claims of participants. With the exception of religious conflicts – where translocal institutions and common religious beliefs facilitated broader coalitions and greater coordination – the actors in these forms of contention seldom moved beyond local or sectoral confrontations or extended them into sustained interactions with authorities or elites.

It was not for lack of organization that pre-eighteenth-century Europeans failed to build social movements. Indeed, when they were aroused or had the opportunity to do so, they could organize powerfully, as the religious wars of the sixteenth and seventeenth centuries showed. Nor were food rioters or funeral marchers "apolitical": The former were not revolting at famine *per se,* but against evidence that authorities were ignoring their inherited rights; while the latter had the political shrewdness to use a legitimate ceremony to air their grievances.

The major constraint on turning these grievances and the collective actions they triggered into social movements was the limitation of the forms and goals of collective action to people's immediate claims, direct targets and corporate memberships. All this would change between the late-eighteenth and mid-nineteenth centuries. The consolidation of national states, the expansion of roads and printed communications and the growth of private associations were largely responsible for this change. But the mechanism for this development was the appearance of a new and more general repertoire of collective action.

THE MODULAR REPERTOIRE

Bloch's axiom embedding particular forms of collective action in specific social structures, perfectly applicable to the estate societies he studied, could not be extended to the societies that began to emerge in Europe and North America in the eighteenth century. In these societies, a new repertoire developed that was general rather than specific; indirect rather than direct; flexible rather than rigid. Centering around a few key routines of confrontation, it could be adapted to a number of different settings and its elements combined in major campaigns of collective action. Once used and understood, it could be diffused elsewhere and employed on behalf of the broader claims of wider social coalitions. The result was to make it possible for even scattered groups of people who did not know one another to combine in sustained challenges to authorities – in social movements.

Of course, inherited forms of collective action of the past like the *charivari*, the serenade, the illumination and violent attack on enemies' houses did not simply disappear. But as new claims were diffused – together with information about how others had put them into practice – and as people gained enhanced capacities for collective action, even these older forms were infused with more general meanings and combined with newer forms. Three examples, from both sides of the Atlantic world of the late eighteenth century, will illustrate what was happening.

From effigies to boycotts in America

The American colonists brought with them a repertoire of collective action from early modern Europe, and as the political conflict with the mother country gathered force in the early 1760s, their first responses were traditional. When the British tried to impose a new and more onerous stamp duty in 1765, the instinctive response of Bostonians was to hang an effigy of the designated stamp distributor of Massachusetts on the future Liberty Tree in Boston's South End. "In the evening a large crowd paraded the effigy, leveled a small building . . . reputed to be the future Stamp Office, then burned the effigy," writes historian Pauline Maier, "while a smaller contingent attacked the stampman's home" (1972: 54).

The solution was infectious and spread rapidly around the colonies, using the forms inherited from the old country. Mock trials for stamps and stampmen were held, "funerals" were staged for liberty, and effigies were paraded in routines that recalled traditional English repertoires (pp. 54 ff.). Serious rioting was a frequent accompaniment of these proceedings. But by September, with the news that the Ministry of George Grenville had fallen, the wave of violence against the persons and policies of the stamp controversy quickly subsided (p. 61).

During the same period there was also the beginning of a more organized, general and nonphysical form of collective action – the boycott.[18] Colonial merchants first made "nonimportation" agreements against the Sugar Act of 1764, calling for reducing the import of luxury goods from England, above all of the mourning clothes and gloves traditionally worn at funerals. "These fledgling efforts," writes Maier, "were systematized in September 1765 [with the Stamp Act controversy] and thereafter nonimportation associations were organized in other commercial centers" (1972: 74).

The boycott became a basic routine for the rebellious colonists, used in response to virtually every effort of the British to reimpose control. For Americans, "nonimportation could constitute an effective substitute for domestic violence," observes Maier; "opposition could retreat from the streets to the spinning wheel" (p. 75). If giving up mourning could contribute to the fall of a British minister, "what may we not expect from a full and general Execution of this plan?" asked a writer in the *Boston Gazette* (p. 75).

Thenceforth, nonimportation and boycotting became the modular weapons of the American rebellion, employed most clamorously in the controversy over tea that exploded in Boston Harbor in the 1770s.[19] The associations that were formed to effect it were the revolution's first social movement organizations – employing a combination of enforcement and agitation. The effectiveness of the tactic was not lost on the British; in 1791, a boycott was employed against the importation of sugar to put pressure on Parliament for abolition of the slave trade (Drescher 1987: 78–9). From a parochial response to new taxes from the periphery of the British empire, the boycott migrated to its core.

From private to mass petitioning in England[20]

The boycott against slave-grown sugar was only an adjunct to the major British innovation of the late eighteenth century – the transformation of the private petition into a tool of national campaigns of collective action. The petition was an ancient form of seeking redress from patrons or from Parliament on the part of individual suppliants or corporate groups. As such, it was a culturally acceptable, lawful part of the old repertoire and was scarcely contentious.

Petitioning spread rapidly in the early eighteenth century on the part of trades claiming injury from the expansion of the excise tax (Brewer 1989: 233). By the early 1780s, petitioning Parliament was still more of a 'private' than a public act, "tied to the claims of specific injured parties or beneficiaries," in Seymour Drescher's words (1987: 76).[21] But during the two decades between 1770 and 1792, the petition was transformed from the tool of private interests seeking redress, to a public act seeking justice in the name of general moral claims. And where earlier petitions were single acts launched by groups of petitioners, by the 1790s they were being regularly launched at public meetings and accompanied by boycotts, newspaper advertisements and lobbying in extended movement campaigns.

Although Wilkes and others had used petitions for political purposes earlier – for example, a petition preceded the outbreak of the Gordon riots of 1780 – it was the antislavery campaign launched from the city of Manchester that effected its transformation into a modular tool of collective action. Manchester's industrialists had used a petition to demand repeal of the government's revenue plans in the early 1780s. They played a leading role in the petition campaign against a customs union with Ireland a few years later (p. 69). These were interest-borne campaigns, but they created the expertise in Manchester that could, in Drescher's words, "open the sluices of enthusiasm" for issues with broader policy or moral content (p. 69). Bustling – and electorally unrepresented – Manchester businessmen extrapolated the skills developed on behalf of their economic interests to lead a national moral campaign.

The Manchester petition raised by a quantum leap the number of petitions and the numbers of signers who were coordinated in a single campaign. In December 1787, eleven thousand people – almost 20 percent of the city's population at the time – signed the first great abolitionist petition (p. 70). But more important, the men of Manchester used Britain's network of provincial newspapers to advertise their petition in every major newspaper market, triggering a diffusion process that found a resounding echo all over the country (pp. 70–2).

In 1792, a new antislavery campaign quintupled the number of petitions over 1788, "the largest number ever submitted to the House on a single subject or in a single session," according to Drescher (p. 80). The process was, by now, entirely modular, with the collection of petitions, quietly guided by a national committee, organized in town after town, followed by the joint presentation of many local petitions to Parliament, coordinated with Wilberforce's deposition of his abolition motion.

By the 1790s, mass petitions were being used by radicals to demand the expansion of the suffrage and protest the curtailment of free speech (Goodwin 1979). Like the abolitionists, the reform societies coordinated the efforts of different local associations, used the provincial press to gain publicity for their cause and linked the signing of petitions in the country with parliamentary efforts. From the plea from a dependent client to his patron, to a lobby's claim of tax relief, the petition had been transformed into a modular form of collective action to put pressure on government for major policy shifts.

By the 1830s, the decorous presentation of mass petitions was being combined with the collective use of public space to demonstrate the reform movement's strength. In presenting their "people's petitions" to Parliament, the Chartists brought thousands of people into the streets. By April 1848, with revolution breaking out all over Europe and the threat of anarchy in Ireland, this was too much for the government which mobilized 150,000 "voluntary" constables to stop the presentation of the Chartists' petition on Kennington Common.[22] From then on, the mass petition gave way to the mass demonstration and the strike as the major expressions of British popular politics.[23]

The urban insurrection in France

Innovations in the repertoire were not limited to the Anglo–American world – although they were probably easier to free from traditional routines there than on the continent. Even before the French Revolution, a repertoire of urban insurrection was forming in France. It was most forcefully implemented on July 14, 1789 in Paris, but, interestingly enough, the model of an urban insurrection was provincial.

In June 1788, triggered by the Crown's attempt to replace the parlements with a new system of national courts, and exacerbated by local economic distress, a disturbance began in the marketplace of Grenoble. What resulted was the "Day of the Tiles," probably the first fully secular urban insurrection in French history, and a foretaste of what was to come a year later. At first, the forms of collective action used by the Grenoblois were familiar, direct and physical. They attacked buildings and officials at the marketplace, and when troops were sent to quell the riot, they showered them with a rain of roof tiles. But soon after, an urban leadership was formed – assembled illegally – and produced a major manifesto that put pressure on the king to call the Estates General.[24]

In the Grenoble events, we see a premonition of something resembling the modern social movement. A variety of forms of collective action were employed in a sequence of contentious conflicts with elites and authorities. A social movement organization emerged at a meeting at the Chateau of Vizelle, in which the claims of upper class *parlementaires,* middle class writers and clerks, artisans, glovemakers and women were merged under a broader umbrella of rights. In the words of the latter group, the main demand was "the return of our magistrates, privileges and the reestablishment of the conditions which alone can make true laws" (Schama: 279).

At first what the Grenoblois sought was no more than continued employment for the army of clerks, writers and lawyers who made their living off the Parlement of Dauphiné and were threatened by the Crown's attempt to circumvent the parliamentary courts, as well as economic relief for the glovemakers. But the doctrine of natural rights that was enunciated in the course of the struggle went much further than posts or gloves. In addition to dignifying and uniting the claims of a coalition of social actors, it established the idea that a wholly unauthorized assembly, acting in the name of "the laws and the people," could demand a contractual relationship with the state that went far beyond parliamentary privilege or economic relief (Egret 1977: 177). By 1788, the rough outlines of a new and modular repertoire facilitating sustained interaction with the state around general claims and solidarities was emerging in France.

The boycott, the mass petition and the urban insurrection: These and other modern forms of collective action had already appeared when the Great Event of the French Revolution broke out in 1789. What they had in common was that they were indirect, flexible and autonomous of the claims and antagonisms of established collective actors. They were facilitated by – and helped to create – movement networks that mounted and diffused collective action in the name of general claims in contentious interaction with powerholders, as can be seen with the case of the revolution that Tocqueville witnessed in 1848.

The social construction of the barricade

The most dramatic and most feared expression of the European movements of the nineteenth century was the armed insurrection on behalf of popular sovereignty and the barricade that became its main instrument. Barricades first appeared in Paris when neighborhoods protected themselves by stretching chains across the road to keep intruders out. The term itself evolved after 1588 when these defenses were reinforced by filling barrels *(barriques)* with earth or paving stones.[25]

At the beginning, writes Marc Traugott, barricades "were the collaborative creations of the members of small-scale communities, often directed against the representatives of constituted authorities" (1990: 3). By the 1830 revolution, they appeared as offensive strongpoints in the streets of Paris where people were recruited on a largely local basis. But by the February Days in the 1848 Revolution, although they occupied much the same positions as they had in 1830 (Traugott 1990: 6), barricades attracted a large number of "cosmopolitans" from other neighborhoods of Paris (pp. 8–9). By this time, they were no longer local, but had become trans-neighborhood instruments of defense and mobilization, erected at the culmination of a march and constructed by groups of demonstrators who came to well-known sites for the purpose.

Like the demonstration, the barricade had an internal as well as an external function. As they faced off against hostile troops or national guardsmen, the defenders of a barricade came to know each other as comrades, developed a division of labor of fighters, builders and suppliers, and formed social networks that would bring their survivors together in future confrontations. As Traugott writes,

from a vantage point atop a barricade, an entire generation of revolutionists was formed in the struggle against the Bourbon and Orleanist monarchies; matured in the struggles of the Second Republic; and saw its political aspirations crushed by the coup that ushered in the rule of Louis Napoleon. (p. 3)

As insurrections spread across Europe in the wake of the February Days, it became clear that the barricade was modular. It was not limited to any particular grievance or social group; it could bring people together on behalf of varied claims; and it attacked the state rather than private targets. If barricades were built to claim the Republic in Paris in February, they were erected in April to express disappointment with the results of the elections in Rouen, by Parisian workers in June to protest the closing of the national workshops, and later, to express outrage at the sending of French troops to suppress the Republic of Rome and put the pope back on his throne.

France was not far ahead of its neighbors. From February to the middle of 1849, barricades appeared as far apart as Madrid and Lisbon, Messina and Milan, Berlin and Vienna (Godechot 1971; Soule and Tarrow 1991). In Vienna, they went up to demand constitutional reform, in Sicily to demand independence from Naples, in Milan and Venice to end Austrian rule, and in the smaller Po valley towns to unite with Piedmont.

The barricade was so well known by 1848, and its use so well understood, that it spread faster than a man could travel by coach from Paris to Milan. As Verdi wrote to Piave on his return to Italy, eager to take part in his country's revolution,

Guess whether I wanted to stay in Paris when I heard the news of Milan's Revolution? I left as promptly as possible, but I arrived only in time to see those fantastic barricades![26]

SMALL CHANGE AND GREAT EVENTS

Great events like the Stamp Act controversy, the abolition of the British slave trade and the French Revolution are the crucibles out of which new political cultures are born (Sewell 1990). Many of the future changes in the repertoire of collective action appeared in such events. But most of them first developed in the interstices of the day-to-day practice of contentious politics – like the mass petition that was first employed by trade associations in Britain, and the barricade that was first used to defend Parisian neighborhoods from thieves.

From the point of view of the repertoire of popular politics, "Great Events" are often only the public stage on which structural changes that have unobtrusively germinated in the body politic become manifest. If we look only at collective action in such events, we may miss the structural changes that occur beneath the surface that are more general, and predate their eruption on the scene of history. The change from the traditional repertoire to the new one is a case in point. Where the old repertoire had been direct, inflexible and corporate based, the new one was indirect, flexible and based on forms of association created for struggle. Where the former segmented grain seizures, religious conflicts, land wars and funeral processions from one another and from elite politics, the latter made it possible for workers, peasants, artisans, clerks, writers, lawyers and aristocrats to march under the same banner and confront the national state in uneasy coalition. These changes facilitated the national social movement and more as well.

The first important effect was on the possibility of sustaining collective action. As the new forms of collective action became known, they helped to overcome the episodic and localized character of popular protest, and facilitated the formation of coalitions across localities and among people who didn't know one another. Through boycotts, mass petitions, marches and demonstrations, strikes and sit-ins, adherents could be mobilized, bystanders impressed, and campaigns organized against opponents for considerable periods of time. Indeed, while it is the single, dramatic "Event" that has captured historians' attentions, it is the capacity of social movements to produce sustained sequences of collective actions against powerful opponents that mark them off from the riots, charivaris and illuminations of the past.

The second great change was the appearance of deliberate movement organizations designed for mounting campaigns, mobilizing people within them and keeping them going without benefit of the material incentives that ordinary secondary associations could offer. Unlike more conventional associations, these rough-hewn organizations were the product of struggle. They specialized in struggle, and they engaged ordinary people in collective action through forms of struggle that excited and amused them and at times transformed their lives.

Each form produced a characteristic organization of collective action: The boycott produced the nonimportation association; the strike the strike committee; the barricade the cadre of defenders, scouts and provisioners; and the demonstration the organizers, speakers and parade marshals who remain the stock-in-trade of social movements today (Favre 1990). Through the efforts of an army of movement entrepreneurs, militants and publicists, the idea and practice of movement spread around the world.

The third great change was the increased capacity of movements to be diffused from their epicenters. This was a function of movement associations and print media as I shall argue in the next chapter. But it was also the result of the known, flexible and inclusive forms of collective action that people learned of and could deploy for a variety of purposes in combination with different allies and against different opponents.

The combination of known forms, movement organizations and diffusion culminated in the movement cycles that recurred at irregular intervals from 1830 on. Based on the elements outlined above, collective action could spread to more groups and localities, and be sustained for much longer than the episodic and cathartic collective actions of the past. As word of successful – and learnable – collective actions spread to other social groups and across national boundaries, movements developed a rolling, spiraling dynamic. On occasion, these cycles combined with economic and international crises and elite cleavages to produce revolutions.

The newly found power in movement had a profound impact on the structure of institutional politics. For if in the short run, people challenging authority frightened elites and brought down repression on their heads, over the longer run the new repertoire increased the leverage of groups within the system to challenge rulers and elevate their own power or privileges. As in the revolutions of 1848, the 1919–21 strike wave and the movements of the 1960s, what began as cycles of protest were usually completed by elites and authorities – sometimes in directions that left their initiators disillusioned, divided or dead.

As for national states, which at first reacted to the new forms of collective action with incomprehension and repression, they eventually developed strategies of social control and accommodation that turned some of the new repertoire into conventional politics. The strike became an institution of collective bargaining; the demonstration was covered by a body of law that distinguished it from criminal activity; and the sit-in and building occupation were eventually treated with greater leniency than ordinary delinquency. Public assembly, though at first repressed and surrounded with legal inhibitions, came to be regarded as a component of modern politics protected by constitutional guarantees.

How did these changes come about and why did they begin when they did? Particular events, to be sure, had profound effects in providing models of collective action and collective consciousness. Although they left their mark on the changes we have identified, we must look beneath the surface of such events for the causes of such powerful changes in popular politics. In the next two chapters, I will turn to the causes of these changes. They were associated with the coming of capitalism, the spread of literacy and the increased availability of cheap newspapers. But more than anything, they were triggered by developments in the formation of the modern state.

3

Print, association and the diffusion of movement

Social movements as we know them today began to appear during the course of the eighteenth century. They drew their substance from structural changes that were associated with capitalism but which preceded widespread industrialization. The major changes were the development of commercial print media and new models of association and socialization. These changes did not, in themselves, produce new grievances and conflicts, but they diffused new ways of thinking about them and helped ordinary people think of themselves as part of broader collectivities and on the same plane as their betters.

Increasingly, popular newspapers and printed songs and pamphlets diffused images of ruler and aristocrat on the same sheets of paper as bourgeois and plebeian, mechanic and tradesman, city dweller and rural notable. Associational forms that first developed around church and commerce were adapted to reading clubs, reform groups and antislavery associations that embodied moral purposes. Latent conflicts between people and their opponents were transposed into pamphlet wars, ribald songs and scatological cartoons and prints. If the Queen of France could be portrayed in print in a compromising position,[1] how long could the King remain sacrosanct? And if aristocrats and commoners could meet in the same coffee shops and reading clubs, how long would it be until they engaged in collective action in common?

In the European past, corporate solidarities and face-to-face communications had nurtured episodic outbursts of collective action. Religious conflicts produced wars and revolutions and broadened the ideological frameworks of peasant uprisings and tax revolts. But from the eighteenth century on, new forms of association, regular communications linking center and periphery and the spread of print and literacy produced a secular change. Print and association made it easier for people in widely scattered towns and regions to know of one another's actions, and join across wide social and geographic divides, diffusing conflict into national social movements.

Western Europe was the crucible in which many of these trends were self-consciously analyzed and their implications propagated: But they first appeared among the Americans who – with characteristic absentmindedness – promptly forgot what they had bequeathed to the rest of the world.[2] As in our own century, when the most sharply drawn contradictions have developed on the periphery of the world system, the reach of the state was weaker, the social contradictions more sharply etched and the prerequisites for a national social movement more well developed in Britain's North American colonies than in Europe, itself, as the following example shows.[3]

When American colonists first began to object to the attempts of the British to make them pay for the cost of the Seven Years' War, their actions resembled traditional forms of English resistance: with burning of effigies in Boston's South End and nearby towns like Newport; with ritual shamings and levelings of future stamp office sites (Maier 1972: 54; Wood 1991: 244–5). But not long after the first mob actions broke out, radicals in commercial centers along the coast began to organize a campaign of opposition centering on the intimidation of officials and the boycott of British goods. And after the Townshend Acts of 1767 provoked a new wave of resistance, organization spread along the coast.

Although the major protests were limited to the coastal towns with few echoes in the western districts, the movement was soon diffused to a wide spectrum of social and economic groups. The groups that formed to concert resistance to the Stamp Act worked self-consciously to broaden their social bases and to limit violence (Maier 1972: 87).[4] Although the social composition of the movement was diverse, its repertoire of collective action was quite uniform. Effigies, marches to designated "liberty trees" and especially the forced resignation of stamp officials predominated. In Georgia, the stampman avoided the humiliation of being forced to resign (p. 55) but the pattern that had been set in Boston spread as far south as Virginia and Carolina. Though intimidation was widespread, violence was abhorred and "criteria of purpose and constraint were applied to extralegal crowd action" (p. 53).

What explains the rapid diffusion, the broad social composition and the tactical uniformity of the anti-stamp tax movement? In part, of course, the nature of the colonists' grievances conditioned the nature of their actions. If stamp duties were to be required for a wide range of legal and colonial documents, an obvious riposte was to assemble a coalition of those who would be affected by the duty and attack the officials charged with distributing the stamps. This, in itself, could produce a common response throughout the colonies.

But there was more than the instinctively similar reactions of aggrieved people involved. For one thing, mechanics and publicans, milkmen and the children of indentured servants – people who might never need to use a stamp – joined in the movement (Countryman 1981: 59). For another, transforming a grievance into a collective action is never automatic; a great deal of communication and conscious planning is involved as well. Both the broad social composition of the movement and its repertoire were the products of print, association and the deliberate diffusion of information and opinion that they allowed, and this made the movement quintessentially modern.

Although much of America was still rural in 1765, the coastal towns were linked by ship, road, newspaper and private correspondence, and news of the stamp controversy spread rapidly by stage, circuit riders and especially through the press. The role of the press in diffusing word of the first crowd actions was most striking. A New York article describing the August 19 events in Boston was quickly reprinted in Philadelphia and Portsmouth. On August 22, the *New York Gazette* was reporting similar actions in New Jersey, while on August 24, a Providence newspaper described the events in Connecticut, and the *Boston Gazette* published letters from Newport (Maier 1972: 56–7).

The Stamp Act controversy also touched off a flurry of pamphleteering in which basic American positions in constitutional theory were staked out for the coming revolution (Bailyn: 1). But it also showed the future role of the press in reporting on and propagating models of collective action. By December 1765, even something like a set of directives for opposing the stamp duty had appeared in the New York and Boston *Gazettes,* calling for restraint, justice, and a unifying focus on the tax (Maier 1972: 65–6).

Association was a complementary source for the rapid spread and tactical uniformity of the movement. The first signs of organization had appeared as early as the August 14, 1765 events in Boston, where a merchants' social club, called "The Loyal Nine," planned the effigies and the march and became the core of the town's future Sons of Liberty (p. 58). Elsewhere as well, preexisting social and political organizations – volunteer fire companies, artillery companies and religious associations – transformed themselves into Sons of Liberty. In the case of the Charleston Fire Company, they simply continued under their original name (p. 85).[5]

As the movement spread, methods for coercing opponents were refined and regularized. Although there were threats and ultimata in New Jersey and Virginia, in most places, concludes Maier, "threats were moderated from violent punishment to ostracism of Stamp Act supporters" (p. 73). Even in Boston, where violence first broke out, so much control was imposed by radical leaders that "even the Governor had to admit that 'the greatest order was observed' " (p. 69). With the development of the strategy of the boycott, associations to enforce it became the major instruments of collective action (p. 74).

In a way, these moves were more frightening than the mobs and rioting that had preceded them. "What alarmed the gentry," writes Gordon Wood, "were the growing ideologically backed claims by ordinary people to a share in the actual conduct of government" (p. 244). By early 1766, a loose network of Sons of Liberty associations had been created to enforce the boycott. These committees dissolved when the act was repealed. But when British obduracy reemerged, a new network of correspondence committees appeared to spread news of British actions and to concert opposition to them. The committees that were formed under the Continental Association of 1774 began in this way but were already agents of revolutionary government.

What can the story of the Stamp Act controversy tell us about the birth of the national social movement? First, it indicates that the mechanisms that created the social movement did not need to await the European Industrial Revolution or the French social one – they were available on the periphery of the European world before either revolution was imagined. Second, it shows how print and association worked together to construct a controversy and give people information about how to deal with it. And third, it shows how printed sources and associations diffused collective action to broad coalitions of social actors who were able to confront an empire in many places at once; and in doing so, build a national social movement.

A REVOLUTION IN PRINT[6]

The spread of literacy was a crucial determinant of the rise of popular politics.[7] Without the capacity to read, potential insurgents would have found it hard to learn of the actions of others with similar claims – except by word of mouth.[8] But literacy *per se* was less responsible for the spread of social movements than was the increasing ownership of books, and readership of newspapers and pamphlets that were spreading to social sectors that had formerly done little reading (Chartier 1991: 69).

Increased demand for reading matter was part outcome and part cause of the changes in the production and diffusion of commercial printing (Chartier 1991: 70ff.; Darnton 1989). While a peasant who could sign his name to a parish register might or might not have the self-confidence to claim his rights, a man who had invested in expensive publishing equipment had a commercial motive to produce news for a mass audience. Out of the audiences for the products of commercial print, invisible communities of discourse were formed.[9] In places like The Hague, Lausanne and Philadelphia, men found both work and profit in the production of books, newspapers, pamphlets and cartoons.

One example of these "new men" was particularly notable. In 1774 a failed English excise worker named Thomas Paine stepped off a boat in Philadelphia with a letter of introduction from Benjamin Franklin to Robert Aiken, a well-known printer in the town. In England, Paine had been an "apprenticed stay-maker, teacher, petty official, tobacconist, journalist and 'an ingenious person.' " But for the American Revolution and his role in it, he would probably have died a failure, or perhaps been remembered only as one of those "inventive spirits" that the Enlightenment produced.[10]

What made Paine's impact on history so great was not only his role in two revolutions – the American and the French – but his extraordinary success as a publicist. He did this, as Hobsbawm observes, three separate times: first in

1776, with the publication of *Common Sense;* then in 1791, with his defence of the French Revolution, *The Rights of Man;* and again, in 1794 in Britain, when "his *Age of Reason* became the first book to say flatly, in language comprehensible to the common people, that the Bible was not the word of God."[11]

Paine arrived in a country that was literally covered in printed paper.[12] It was in the form of pamphlets that the democratic implications of print appeared. "Highly flexible, easy to manufacture, and cheap, pamphlets were printed in the American colonies wherever there were printing presses, intellectual ambitions and political concerns" (Bailyn: 4). More than four hundred pamphlets bearing on the Anglo-American controversy were published between 1750 and 1776 (p. 8). By the time Paine arrived in the colonies, pamphlet wars were a familiar part of the political landscape.[13]

The new journalism was *obliged* to appeal to a mass market in order to compete economically. When the *Pennsylvania Magazine* increased its subscriptions, Paine wrote to Franklin with satisfaction. When Part Two of *The Rights of Man* sold well, he invested his royalties in a cheaper edition to sell more copies. "Political independence and increased circulation were . . . the chief leit–motifs of Paine's career," concludes Elizabeth Eisenstein (p. 198). The same could be said of the whole new enterprise of commercial printing. "In a rather special sense," writes Benedict Anderson, "the book was the first modern-style mass-produced industrial commodity" and the newspaper "a book sold on a colossal scale . . . a one-day bestseller" (1991: 34–5).

By the middle of the eighteenth century, there began a "drive to tap new print markets, which differentiated the profit-seeking printer from the manuscript book dealer" and "worked against elitism and favoured democratic as well as heterodox trends."[14] After 1760, French booksellers began to open *cabinets de lecture* which "enabled subscribers to read extensively while spending little and made prohibited titles discreetly available" (Chartier 1991: 70). If reading increased commerce, the converse was also true: In America, notes Gordon Wood, "the strongest motive behind people's learning to read and write, even more than the need to understand the scriptures, was the desire to do business" (p. 313).

The francophone press that was established outside the borders of France typified the intersection of profit and politics. On the one hand, clandestine publications intended for the French market allowed the small principalities and city–states on France's borders to enrich their coffers; on the other, printers and publishers had a free hand to produce books that were too subversive to be published in France. The "neutrality" of these entrepreneurs was as subversive as capitalism, and for the same reason – in the name of profit, it nurtured indifference to the claims of any religious creed or dynastic cause (Eisenstein: 194). When French booksellers asked for works of philosophy from the Société Typographique de Neuchâtel, the Swiss publisher responded; "We don't carry any, but we know where to find them and can supply them when we are asked to."[15]

Communities of print

The expansion of commercial publishing for a mass market triggered a competitive capitalist cycle. Editors and publishers competed to attract new audiences, vying to involve readers in their enterprises and creating invisible communities of print. "By means of letters to the editor and other devices," writes Eisenstein, "the periodical press opened up a new kind of public forum" and helped to create something like a public opinion – well before the French Revolution broke out (pp. 196–7). The *Encyclopédie* was only the most successful of a number of networks that linked publishers and readers, intellectuals and lay people, metropole and provinces. Such journals as the English *Present State of the Republick of Letters,* which imitated Pierre Bayle's *Nouvelles de la République des Lettres,* "extended lifelines to isolated subscribers" and "conveyed a new sense of forward movement to their readership" (p. 196).

A new kind of social life developed around the reading and exchange of books and printed papers. In France, even provincial cities like Besançon had public libraries and reading clubs. Small towns, like Saint-Amour in the Beaujolais, asked permission of the authorities "to rent a room where they could meet, read gazettes and newspapers and indulge in games of chance." Even in conservative Franche-Comté, the clergy was busy promoting the distribution of religious publications among the peasantry (Vernus 1989: 127).

If books were the first mass-produced commodity, newspapers were its most subversive extension. If a man could read about a great event on the same day as thousands of others he didn't know, he and they were part of the same invisible community of readers. And if a newspaper described the actions of rulers and dignitaries in the same language it used to discuss the doings of merchants and traders, the status of rulers and readers was brought closer together.

Rather than emanating authoritatively from above, newspaper information circulated horizontally. "Newspapers spoke polyphonically," writes Anderson of a later time and place, "in a hurly-burly of editorialists, cartoonists, news agencies, columnists . . . satirists, speech-makers, and advertisers, *amongst whom* government order-givers had to jostle elbow to elbow" (1991: 31, 34–5).

First created in the capital, newspapers spread to the provinces to report on doings in the metropole. "Such provincial newspapers," writes Donald Read, "helped to build up knowledge outside London of parliamentary and London politics, filling their columns not so much with local news as with news and comment copied from the London press, especially from the lively journals of the Opposition" (p. 19). But the provincial press soon became a vehicle for reporting on local news and expressing local attitudes. As a result, by the 1760s, provincial readers were well schooled in opposition politics, and this helps to explain why so many rose up in support of Wilkes in the 1770s and responded so rapidly to antislavery a decade later.

By the early nineteenth century, there would even be a modest attempt to found a "pauper press" in London. Given the economic and educational impediments that these papers faced, the number of copies they sold was modest, but the habit of reading aloud in groups meant that their influence extended well beyond their circulation. Their main period of growth in England was during the 1830s, when middle class reform movements were particularly active.[16] Their titles reveal their inflammatory nature: "Destructive," "Gauntlet," "Working Man's Friend," "Slap at the Church" were some of the most sensational (Hollis: ch. 7).

Revolutionary episodes were fertile ground for the creation of new journals. The campaign for the Estates General in France loosed a torrent of publications. The catalogue of the Bibliothèque Nationale lists 184 periodicals publishing in Paris, alone, in 1789 and 335 in 1790 (J. Popkin: 150). The February 1848 Revolution had a similar effect, but on an international scale. It spawned some 200 new journals in Paris, a wave of new newspapers in German – many as far away as the United States – and in Italy, over one hundred journals were registered in Florence alone.[17] While newspapers circulated the idea of movement, movements expanded the market for print.

By their very mastheads, newspapers announced themselves agents of movement. As Anderson discovered for Java in the early twentieth century, the founding of a journal called "The World on the Move" was rapidly followed by that of "Islam on the Move," "Workers on the Move" and "The People on the Move" (1990: 32). Through print, people as far apart as Messina and Warsaw, St. Petersburg and Beijing could imagine themselves not only as Italians, Poles, Russians and Chinese, but as Jacobins and *sans-culottes,* radicals and communists, and their enemies as the feudatories and rentiers, aristocrats and capitalists who were being trounced a world away.

The popular press did not so much make rebellion heroic as make it ordinary. If Philadelphians in 1773 could read in the New York papers about the rebellion brewing up North, rebellion became thinkable in the Quaker colony (Ryerson: 43–4). If Norfolk's citizens could read how thousands in Manchester signed petitions against slavery, it became intolerable to allow slavers to go unblamed in Norfolk (Drescher 1982). And if a man could read in his national press about how insurgents in another country overthrew their ruler, ruler overthrow became conceivable everywhere. As Anderson (1991) writes of the French Revolution,

. . . once it had occurred, it entered the accumulating memory of print. . . . The experience was shaped by millions of printed words into a 'concept' on the printed page, and, in due course, into a model. (p. 80)

ASSOCIATIONS AND MOVEMENT NETWORKS

People have always come together in associations, both religious and secular. But until the late eighteenth century, corporate and communal organizations predominated in European society. These, as William Sewell argues for the case of France, were aimed more at the defense of established and communal privileges than at the acquisition of new rights and benefits (1980; 1990). Rather than bringing people together on behalf of emergent or contingent interests, corporate and communal ties divided them into insulated pockets that emphasized identities and differences and not broader solidarities and common interests. In any case, these corporate ties were limited to solid burghers, trade guilds and clerics and left most of the poor outside their protection.

During the eighteenth century, a new kind of association developed to help occupational groups protect themselves against state pressure, and to influence the passage of legislation in their favor. In England, the expansion of the excise tax stimulated such groups as early as 1697 for the leather trades, 1717 for tanners, and for glassmakers and brewers by the 1760s. "The levying of indirect taxes," writes John Brewer of these groups (1989: 233), "encouraged the emergence of organizations which transcended local and regional boundaries."

By the last quarter of the eighteenth century, a rich and varied associational life was developing in both Europe and North America. In England, there were religious associations, such as the Quaker London Meeting and the nonconformist Protestant Dissenting Deputies; trade associations, like the Society of West India Merchants or the Virginia Merchants; and commercial, industrial and manufacturing lobbies, like the Midland Association of Ironmasters: All of these had permanent agents and meeting places (p. 231). Government officials came to depend on them for information, and they, in turn, cultivated contacts with ministers and members of Parliament to improve their chances of gaining favorable treatment (pp. 232–4). But association would not remain within such narrow precincts for very long.

The modularity of association

Once developed, the private secondary association could not be limited to religious or commercial purposes. England, where new forms of association grew out of earlier commercial and religious models, was way ahead of the continent. The antislavery agitation of the 1780s first appeared among the dissenting sects before spreading to Manchester's industrial interests (Drescher 1987: 61–3). The Yorkshire Association expanded the use of correspondence committees like those which had been used earlier by the commercial lobbies (Read 1964). O'Connell's Catholic Association adopted the subscription tactic of the lobbies, asking members to contribute a penny a year for emancipation. The Catholics' success was not lost on the parliamentary reformers, who used subscriptions to finance the Political Unions that extracted the Reform Act of 1832 (Tilly 1982). The special purpose association had become a modular form of social organization.

England's American colonies were in advance of the metropole in the spread of movement organizations. With the hardening of British financial policy towards the colonists in the 1770s, a new wave of committees and associations were formed to resist British pressure. Association was no longer limited to merchants and traders; in 1772, the mechanics of Philadelphia formed a Patriotic Society, which Wood describes as the first organized nonreligious public pressure group in Pennsylvania's history (p. 244). This was followed by similar moves in New York and Massachusetts in 1773, culminating in the formation of the Continental Association of 1774.[18] By the time the guns were fired at Lexington and Concord, a national network of associations, couriers and spies was in place and word of the confrontation spread astonishingly quickly up and down the coast.[19]

As in England, in America religion was a cradle for associational development. Habits and forms of association that were learned in prayer meetings were applied to moral crusades and then to civic and social movements. This can be seen in the militant evangelical protestantism of the Second Great Awakening. When historian Paul E. Johnson examined the social structure of the newly established city of Rochester, he found that by 1830, it already possessed a rich network of religious associations (1978).

What was interesting in Rochester was not that a new town on the Erie Canal already had a large number of churches. After all, churches had been the organizing matrices of local society in New England for two hundred years. What was remarkable was how easily special-purpose associations were formed across denominational lines for secular purposes.[20] Such temporary coalitions would be instrumental in the moral crusades of the later nineteenth century. It was from the associational crucible of evangelical protestantism that such movements as anti-masonry, sabbatarianism, temperance, evangelical revivalism and its most revolutionary product – abolitionism – arose.[21] The newest social actors in American popular movements – women – first organized in church groups and then gained experience in movements like temperance, abolitionism and feminism (Cott 1977).

Movement networks

The informal social networks that lay at the heart of these associations were potential centers of collective action. This was even more important in France, where legislation dating from the revolutionary *Le Chapelier* law restricted combination. French guilds and corporations had been legal bodies, regulating trade and restricting practices; but workers' corporations and *compagnonnages* were illegal. With the liquidation of guilds by the Revolution, the workers' combinations remained, but outside the law. It was only in the 1830s – and then briefly – that they took legal form, and their repression after 1834 left the workers to organize in clandestine networks until 1848 opened up new opportunities (Sewell 1986).

The same was true in rural areas. Like the English coffee houses, the *chambrées* that developed in the Midi in the 1840s were places where a man could drink with his friends without having to pay the hated tax on alcohol. Never a formal system of association, they were rather a set of similar informal groupings modeled on the social *cercles* of upper status Frenchmen. Though not organized for political purposes, they had enough in common to permit them to become centers of collective action when the opportunity arose. In such settings, republican newspapers could be read, a sense of solidarity developed and the occasional traveler dropped by with news of what was happening in the wider world.

At first tolerated by authorities, the *chambrées* came to be feared as potential sites for the instigation of collective action. "For the lower classes of Provence," concludes Maurice Agulhon, "to set themselves up as a *chambrée* was, just as much and perhaps even more than learning to read, to become accessible to whatever was new, to change and to independence" (p. 150). The *chambrées* would prove to be key centers of recruitment for the Montagnard societies that sparked the 1851 Insurrection against Louis Napoleon's coup d'état (Margadant 1979).

Informal groups like the *chambrées* help us to understand the subversive role that movement networks played in spreading models of collective action. Painites, radicals and reformers in England; Whigs and radicals in the American colonies; liberals, republicans and *montagnards* in France; *carbonari* and freemasons in Italy: They used the tools of association developed by commercial, religious and reformist groups when they were legal but could relapse into informal networks in times of demobilization.

Less easily infiltrated by the police than formal associations and less subject to factionalization, movement networks had advantages during a time when governments were becoming increasingly wary of combination. They could develop and reside within friendship and family networks, "lying low" during times of repression and emerging actively during times of stress or opportunity.[22] They were difficult to repress and control, for who could complain if a man wanted to drink with his friends in a private house or in back of a café?

The persistence of such groups and networks during periods of repression suggests that – even where open organization was permitted – what counted was the interpersonal solidarities that underlay these organizations rather than the organizations themselves. Even a well-organized group could quickly collapse if it was not based on a well-woven network of militants, while a network of militants held together by ties of sociability could carry a movement through hard times without benefit of organization. The role of informal movement networks helps to explain why even the most formidable movement organizations today can quickly collapse, and how movements can arise with no obvious organizational framework, as we will see in Chapter 8.

COMMUNITIES OF PRINT AND ASSOCIATION

If print and association were complementary channels in which movement networks could develop, together they made for an explosive combination. As Eisenstein notes of the reading clubs and corresponding societies of the eighteenth century, they had no fixed numbers of members and, in the case of informal gatherings, no membership at all. But readers of the *Encyclopédie* and other such periodicals were conscious of a common identity.[23] To subscribe to such a journal linked them to unknown others with similar views in invisible communities whose amplitude could only be imagined and could easily be exaggerated – as their publishers had ample reason to do.

By the time of the French Revolution, this intersection between print and association was explicit. Eisenstein observes that "to a greater extent than is often appreciated, the events of 1788–9 in France hinged on both a suspension of governmental controls over the printed word and on the freeing of associations" (p. 191). At the same time as the government was convoking the Estates General, it legalized Parisian clubs and freed a number of booksellers and printers from jail, resulting in what Lefebvre calls "an outpouring of pamphlets that astonished contemporaries."[24] What followed was the first deliberate public opinion campaign in history.

England was both more pacific and more advanced in the use of print to propagandize associational causes. By the late eighteenth century, reform associations were becoming skilled in using the press to advance their views. As a strategic directive from the London to the Sheffield Corresponding Society put it:

... if every [reform] society in the island will send forward a petition, we shall ultimately gain ground, for as much as it will force the members of the senate repeatedly to discuss the subject, and their deliberations, printed in the different newspapers, will most naturally awaken the public mind towards the object of our purpose. (Read: 45)

The link between print and association was, if anything, even more explicit in America. For example, according to Maier, during the Stamp Act controversy, the Sons of Liberty in Connecticut "instructed local groups to 'publish their proceedings in the *New London Gazette*.' " The same was true in Rhode Island and New York. Printers were active members of the Sons of Liberty in Boston, Rhode Island and Pennsylvania. Long after the Sons were dissolved in 1766, "these papers and others like them . . . remained a forum for public discussion" (Maier 1972: 90–1).

DIFFUSION BY SOCIAL COALITION

The role of print and association in the diffusion of collective action helps to put in a different light the role of social class in the first social movements.

Observers of nineteenth century movements have had a fixation on their class basis – first with respect to the French Revolution, which had to be either "bourgeois" or not based on class at all (Furet 1981); and then, with respect to the formation of the modern English working class. Early English workers were not easy to distinguish from their artisan and journeyman antecedents: When the two groups cooperated in the popular movements of the late eighteenth and early nineteenth centuries, either the coincidence was thought to be accidental – like ships passing in the night – or the result of a "declining" social formation being absorbed into its "rising" successor.

The result has been the same in both cases: to obfuscate the important degree of *interclass* coordination of collective action among diverse and often divergent sectors of the population. It was through the diffusion of information that claims were coordinated and collective action co-occurred among social groups with different social interests and identities. Both print and association played a key role in this diffusion process.

Karl Marx was the first to propagate the view that *the* social movement of the nineteenth century would be class based. He thought that as capitalism produced a more and more socialized mode of production, the resulting homogeneity of the working class would counteract its tendency to fractionation and competition. When intellectuals joined their efforts to those of the workers, they were "leaving" their class of origin as a sign of the coming collapse of capitalism (Tucker, ed., p. 481). When different classes formed coalitions – as in the *Eighteenth Brumaire of Louis Bonaparte* – it was the result of an intermediate stage of development that History would soon render provisional (pp. 604 ff.).

But the societies that produced the movements we have encountered in this and the last chapter were not yet the homogeneous industrial societies that Marx saw in the future of capitalism and were no longer the estate societies that preceded them. How did they produce such powerful social movements as British abolition, American independence and French revolution without the cleavages produced by industrial capitalism or the solidarities produced by class? The answer is that the loose ties created by print and association, and by newspapers and informal social networks, made possible a degree of coordinated collective action that the supposedly "strong ties" of social class could not have accomplished.

Weak ties and strong movements

It is not that the strong ties of homogeneous groups of workers or artisans at the base of social movements were unimportant; in institutional settings like the factory or the mine, class could be the basis of the primary solidarities of a social movement. The problem is that, when it came to forming broader social movements, class homogeneity was rare and what movements needed were *networks of ties among different and interdependent social groups and localit-*

ies. Class solidarity was a tool in mounting strikes, but it was much less important – and it could be even counterproductive – in the sustained interactions with authorities that successful movements required.

Even in relatively homogeneous England, it was not dense concentrations of industrial workers that produced the most militant movements of the early nineteenth century, but heterogeneous communities of artisans, mechanics and craftsmen.[25] In colonial America, the patriot movement deliberately broadened its ranks to include representatives of different religious associations, mechanics and even ethnic representatives (Wood p. 245). In France the sans-culottes were an interclass collection of "tradesmen, wineshop intellectuals, lawyers, officials and professionals and occasional wage earners" (Schama: 901), and not the homogeneous lower class grouping that earlier scholars had imagined (Soboul 1964).

By emphasizing the internal development of class, the Marxists misspecified a crucial factor in the great movements of their time: That they were interclass networks of democratic workers, literate artisans and middle class radicals whose power came from the fact that they could challenge authorities from different angles. To put this in more sociological terms, Marx thought the socialist movement needed to be based on the strong ties of a homogeneous working class. But the ties of homogeneous groups are more likely to produce cliques and factions – inimical to the process of broader mobilization – than large-scale collective action (Granovetter 1973). Weak ties among social networks that were not unified, but were in some way interdependent, produced a broader matrix for national movements than even the strongest ties of workbench or family.[26] Print and association helped to weave those ties into national social movements.

CONCLUSIONS

Primary associations and face-to-face contacts provide solidarity for collective action among people who know and trust one another. But print, association and coalitional campaigns of collective action build solidarity among larger numbers of people and help to diffuse movements to new publics. They thus permit the formation of loose, often contingent social coalitions, sympathetic or parallel issues and broad movement cycles.

Because of their narrower range, it is easy for historians to characterize the localities and the actors found in earlier waves of collective action. Thus, geographer Andrew Charlesworth was able to characterize English riots from 1548 to 1900, delimiting their social actors and pinpointing their geographical sites with great accuracy (1983). The reason for this is that most of these encounters involved a particular social category of people living in a limited territorial space, and making a distinct set of claims on others. Their local or corporate ties gave them the confidence and the communications to attack others simultaneously or in a rapid series of assaults. But the same strength of local or corporate ties limited their capacity to spread elsewhere or to form coalitions with other social categories.

Sometime during the eighteenth century, we begin to see a broadening of claims, a more sustained capacity to mount collective actions and a wider geographic and social reach. Pauline Maier found it in the cross-class and intercolonial spread of tax resistance in America in the 1760s (1972: 69, 87). Seymour Drescher observed it in the antislavery agitation in England (1987: 80–1); Ted Margadant saw it in the urban and rural, middle and lower class interaction in the 1851 insurrection in France (ch. 7–8). It was print and association – and especially the two in combination – that made possible such sustained campaigns of collective action on the part of broad coalitions of social actors against elites and authorities: And these created the national social movement.

But national movements needed more than the "push" provided by print and association to develop; they needed the pull of a common target and a fulcrum for their claims. They found these through the expansion and consolidation of the national state and in reaction to its demands and incentives. Social movements grew up around the armature of the expanding national state, as we shall see in the next chapter.

4

States and social movements[1]

National states are so central a focus for the mobilization of opinion today that we often forget that this was not always so. The major change took place between the late eighteenth and the middle of the nineteenth centuries.[2] Alexis de Tocqueville was the first to theorize about the implications of the change for collective action. In his *Democracy in America* and *The Old Regime and the French Revolution,* he argued that differences in state centralization produced differences in the opportunity structure of social movements. The coming of the national state coincided with the birth of national movements.

Tocqueville's perspective was implicitly comparative and, as a result, he has been interpreted mainly as a theorist of the effects of different kinds of state structure on behavior. Centralized states (i.e., France), he argued, aggrandize themselves by destroying intermediate bodies and reducing local autonomy. This discourages institutional participation and means that when confrontations break out, they are violent and likely to lead to despotism. In contrast, in weak states(i.e., the United States), in which civil society and local self-government are stronger, participation is both regular and widespread, diffusing confrontation into a thousand rivulets and allowing democracy to flourish.

Most of those who have followed in Tocqueville's footsteps have emphasized these comparative elements in his theory but ignored the dynamic implications of his analysis: *That state-building creates an opportunity structure for collective action of which movements take advantage.*[3] The dominant model is: Strong states plus weak civil societies lead to constrained participation, punctuated by violent outbursts of movement, while weak states in strong civil societies lead to open participation and conventional collective action. But underneath these differences, all state development provided opportunities for collective action. Even if some states were more centralized than others, it was the appearance of consolidated states as targets and fulcrums of collective action that provided the framework for the social movement; and, once the social movement was created, its challenge shaped the future relations between states and collective action across state boundaries. States learned from other states, and movements from other movements. The ultimate result was to limit the impact of any particular state structure on its social movements, as I will subsequently argue.

CENTRALIZATION AND EXCEPTIONALISM

Tocqueville's vision provides a convenient starting point for examining the role of state-building in the rise of national social movements. He began by asking why the French Revolution should have broken out in France – where the peasantry was far removed from feudalism – and not in more backward countries of Europe (1955: x). His answer was that in France, state aggrandizement had denuded the aristocracy and other corporate groups of their positive functions, reducing them to parasitic weights on society. Because a society stripped of intermediate bodies lacks a buffer between state and society, Frenchmen became "self-seekers practicing a narrow individualism and caring nothing for the public good" (p. xiii).

The result was jealous egalitarianism, sporadic and uncontrolled mobilization and, ultimately, the 1789 Revolution: "a grim, terrific force of nature, a newfangled monster, red of tooth and claw" (p. 3). The stronger the state, the weaker its encouragement of institutional participation and the greater the incentive to violence when collective action did break out. No one would want to live in such a state; and, after a decade of terror and chaos, a despotism more absolute than the Old Regime ensued.

But both Tocqueville's image of the Old Regime and that of the governments that followed were painted with too broad a brush. With respect to the Old Regime, we know now that he exaggerated both its strength and how thoroughly it had eviscerated France's intermediate bodies. After all, aristocrats and provincial parlements were among the strongest forces to act against the monarchy in 1789, and the corporate spirit – if not the structure – of the guilds and other intermediate bodies remained alive long after the Revolution (Sewell 1980; 1986).

With respect to the regimes that followed, Tocqueville generalized to all centralized states the obsession with the indivisibility of popular sovereignty that characterized only the Jacobin phase of the Revolution. It is true that the Revolution ended feudalism, destroyed the guilds and passed the Le Chapelier law suppressing association. But corporatism remained in spirit, and often in practice, the language of labor in the regimes that followed. Workers and peasants, masons and notaries retained a strong spirit of association that emerged in their collective action and during every regime crisis (Perrot 1986; Sewell 1986).

For Tocqueville, the process of state-building that began soon after the Revolution was no more than the continuation of the Old Regime's centralization. He thought that centralization deprived the country of the fiber in its civil society necessary to channel discontent into positive interactions and moderate the strivings of an acquisitive society.[4] He forgot that citizenship was being invented at the same time, and that the modern nation–state resulted from the interaction between states and citizens.

Where would Tocqueville find this fiber? In both state and society, Jacksonian America showed him a picture of a weak state and strong civil society that contrasted vividly with his image of his native land. What he so admired in his travels through the United States was that no strong central state had emerged to constrain its vigorous associational life and flourishing civil politics. To be sure, America had never had the traditional corporate bodies whose passage Tocqueville regretted in France. But it had a functional equivalent in the churches, interest groups and local assemblies that provided Americans with self-help and a buffer against state expansion (Tocqueville 1954: ch. 16). With its weak state and its flourishing associations, American democracy could avoid the extremes of egalitarianism and statist despotism that France was suffering.

But if Tocqueville's image of a France bereft of intermediate bodies exaggerated both societal atomization and state strength, his glowing picture of Jacksonian America glossed over the relationship between state-building and collective action. For one thing, the bucolic image he drew of America left the relationship between association and mobilization in the shadows. For another, he mistook the non-European character of the early American state for the absence of a state *tout court.*

To begin with the second point, although the nineteenth-century American state was not centralized, neither was it a *non*-state. The Federalists had constructed what was for the late eighteenth century an effective state for their purposes – one of fiscal consolidation, debt reduction, diplomatic maneuver and westward expansion (Bright: 121–2). The state that Tocqueville found in his travels was weak; but it had been weakened, not by Americans' inherent love of freedom or by a native genius denied to others, but by a political stalemate between two expanding, sectionally based socioeconomic systems, North and South (pp. 121, 134). State weakness was a *historical,* and not a characterological property of the American state. As Charles Bright observes; "the periods of greatest paralysis in federal policy corresponded with the periods when party mobilization was the fullest and the margins of electoral victory the slimmest" (p. 136).

What of American collective action? Here, too, Tocqueville's vision was clouded by the Reign of Terror that had decimated his family and his class. The United States in the late eighteenth and early nineteenth centuries was positively bursting with collective action – much of it violent and contentious. The sabotage of British rule and the raising of a popular army in the 1770s; the local rebellions which followed the Revolution and required troops for their suppression; the national debate around the passage of the Constitution; popular opposition to and support for the 1812 war; the frontier mobilization that produced Jackson's presidency; the religious fervor of the Second Great Awakening that "burned over" wide swatches of newly settled territory: These episodes escaped the neat institutional pluralism that Tocqueville thought he saw in his travels through America.

The center of gravity of American social movements was still local in 1832, and this fit the Tocquevillian paradigm. But even before industrialization, there was a lively urban workers' movement with a strong dose of Painite republicanism in the cities of the Atlantic coast (Wilentz 1984; Bridges 1986). Already, regional and national movements were developing a capacity for collective action in a rough dialectic with the national struggle for power, and were laying the groundwork for temperance, abolitionism and, indirectly, for the world's first feminist movement. The sectional conflict that had begun by paralyzing the development of national policy ended in the most cataclysmic episode of collective action in the nation's history – one that would remake the American state into a modern Leviathan (Bensel 1990).

The differences that Tocqueville found in state centralization, association and collective action between France and the United States were real. But in both countries, state-building was providing an opportunity for social movements. America was not as exceptional – nor was France as centralized – as Tocqueville thought. He found in the United States what he thought France had lost – a flourishing associational life that he mistook for a functional equivalent of a lost corporate order. Praising the weak American state whose presence could be barely seen at the grassroots, and ascribing associational development to that absence, Tocqueville overlooked in America how a contentious – and often ugly – mass politics in rough dialectic with the state was shaping how people acted collectively. It was the expansion and consolidation of the national state that prodded the social movement into existence, and this was true all over the West, regardless of the degree of state centralization.

Tocqueville's institutional persuasion also led him to miss two dynamic elements. The first one was short term; while movements are shaped by state structures, which are more or less stable, they are triggered by quite short-term changes in political opportunity. The second was long term; once movements are created, whether in the context of one state structure or another, they became models for collective action in other states with very different structures. In this chapter, we will examine how state-building provided opportunities for social movements during the phase of state consolidation before turning, in the next chapter, to the effects of political opportunities on movement construction and strategy today.

STATE-BUILDING AND COLLECTIVE ACTION

Even before the French Revolution, and in places more pacific than France, the national state was gaining unprecedented power to structure the relations among citizens and between them and their rulers. Expanding states made war, and needed roads and postal networks, armies and munitions factories to do so. In financing such great improvements, states could no longer rely on a surplus extracted from the peasantry, but depended on the growth of industry and commerce, which in turn required that law and order be maintained, food be supplied, associations be licensed and a citizenry be developed with the skills necessary to staff the armies, pay the taxes and turn the wheels of industry.

These efforts at state building were not intended to support social mobilization – quite the contrary. But they provided expanded means of communication through which opinion could be mobilized, created a class of men experienced in public affairs and led to financial exactions on citizens who were not always disposed to pay them. In addition, states that took on responsibility for maintaining order had to regulate the relations between groups, and this meant creating a legal framework for association as well as providing more subtle mechanisms for social control than the truncheons of the army or the police.

By these efforts, the state not only penetrated society – it integrated it. By producing policies intended for large populations and standardizing the procedures for citizens to use in their relations with authorities, states provided targets for mobilization and cognitive frameworks in which challenging groups could compare their situations to more favored constituencies and find allies. Expanding states attacked the corporate institutions of the past and tried to impede new kinds of association. But their activities provided a matrix in which new identities, new associations and broader claims developed. Within this matrix, citizens not only contested state expansion, but used the state as a fulcrum to advance their claims against others.

The most obvious example was the extension of the suffrage, and the legalization of public gatherings that it fostered. Liberal states might not wish to see workers marching or peasants milling around the village square. But even under a restricted suffrage, the meeting and drinking that attended election campaigns provided umbrellas under which less desirable social actors and more contentious forms of collective action found shelter. Even without elections, as Raymond Grew writes, all states, "as if by irresistible mandate, encouraged easier nationwide communication and a minimal universal education. . . . Once citizenship became a formal matter of birth or oaths registered by the state, it remained so even though specific criteria could be altered" (p. 94).

Three basic policies – making war, collecting taxes and provisioning food – were part of the struggle waged by expanding states to assure and expand their power. While they began as pressures on citizens and as efforts to penetrate the periphery, each produced new channels of communication, more organized networks of citizens and more unified cognitive frameworks within which people could mount claims and organize. In states as different as liberal constitutional Britain, absolutist France and colonial America, these policies shaped arenas for the construction of social movements; and these movements – or the fear of movements – shaped the way the national state evolved.

War and movement in Britain

The most portentous changes were produced by war-making and colonization; not only because they raised taxes and granted governments more power, but because they mobilized people and provided opportunities for collective action. Mobilization to make war had been a limited affair until, in trying to realize their ambitions, rulers built larger standing armies than noblemen could lead or mercenaries could staff. The growth in the size of armies became geometric in the eighteenth century,[5] as did the financial and logistical requirements for putting men in the field. From multinational collections of mainly mercenary battalions, armies became national.[6] And national mobilization – while it came nowhere near twentieth-century levels – was great enough to cause severe social and financial dislocation – and sometimes even revolution (Skocpol 1979).

It may seem odd to choose peaceful England in the late eighteenth century, where patronage was still the milk of politics, as the place to demonstrate the link between war and movement. But it is always a mistake to separate collective action from politics, particularly in the eighteenth century. Patronage generated intra-elite conflicts between opposition Whigs and governing Tories, leading the former to try to stimulate an extra-parliamentary opposition "out-of-doors."[7] Among other things, this meant that public opinion was mobilized around the themes of parliamentary debate. Issues like increasing tariffs on cider in the West country, "economical" and parliamentary reform, as well as the public scandal of Wilkes' exclusion from the Commons, were used to mobilize people out of doors.

Both the formation of the party system and opportunities for social movement formation were advanced by the most aggressive activity of the British state – colonization and waging war. The reform movement of the eighteenth century, with themes that were largely domestic, was given a boost by the agitation in the colonies. During the first years of the American troubles, rebellious colonists hoped that the outcome of their efforts would be a reform of British politics. In their contacts with Wilkes they encouraged the English radicals to argue that "the cause of Liberty . . . is one common cause" (Maier 1972: 198).

The early years of the colonial war produced a typical increase in public support for the government. The later war years, however, brought disillusionment, financial strain and the public's fear of French invasion, leading to continuous attempts to mobilize opinion. These were at first elite led and centered on London. But after failing to find a new basis for political organization in the 1760s (Brewer 1976: ch. 5), the Whig opposition encouraged a broad-based and continuous attack on ministers on the basis of economic reform. Instead of carping on individual issues, Lord Richmond urged merchants and others who opposed the government's policies to "come forth and give general opposition to men they feel are ruining them and the Country" (Read: 10–11). It was in this context that Wilkes made his famous plea connecting the war to parliamentary reform: "The American war," he argued, "is in this truly

critical era one of the strongest arguments for the regulation of our representation'' (Christie 1982: 65).

The most portentous change began far from London – in Yorkshire. As the
cost of the war increased and the probability of defeat grew stronger, a cry went
up for a reduction of waste and corruption by a government that based its power
on the buying of votes through pensions, sinecures and the like. Much of the
opposition came from sectors of the country – like Yorkshire – where trade was
badly hit by colonial boycotts of English goods and then by the British blockade
of American ports.

The Yorkshire Association began its activities with a platform combining a
call for economic and parliamentary reform with an attempt to build a national
network of county associations. Led by a substantial Anglican clergyman–
landlord, Christopher Wyvill, it called for nothing less than ''opposition to that
mercenary phalanx'' that ruled the country through the formation of ''associations in the several districts of the kingdom, acting by their respective Committees, and by general deputation from the Associated Bodies'' (Read: 12). Wyvill's association drew up a petition which gained nearly nine thousand
signatures in Yorkshire and elected a committee of correspondence to keep up
the pressure for reform.

Forming a committee to manage a petition was nothing new in the England of
1779, as we have already seen. What *was* new was that the Yorkshire committee
was designed to maintain a sustained pressure for reform (Read: 13). Wyvill
wanted to ''keep a foot on machinery in Yorkshire for promoting his political
program'' (Christie: 76). His example was followed in Middlesex, Westminster
and Gloustershire, where Wyvill had correspondents and where similar committees were being formed. No wonder the Tory government condemned the effort
as an attempt to imitate the ''seditious'' American Continental Congress.

The Gordon riots of June 1780 produced a reaction against extra-parliamentary association, and the Yorkshire and other branches of the movement petered
out in the early 1780s (Read: 14–16). The reaction was intensified when the
Jacobin phase of the French Revolution appeared to threaten British institutions
(Goodwin 1979). But while Jacobin and Painite agitators were suppressed, the
movements for economic and parliamentary reform firmly established the future
form of association in English politics. War, and the domestic strains it created,
provided opportunities for a form of mobilization that became central to British
political culture. ''War made the state and the state made war,'' writes Charles
Tilly (1975: 42). But making war also made space for movements.

Provisioning food in France

Collective actors directed their claims and joined together around more routine
activities of national states as well. A traditional need of European states was to
regulate the supply and the price of food – in part, to tax it, but also to assure

subsistence and public order. In the past, the battle had been fought mainly by urban elites trying to gain control of their hinterland. But as cities grew, states expanded and markets became international. National states became responsible for guaranteeing food supply and were held responsible when it failed.

The provision of food was never wholly free of public control. For example, the insistence that trading and weighing food take place in public was not only a way of insuring its taxation, but also of assuring minimal standards of quality and price (Kaplan 1984: 27ff.) At one time or another, communities, manors, churches and states were all involved in controlling food supply. But "only states unequivocally acquired greater power to intervene in the food supply over the long run" (Tilly 1975: 436).

Under the French monarchy, the connection between provisioning food and preventing disorder was explicit. According to an eighteenth century administrator, the prerequisite for order "was to provide for the subsistence of the people, without which there is neither law nor force which can contain them."[8] Indeed, the obligation to assure subsistence came to be seen as a major responsibility of paternal kingship, for "what more solemn duty could a father have than to enable his children to enjoy their daily bread" (Kaplan 1984: 24).

Though conflicts over food frequently occurred when people felt their right to subsistence was threatened, this situation was generalized "when states began to assure the subsistence of those populations most dependent upon them and/or threatening to them." This included, most notably, the armed forces, state administrators and the populations of capital cities (Tilly 1975: 393). Since all three of these grew rapidly in the eighteenth century, it is no accident that subsistence crises and food rebellions punctuated much of that century – most notably in the years before and after 1789.

With the spread of physiocratic ideas after the middle of the century, the liberal idea of freeing the price of grain came up against the paternalistic policy of assuring subsistence to the cities – and especially Paris. This was a source of a major contradiction in the late eighteenth-century French state; for while "high officials of the Crown worked increasingly to promote the free flow of grain out of the provinces" and "to overrule the frequent resistance of the provincial parlements to the dismantling of the old local regulation of the grain trade" (Tilly 1975: 448), an entire "police," or state regulation of food supply, developed to make sure that the teeming city of Paris was fed.

Provisioning Paris was seen as a special state responsibility, not only because of the city's enormous population, but because it was assumed that Parisians were quite capable of overthrowing the government. The police made it their business to assure not only the amount of food supplied to Paris, but also its quality.[9] It was not only bread that picky Parisians craved, but high quality white bread. Even the radical Babouvists would later call for "liberty, bread and *good* bread!" (Kaplan 1984: 58).

The deepest conflicts arose in times of dearth between Parisian officials and the local communities that produced the grain and competed for its supply. "The fiercest intercommunity struggle for subsistence," writes Kaplan, "opposed the local market town to the vulturous capital" (p. 39). This was no simple conflict between expanding state and recumbent society; although they talked breezily about the virtues of free trade, the Parisian police interpreted this doctrine as the imperative to feed the capital, while local officials who cried out against the stranglehold of Paris might be protecting the needs of consumers, miller–merchants or even their own investments in the grain market (Kaplan 1982: 64).

Grain seizures were seldom a straightforward matter of the local plebs demanding that grain be retained for local markets. Provincial parlements, seigneurs and local officials and the police would often weigh in on the side of the hinterland and against the capital, using mass resistance as "a powerful pretext to take drastic action to marshal supplies" (p. 39). "In some instances," writes Kaplan, "the people took their cue from the police" (1982: 64).

Resistance took both physical and legal form. During grain shortages, while consumers were blocking the export of grain and demanding a "just price" for bread, local officials were barring Parisian suppliers from the local trade, causing long delays at the marketplace, requisitioning Paris-bound merchandise and working out clandestine routes of supply and reserves (Kaplan 1984: 39). This encouraged recurring uprisings "affirming the intensely felt right of the community to its subsistence" (p. 39).

The French Revolution, although it was triggered by broader conflicts over taxation and parliamentary power, showed how deeply the national state had become imbricated in conflicts over food. When the women of Paris marched on Versailles in 1789, it was bread that they demanded. Even the Jacobins, fearing to be outflanked on their left, found it convenient to set maximum prices on bread and sent revolutionary armies scouring the provinces for grain. The municipal insurrections that followed the news of the fall of the Bastille were in some places radicalized by the cry of "bread at two sous" (Lefebvre 1967: 125). From a set of local, parochial and episodic conflicts over subsistence, food provision became a pivot for the spread of revolution. It would remain an important element in each revolutionary cycle in French history right up to 1848.

Levying taxes in America

The common denominator of all of the modern state's policies is its ability to raise revenue to support its activities. The result is that fiscal problems, writes Gabriel Ardant,

are to be found in the beginnings of great social changes, such as the liberation of the serfs of Western Europe, the subjugation of the peasants of Eastern Europe, wars for independence (that of Portugal as well as that of the United States), revolutions, the creation of representative governments, etc. (p. 167)

The growth of the modern state was most often contested in revolts against the burden of taxes. The hated *gabelle* in France and the *dazio* in Italy led to revolts which flared up for years. A ruler's habit of selling the right to collect taxes to tax farmers increased people's resentment against the burden while making it easier for them to assault the collector. Tax revolts rose and fell – more common in peripheral than in core areas – but were by no means limited to the lower classes, as the history of the relations between the French monarchy and the provincial parlements shows.

But it was only in the late eighteenth century that tax revolts became sufficiently broad based and well organized to feed into national movements. If the states of eighteenth century Europe had a new fiscal problem, it was because the scope of their ambitions required a degree of financial universalism that was contradicted by their dependence on the privileged classes. The latter paid few or no taxes, regarding the military role of the nobility and the spiritual one of the clergy as sufficient service to the state. Rulers who toyed with equalizing the burden of taxes had to face the prospect of losing the support of one or the other of their major allies (Ardant: 213).

England's difference from the continental powers was that basic reforms in its tax system were never attempted and because the effective center of the British state was a Parliament that would have had to approve such reforms (Ardant: 207). Both differences were due to the same factor; since 1688, Parliament had been the center of the British state and revenue collection weighed relatively lightly on the land on which the wealth of the parliamentary elite depended.[10] Instead, it weighed heavily on trade – particularly on trade with the colonies, which were seen as a cash cow to finance the wars that were necessary to acquire and maintain them.

As we saw in the last two chapters, the rebellion that led to the American Revolution began in a controversy over Britain's attempt to increase its revenues. In one sense, London was taking what seemed the easy way out. As Gabriel Ardant writes, the American Revolution "was touched off by the lack of fiscal daring on the part of the English who had thought it possible to lighten their (domestic) financial burden at the expense of men who had not consented to taxation" (p. 204). This was justified by the argument that the war in North America had been fought for the benefit of the colonists and it was they who ought to pay for it.

But such a fiscal strategy was foolhardy. For the American colonists lived an ocean away and had their own provincial governments which depended on much the same mix of revenues as the mother country.[11] The new imperial fiscal policy was not only offensive and difficult to collect; it threatened the autonomy of the colonial political system that was an instrument of indirect rule.[12]

In forcing the British government to revoke the Stamp Act, the colonists stopped the financial strategy of the most powerful empire of the time in its tracks. Had the act been no more than an attempt to make unrepresented colonists pay for a war supposedly fought on their behalf, it would have remained a minor chapter in British colonial history. It led to a revolution because the British refused to desist. But why did they refuse to desist and keep coming back with increasingly outrageous acts against American commerce?

The simplest reason was that they wanted the money, and thought they had the right to demand it. But the second was the fear of diffusion; if a bunch of ragged colonists living on the fringes of civilization could successfully challenge the British Empire, their example might be followed in Ireland – where revolt would be far more dangerous and resisters might easily link up with France. It was from Ireland, after all, that the slogan, "No Taxation without Representation," had come.

But there was a still more fundamental reason for Parliament's obduracy; in refusing to finance a war that had supposedly been fought for their benefit, the colonists were challenging nothing less than the expansion of the British state. Parliament, as the core of that state, was "inherent and inseparable from the supreme authority of the State," in Lord Dartmouth's words (Maier 1972: 233). If Parliament could be challenged on this issue, the state might face even greater challenges at home. The first major colonial revolution in history was a response to state-building, indicated its limits and demonstrated the international power of movement.

THE STATE AS TARGET AND MEDIATOR

Much of the literature on state-building focuses on the imposition of state authority on areas that were previously free of central state control or were ruled indirectly. Activities like making war, provisioning cities and levying taxes stimulated new and more sustained episodes of collective action in reaction to them. But as the activities of national states expanded and penetrated society, they also caused the targets of collective action to shift from private and local actors to national centers of decision making. The national state not only centralized the targets of collective action; it involuntarily provided a fulcrum for the standard forms of collective action discussed in Chapter 2. Henceforth, these could be employed against social or political antagonists through the mediation of the state.

During much of the eighteenth century, as we learn from Charles Tilly's recent research on Britain, the targets of the prevailing forms of contention were millers and grain merchants, local gentry, members of the community and peripheral agents of the state like tollgate managers. But from the late eighteenth century on, with a brief reversal between 1789 and 1807, Tilly finds a decisive movement of collective action away from such private targets and towards the use of public meetings, with Parliament as their main target. By the 1830s, Parliament had become the object of approximately thirty percent of the contentious gatherings in Southeast England (1993a: fig. 2).[13]

State-building not only made the national government a target for citizens' claims; it led to broader framing of citizen actions. The standardization of taxation, of administrative regulations and of census categories encouraged the formation of coalitions of groups which had been previously opposed or indifferent to one another's existence. The state's classification of citizens into what started out as artificial groupings (e.g., payers of a certain tax, residents of statistical classes of cities, soldiers conscripted in particular years) constructed new social identities or at least laid the bases for broader coalitions.

The French *départements* created during the Revolution were an archetypical case. Constructed out of mapmakers' calculations and named for whatever river happened to flow through them, the departments were designed to break up the old provincial loyalties, especially in areas of late integration that had been indirectly governed by the monarchy. But they eventually gave rise to administrative, and then to political, identities in reaction to the state's territorial policies.

We see this integrative outcome most clearly in the effects of taxation on collective action. As taxes shifted from a congeries of disparate duties on different classes of citizens, to simplified national taxes collected by a central bureaucracy, tax revolts could unite diverse social groups and localities. Conscription had a similar effect – especially when resistance was backed by ideological or religious objections. The Vendée Rebellion, which followed the French Revolution, was only the first in a series of movements, ending in the opposition to the Vietnam War, for which the trigger for broader mobilizations was resistance to the draft.

These trends meant more than the centralization of political life that had worried Tocqueville, and they extended to less centralized states than France. They coincided with the spread of the new modular repertoire and provided a fulcrum for pressure on the state by combinations of social and political actors. Through mass petitions, public meetings and demonstrations aimed at the state, disaffected groups with claims against others had an alternative to attacking their enemies directly: Henceforth they could use the state to mediate their conflicts with those they opposed.

For example, if the petition could be used to pressure Parliament to pass a reform law, it could also be used to make Parliament a *fulcrum* to pass resolutions against slave traders, Protestants, Catholics and employers. If the barricade could be used to overthrow a monarchy, as it was in February 1848, it could be used against the parliamentary Republic in June of the same year and to protest the sending of French troops to Rome the year after. For the emerging social movements of the late eighteenth and early nineteenth centuries, the expanding state provided opportunities for contention against others. These state-created opportunities for mobilization were both short term and long term, as the following examples from France and America suggest.

Short-term opportunities:
the coming of the French Revolution

The 1780s had been marked, in France, by a series of increasingly desperate attempts by the state to cover its mounting debts by reforming its fiscal system – in part, at the cost of the aristocracy. When the attempt to create a system of national courts failed in the spring of 1788, the result was the decision to open up the system to broader participation than had ever been the case before. During the year following the King's announcement of a forthcoming Estates General, networks of friends and acquaintances became political, a propaganda campaign was launched and public assemblies were called throughout the country to discuss people's grievances and elect delegates to the forthcoming Estates. These short-term opportunities to mobilize consensus laid the groundwork for the Revolution.

The King's motivation was not his sympathy for his people – far from it. The state was nearly bankrupt, the aristocracy had mounted effective blocking maneuvers against new taxes and there was widespread hunger and disorder in the country. Calling for a debate to prepare a new Estates General was an opportunistic strategy for a state in search of societal allies to counter the recalcitrance of its opponents to provide new sources of revenue.

But nothing like the assemblies of the spring of 1789 had occurred in living memory. With official sanction, local notables, lawyers and professional men – and even the occasional peasant – could stand up in public and declaim publicly about what was wrong with the existing system (Lefebvre: ch. 4; Palmer 1959: 459 ff.). Once the Estates were called, local assemblies kept in touch with their delegates, sending them instructions on how to vote and following events in Versailles through their reports (Lefebvre 1967: ch. 6). The rebellions of the summer of 1789 were the result of many factors, but they would have been unlikely had it not been for the short-term opportunities opened up by the state during the previous months. Changing opportunities were the cause of the greatest social movement in French history.

Long-term opportunities:
the making of the American working class

But long-term changes in state structure also affect the prospects and strategies of social movements. For example, the French Revolution and its Napoleonic aftermath had a major effect on the stabilization of small and midsized peasant farming in France. In combination with a low birth rate, this offset the exodus from the countryside, slowing the rate of industrialization considerably (Perrot: 72). The result was to help rural industry to survive well into the twentieth century, and to retain an artisanal base for much of the working class (Sewell 1986).

In America, the pattern of early state-building had an equally long-term effect on the workers' movement. The fundamental facts about American workers in the early nineteenth century were that they were urban – in contrast with much of the European working class during that period – and that they were given the vote much earlier than workers in Europe. This not only meant that workers' collective action was directed at the ballot box; it meant that workers' participation was territorially oriented. And since the bulk of the American working class was urban, this directed their collective action towards urban politics where political machines could make use of their votes and provide channels for upward mobility.

These institutional factors structured the nature of working class collective action in a way that made the American working class different than the one that was appearing in Western Europe at the same time. In 1830, the American working classes shared with their English cousins an artisan republicanism. They understood the coming of the industrial system in similar ways, and used the same language of master and slave (Bridges: 158). But their urban setting, and the fact that they voted in a decentralized and electoralized state, "changed the arena in which the newly created working classes struggled to achieve their goals" (p. 161). As Bridges concludes, "sheer numbers, the search for allies, geographical dispersion or concentration, and the rules of the electoral dispersion or concentration, and the rules of the electoral game all affected the political capacity of the working classes" (p. 161).

Thenceforth, the loyalty of the waves of immigrants who fed the American industrial machine was shared between the unions, which organized workers on an occupational basis, and the urban machines, which sought their vote on territorial lines (Katznelson: 45–72). "Class" as an organizing category had to compete for workers' loyalty with territory and ethnicity. This could only be matched in England in geographically concentrated industries like mining, or where dense concentrations of Irish settled in particular localities and trades. The long-term institutional trends created by the revolutionary settlement created – and foreclosed – political opportunities for American workers for generations to come.

Repression and citizenship

Not all the long-term changes in state structure created opportunities for challengers, and many were designed to check them. For once the idea of combining on behalf of collective goals became widely diffused, the fear of movements led national states to strengthen the police force and pass draconian legislation restricting assembly and association. It does not seem accidental, for instance, that the British created a professional national police in 1829; just as a major cycle of protest was unfolding, and before the first major expansion of the suffrage.[14] A major strengthening of police forces also coincided with the increase in labor disputes, particularly when the mass strike developed towards the end of the nineteenth century.[15]

In France, each wave of revolutionary agitation led to new attempts to restrict collective action. For example, the barricades that had sprung up during the 1830 and 1848 revolutions corresponded to a particular period in the balance of technical power between urban insurgents and authorities. By June of 1848, the Parisian barricades could no longer resist the determined firepower marshalled by the army, and most were blown apart by artillery.

The restructuring of Paris by Baron Haussmann under the Second Empire spelled the barricades' doom as a defensive weapon. For the tangled warren of streets in the old quarters of Paris, Haussmann substituted today's broad boulevards to facilitate the reduction of future insurgencies. Though we find them as late as May 1968 in France, by then they had become a symbolic means of building solidarity and focusing the attention of the media on the Latin Quarter.[16]

As movements learned to use the apparatuses of national communication and consolidated states, governments grudgingly had to accept the legitimacy of some forms of collective action that they had earlier resisted. The English leaders who condemned as subversive the petitions of the 1760s in favor of Wilkes, and who linked the Yorkshire Association to the Continental Congress in the 1770s, were forced to accept as legitimate the mass petitions and political associations of the 1780s. There was a reaction during the war with France, but by the early 1800s, voluntary associations were so common in England that innkeepers routinely kept their funds and papers in locked boxes (Morris: 95–118). By the 1830s, the private association for group purposes was a familiar part of the political landscape (Tilly 1982).

We should not think the progress of the social movement was smooth, even in liberal Britain. For once revolution had broken out on the continent, even mild reform movements like the British one raised suspicions of sedition among frightened elites. Books and pamphlets were censored, radical associations were banned and even moderate ones lost membership. "The result of this confusion and the inexpedient policies that flowed from it," observe Malcolm Thomis and Peter Holt, "was often the creation of revolutionaries where none had previously been." Governments, they conclude, "helped to create and sustain that very danger to themselves that they supposedly wished to avoid" (p. 2).

By the second half of the nineteenth century, movements and their potential for disruption had led national states to broaden the suffrage, accept the legitimacy of mass associations and open new forms of participation to their citizens. In a very real sense, citizenship emerged through a rough dialectic between movements – actual and feared – and the national state. Many of the reforms of the modern state – from the factory legislation of the 1840s to the unemployment and health reforms of Prussia – were either direct responses to movement demands or attempts to preempt their development. As Bright and Harding point out, "contentious processes both define the state vis-à-vis other social and economic institutions and continually remake the state itself'' (p. 4).

As movements developed in different directions and encountered resistance and support, state responses to them became internally differentiated. Some groups were welcomed into the fold of citizenship, while others were excluded; some kinds of collective action were accepted, while others were suppressed; some sectors of the state accepted the claims of citizenship, while others denied it. It is only in the most extreme cases – or when history is examined from too far away – that an abstraction called "The State" can be said to have been monolithically arrayed against "society." More commonly, state elites chose their allies and attacked their enemies, and the state provided opportunities to some groups and not to others. Under the vast, expanding umbrella of the national state, challengers found opportunities for collective action, and states structured social movements.

Nor could these changes be limited to single states – although stronger states resisted longer. By 1848, the same movements, making remarkably similar claims through nearly identical forms of collective action, sprung up all over Europe within a matter of months. When the suffrage was expanded, this occurred in short, transnational bursts as the different structures of "stable" electoral opportunity gave way to intense transnational pressures (Rokkan: ch. 4). By the 1880s, the European working class movement was becoming effectively internationalized, developing similar forms and similar ideologies all over Western Europe.

Tocqueville's insight remains true today: The territorially centralized French state structures collective action differently than the functionally centralized British state or the federal American one. But it was the general process of state expansion and consolidation all across the West that provided the basic opportunity structure in which social movements could develop. Within that structure, movement emergence was triggered by changes in opportunity, both short-term and long-term, national and trans-national. While comparative differences in state centralization and state strength structured movements, it was the changes in opportunity that allowed them to emerge and that shaped their dynamic once they did so.

CONCLUSIONS

It is time to recapitulate what has been argued in the last three chapters. Collective action has characterized human society for as long as there has been social conflict – that is to say, from whenever human society can be said to have begun. But such actions usually expressed the claims of ordinary people directly, locally and rigidly, responding to immediate grievances, attacking opponents and almost never finding allies among other groups or among political elites. The result was a series of explosions – seldom organized and usually brief – punctuated by periods of passivity.

Sometime in the course of the eighteenth century, a new and more general repertoire of collective action began to develop in Western Europe and North America. Unlike the older forms, which expressed people's immediate grievances directly against their antagonists, the new repertoire was national, autonomous and modular: That is, it could be used by a variety of social actors on behalf of a number of claims and serve as a bridge among them to strengthen their hand and reflect broader and more proactive demands. Even inherited forms, like the petition, were gradually transformed from the tool of individuals seeking grace from superiors into a form of mass collective action.

The root causes of this change are difficult to tease out of historical records collected by those whose job it was to repress rebellion. But as we saw in Chapter 3, two main kinds of resources helped to empower these early movements: print and association. Both were expressions of capitalism, but both expanded beyond the interests of capitalists to fuel the spread of social movements.

The commercial press not only diffused information that could make potential activists aware of one another and of their common grievances; it also equalized their perception of their status with that of their superiors, and made it thinkable to take action against them. The private association reflected existing solidarities, helped new ones to form and linked local groups into broader networks that could contest the power of national states or international empires. Social coalitions, sometimes purposefully constructed, but often contingent and provisional, concerted collective action against elites and opponents in the name of general programs. The escalation of specific group demands into general programs was, itself, a product of the need to raise common umbrellas above a plethora of petty claims.

Although the new movements often aimed at other groups in society, the framework for their actions was increasingly the opportunities for collective action provided by the national state. In making war, provisioning cities and raising taxes, as well as by building roads and regulating associations, the state became both a target for claims and a place to fight out disputes among competing groups. Even where access to some groups was denied, the standardizing and unifying ambitions of expanding states created opportunities for less well endowed people to mimic and adapt the stratagems of elites.

In a world that was simple to interpret, either the poor would revolt when their economic conditions became intolerable, or the nonpoor would organize on the basis of their internal resources. But when we factor in the different structure of political opportunities, short-term and long-term changes in opportunity structure and transnational communication between both states and movements, the equation changes: Because the conditions for protest depend not on configurations of social or institutional structure, but on changing configurations of political opportunities, it becomes more difficult to predict who will protest – and when – on the basis of ''objective'' factors alone, as I will argue in Part II.

PART II

The powers of movement

5

Seizing and making opportunities[1]

Why do ordinary people at times pour into the streets, risking life and limb to lay claim to their rights or attack others? The question has fascinated observers and frightened citizens and elites since the French Revolution. Outraged by the excesses of the mob and the dislocations of industrial society, early scholars saw collective action as the expression of a crowd mentality, of anomie and deprivation.[2] But even a cursory look at modern history shows that outbreaks of collective action cannot be derived from the level of deprivation that people suffer or from the disorganization of their societies; for these preconditions are more constant than the movements they supposedly cause. What varies widely from time to time, and from place to place, are political opportunities, and social movements are more closely related to the incentives they provide for collective action than to underlying social or economic structures.

For example, when David Snyder and Charles Tilly looked at the peaks and valleys of French violence after 1830, they found that these were more closely related to electoral opportunities and to changes in regime than to hardship or deprivation (Snyder and Tilly 1972). Collective action increases when people gain the resources to escape their habitual passivity and find the opportunities to use them. Because people act on opportunities, as Tocqueville wrote, "the most perilous moment for a bad government is one when it seeks to mend its ways" (1955: 176–7).

Not only when reform is pending, but when institutional access opens, when alignments shift, when conflicts emerge among elites and when allies become available, will challengers find favorable opportunities. In the next three chapters I will examine how movements utilize repertoires of contention, construct meanings and mobilize social networks into action. But these resources come into play only when there are visible incentives for activism in the relations between potential movements and their opponents. Movement formation, I will argue in this chapter, is the product of people seizing and making opportunities.

Of course, changing opportunities must be seen alongside more stable structural elements – like the strength or weakness of the state, the forms of repression employed by it and the nature of the party system – all of which condition collective action. And opportunity structure applies not only to the formation of movements. Movements *create* opportunities for themselves or others. They do this by diffusing collective action through social networks and by forming coalitions of social actors; by creating political space for kindred movements and countermovements; and by creating incentives for elites to respond. Challengers who seize and make political opportunities are the catalysts for the cycles of protest and reform that break out periodically in modern history. Before turning to the structure of political opportunities, it will be useful to see how the concept developed out of the movement cycles of the 1930s and the 1960s.

FROM THE THIRTIES TO THE SIXTIES

The extremist movements of the interwar years revived the nineteenth-century tendency to see collective action as the product of anomie and deprivation. Embittered by fascism and Stalinism, writers like Erich Fromm (1969) and former militants like Eric Hoffer (1951) saw these movements drawing on marginal people's desire to "escape from freedom" into new identities and utopias. For psychologist Wilhelm Reich, the masses had "become apathetic, incapable of discrimination, biopathic and slaves as the result of the suppression of their vital life" (1970: 208). For philosopher Hannah Arendt, fascism was the outcome of the encounter of mob and capital; Stalinism the product of the mob and intellectuals (ch. 10).

After the war, reconstruction produced what many saw as an "end of ideology."[3] But this was a brief and ephemeral moment of demobilization, and by the 1960s, a new wave of movements appeared that was more closely related to affluence than to deprivation, more redolent of hope and aspiration than of fear and hatred. In the United States, these movements stimulated a paradigm that placed a greater focus on people's resources than on their alienation, more emphasis on affluence than on deprivation; while, in Western Europe, it produced a theory of "new" social movements.

The differences between the two schools of thought grew out of each culture's dominant intellectual traditions – individualist in America, structuralist in Europe. Many American scholars observed the new wave of movements from a standpoint that gave precedence to the individual citizen's attitudes and dispositions. If affluent students, tenured intellectuals and comfortable white collar workers supported new movements, their support might arise more from affluence than from dislocation, alienation or anomie. As recorded in surveys, the public's changing attitudes to protest appeared to support the reasoning of these scholars. Especially among the young, attitudes seemed to be shifting from largely material claims to postmaterial concerns.[4]

Western European scholars, many of whom came out of a Marxist tradition but were disillusioned by the failure of the working class to rise to the challenge of 1968, looked to structural factors as the explanation for the new movements. For them, the co-occurence of the student, peace, ecological and women's movements in the 1960s and 1970s showed that changes in welfare capitalism were the sources of unconventional collective action.[5] Rejecting the simplicities of classical marxism, these "new" social movement scholars argued that the needs of both declining and new middle classes were converging to produce a generation of movements that were no longer centered on class. Where American scholars looked to the internal resources of actors and movements – what Melucci (1988) called the "how" of social movements – Europeans looked to their "why", asking how features of contemporary states and societies were drawing people – mainly middle class people – into movements designed to protect and enhance their "life-spaces."[6]

Both of these perspectives – each of which quickly found advocates on the other side of the Atlantic – added a great deal to our understanding of the new wave of movements. But taken on their own, neither affluence nor the displacement of life spaces could explain why people lend support to movements during some periods of history and not others. To do that, it would be necessary to trace how underlying social structure and mobilization potential are transformed into action.[7] The problem was that both the American and the European schools left out the crucial intervening variables of political structure – the "when" of social movement formation.

Nor did either school have any explanation for the wide differences that were found in the new movements from country to country. If post-materialism and the Keynesian welfare state were their causes, there ought to have been a demonstrated correlation between the extent of these in each country and the social movement activity that developed there. But such a showing was never made by the adherents of either school – and for essentially the same reason: neither included in their analyses the political opportunity structure in which social movements emerge.[8] Had they done so, it might have been possible to predict the decline of these movements in the 1980s as well as their rise in the preceding decades.[9] Before employing this concept to account for the rise and fall of social movements and cycles of protest, we need to examine its dimensions and ask how opportunities provide incentives for collective action.

Business cycles and the ends of wars

The economic depression of the 1930s gave rise to a number of social movements in Europe and the United States. But the economic affluence of the 1960s raised people's consciousness above their material needs and caused collective action, too. Both arguments, though contradictory, run from variations in the economic environment to increases in collective action. How can we explain this apparent contradiction?

Consider strike behavior. Other things being equal, workers are more likely to go on strike in boom times than in depressions.[10] The logic of the connection is fairly clear. Economic prosperity increases employers' needs for labor just as tight labor markets are reducing competition for jobs. As workers learn this – and they learn it quickly – they demand higher wages, shorter hours or better working conditions. As a result, the strike rate follows the curve of the business cycle upward when a declining unemployment pool leaves employers prey to the pressure of the labor market and downward when the demand for labor declines.[11]

But industrial workers sometimes produce major strike waves during troughs in the business cycle – as many did in France and the United States in the 1930s. While workers in Britain languished through most of the Great Depression and German workers were brutally repressed by the Nazis, French and American workers reacted to the crisis with unprecedented levels of collective action, and developed a new type of movement – the factory occupation. How can we explain the increase in industrial insurgency by workers hard pressed during the depression, as well as the cross-national variations among these insurgencies?

The answer, I propose, lies in the changes in the political opportunity structure surrounding French and American workers. There were strike waves in France and the United States in the 1930s, and not in Germany or Britain, not because economic distress was greater in the first two countries than in the latter but because reform administrations came to power – in France in 1936 and America in 1933. Each showed a willingness to innovate in political–economic relationships, and an unwillingness to support the suppression of the labor movement. It was the political opportunities opened by the French Popular Front and the American New Deal that caused the surge of labor insurgency in a poor labor market, and not the depth of workers' grievances or the extent of their resources.

The ends of both world wars produced similar expansions in collective action. But these cannot be explained by economic incentives alone. The social movements of the post-World War I period, ranging from factory occupations to women's suffrage to attempted revolutions, were the joint outcome of economic pressures, the release of pent up political energy and increased political opportunities. The end of World War II produced both a second strike wave and a decolonization movement around the world. If the end of World War I produced more and more energetic movements than the end of World War II, the international incentive of the Bolshevik Revolution had much to do with it.

Writing of the period after the Second World War, Ernest Mandel attempts a largely economic explanation of the increasing rise of industrial conflict after wars (p. 50). With the decline of wartime mobilization, he reasoned, investment in new plant and equipment – and, thus, employment – would decline, and the capitalist countries would be caught in a spiral of withering competition and social conflict. This would lead to a cumulative and linear increase in collective action.

But Beverly Silver made a comparison between Mandel's estimate of postwar industrial conflict and the actual strike data that she and Giovanni Arrighi collected from the *London* and *New York Times*. Her data show that Mandel was projecting a long wave of conflict from short-term postwar variations (Silver 1992a: 286). While Mandel saw a progressive increase in class conflict from 1945 on, Silver finds a peak of conflict in the postwar years, tapering off by the 1950s, and never again rising to such a high level.[12]

We can explain the differences between Mandel's theory and Silver's findings through the intervening variables of political opportunity structure. After both world wars, mobilization for war and promises of peacetime prosperity were followed by rapid demobilization and by the desire to see wartime promises kept. As governments adjusted their economic policies and repressed extreme forms of protest, people settled into postwar niches, economies cooled off and the workers tired of mobilizing. The decline in collective action after both world wars that Silver found would seem to fit better with the changing nature of political opportunities than with Mandel's purely economically driven prediction.

DIMENSIONS OF OPPORTUNITY

By political opportunity structure, I mean consistent – but not necessarily formal or permanent – dimensions of the political environment that provide incentives for people to undertake collective action by affecting their expectations for success or failure. Theorists of political opportunity structure emphasize the mobilization of resources *external* to the group.[13] Although political opportunities are unequally distributed, unlike internal resources such as money, power or organization, even weak and disorganized challengers can sometimes take advantage of them.

Political opportunities sometimes widen for an entire citizenry – as they did in Eastern Europe in the late 1980s. Their effects are sometimes centered on particular groups – as when African Americans were helped by the changing political realignments in the 1950s and 1960s (Piven and Cloward: ch. 4). Sometimes they are localized in particular regions or cities but not in others – as they were for republican organizations in parts of France in 1848 (Aminzade 1993), and in "unreformed" local governments, but less so in "reformed" ones in the United States in the 1960s (Eisinger 1973).

The concept of political opportunity structure helps us to understand why movements sometimes gain surprising, but temporary, leverage against elites or authorities and then quickly lose it despite their best efforts. It also helps to understand how mobilization spreads from people with deep grievances and strong resources to those in very different circumstances. By opening challenges to elites and authorities, "early risers" expose the vulnerability of powerholders to attacks by others. By the same token, the latter groups more easily collapse because they lack the resources to sustain collective action when opportunities close.

The most salient changes in opportunity structure are four: the opening up of access to participation, shifts in ruling alignments, the availability of influential allies, and cleavages within and among elites.[14] Let us briefly survey and illustrate each of them before turning to the relations between contemporary states and opportunities.

Increasing access

Rational people do not often attack well fortified opponents when opportunities are closed. But gaining partial access to power provides them with such incentives. As Tocqueville pointed out, it was the opening of opportunities for the Third Estate by the agitation of the aristocratic parlements against the king that helped to undermine the French Old Regime. The same was true of the power of the Parisian little people as the Revolution gathered force.[15] Access to participation is the first important incentive for collective action.

France's revolutionary populace never had more than fitful or marginal power to influence events. But are people who possess full political rights more likely to engage in collective action? Peter Eisinger argues that the relationship between protest and political opportunity is neither negative nor positive but curvilinear: Neither full access nor its absence encourage the greatest degree of collective action. Taking his cue from Tocqueville, Eisinger (p. 15) writes that protest is most likely "in systems characterized by a mix of open and closed factors."[16]

The idea that partially opened access encourages protest was dramatically supported by the movements for liberation and democratization in the former Soviet Union and Eastern Europe in 1989. As Gorbachev's Perestroika and *Glasnost* opened new opportunities for political action, protest movements that could both take advantage of these opportunities and go beyond them developed (Beissinger 1991). Although Beissinger found that violent protest was *not* closely connected with the opening of opportunity structure, nonviolent protests were clearly related to expanding opportunities, a finding that dovetails with Eisinger's finding for democratic systems.

Expanding access is expressed most obviously through elections, but in authoritarian systems it reveals itself in informal ways as well. Access to the transnational information network created by the Helsinki treaty helped Eastern European dissidents to keep track of the progress of Helsinki Watch groups during the 1980s (Thomas in preparation). In Czechoslovakia, the appearance of a Student Press and Information Center (STIS) gave students from different faculties a site in which they could make contact and the assurance that political action would be tolerated (van Praag Jr.: 12 ff.).

Movements that seek to expand their access to institutions may find that long-term relations of exchange with political opponents cut them off from their base, as Frances Piven and Richard Cloward found in the case of the American welfare rights movement in the 1960s (ch. 5). But movements which seek access rather than demanding new advantages may be placed in a position where they can seek further opportunities. The American women's movement may have gained far more in new advantages by increasing its electoral access than it would have gained by directly demanding the same advantages (Mueller 1987).

Unstable alignments

A second aspect of opportunity structure that encourages collective action is the instability of political alignments, as indicated in liberal democracies by electoral instability. The changing fortunes of government and opposition parties, especially when they are based on new coalitions, create uncertainty among supporters, encourage challengers to try to exercise marginal power and may induce elites to compete for support from outside the polity.

The importance of electoral realignments in opening political opportunities can be seen in the American Civil Rights movement. Throughout the 1950s, racial "exclusionists" in the southern wing of the Democratic Party were weakened by defections to the Republicans, while the number of Democratic "inclusionists" grew stronger (Vallely 1993). Both the decline of their southern white vote and the movement of African American voters to the cities increased the incentive for the Democrats to seek black support. With its razor-thin electoral margin, the Kennedy administration was forced to move from cautious footdragging to seizing the initiative for civil rights, a strategy that was extended by the Johnson administration to the landmark Voting Rights Act of 1965.[17]

But as peasant uprisings in undemocratic systems show, not only in representative systems does political instability encourage collective action. Peasants are most likely to rebel against authorities when windows of opportunity appear in the walls of their subordination. This is what Eric Hobsbawm found when he looked into the history of Peruvian land occupations (1974). The same was true of the peasants who occupied parts of the southern Italian *latifundia* after World War II. Their land hunger and resentment at landlord abuses were age-old; but it was the collapse of Mussolini's Fascist regime, the presence of reform-oriented American occupiers and changing partisan alignments that transformed their habitual resentment into a struggle for the land (Bevilacqua 1980). When the party system stabilized around a strong Christian Democratic pole and isolated the Communist–Socialist opposition, the peasants relapsed into their traditional lassitude (Tarrow 1967).

Influential allies

A third aspect of opportunity structure is the presence or absence of influential allies (Kriesi, et al. 1992). Challengers are encouraged to take collective action when they have allies who can act as friends in court, as guarantors against repression or as acceptable negotiators. There is historical evidence from William Gamson's research in the United States of a strong correlation between the presence of influential allies and movement success. In the fifty-three "conflict groups" that Gamson studied, the presence or absence of political allies ready to help them out was closely related to whether the groups succeeded or not. That success hinges on having "friends in court" does not prove that people mobilize *because* they have such friends; but it does suggest that links between challengers and members of the polity can produce a greater chance of success for outsiders (Steedley and Foley 1979).

Alliances seem to be more explicitly constructed by recent social movements than by movements in the past. For example, comparing the American farmworker movements in the 1940s and 1960s, Jenkins and Perrow found that the advantage of the United Farm Workers in the 1960s lay in the presence of external constituencies that its predecessors lacked: urban liberals who boycotted lettuce and grapes to assist the UFW in its struggle for union recognition; the organized labor coalition that supported it in the California legislature; and, a new generation of sympathetic administrators in the U.S. Department of Agriculture (1977).

Influential allies have proven especially important for movements in nondemocratic systems. For example, in Central America peasant movements profited from external allies, particularly religious workers, union organizers, revolutionary guerillas, political party activists and development workers (Brockett: 258). In state socialist regimes, the Catholic Church in Poland and the Protestant churches in East Germany helped to incubate resistance and protect activists from retribution during the 1980s. Allies are an external resource that otherwise resource-deficient social actors can sometimes depend upon.

Divided elites

Conflicts within and among elites are a fourth factor which encourages unrepresented groups to engage in collective action. Divisions among elites not only provide incentives to resource-poor groups to risk collective action; they encourage portions of the elite that are out of power to seize the role of "tribunes of the people." The liberal aristocracy in Old Regime France – people like Lafayette and Mirabeau – followed just such a pattern. Although its disputes with the Crown began over parliamentary prerogatives and taxes, a portion of that class made common cause with the lower clergy and the Third Estate to create a constitutional monarchy.

Splits within the elite played a key role two hundred years later in Eastern Europe, especially after Gorbachev warned his Communist allies in the region that the Red Army would no longer intervene to defend them. This was understood by both citizens and insurgent groups in Eastern Europe as a serious division in the elite and as a signal to mobilize. Splits within the elite were also important in the transitions to democracy in authoritarian Spain and Brazil in the 1970s and 1980s, where divisions between softliners and hardliners provided openings for opposition movements (O'Donnell and Schmitter 1986: 19).

These aspects of opportunity structure are arrayed differentially in various systems and change over time, often independently of one another, but sometimes in close connection. Splits among elites and political realignments can work together to induce disaffected elites or even governments to seek support from outsiders. When minority factions of the elite become the influential allies of outside challengers, challenges from outside the polity combine with pressure from inside to create incentives for political and institutional change. A frequent result is the cycles of protest we will examine in Chapter 9; a less frequent outcome is revolution.

STATES AND OPPORTUNITIES

The aspects of opportunity structure analyzed above are specified as *changes* in opportunity; but, there are stable aspects of opportunity structure that condition movement formation and strategy, too. As authors like Peter Eisinger, William Gamson and David Meyer in the United States, and Hanspeter Kriesi and Herbert Kitschelt in Europe have argued, stable aspects of institutional structure shape the differences in movement formation and strategy in various countries and institutional settings.[18] Comparative research, like the essays collected in Mary Katzenstein's and Carol Mueller's *The Women's Movement of the United States and Western Europe,* provide strong evidence for the impact of different structures of political opportunity. One version of this comparative argument proceeds from the concept of "state strength" and deserves particular attention.

The strength of the state

In its most common form, the "state strength" argument owes its origins to Tocqueville but was revived during the 1970s and 1980s in American political sociology.[19] The argument runs that centralized states with effective policy instruments at their command attract collective actors to the summit of the political system, while decentralized states provide a multitude of targets at the system's base. Strong states also have the capacity to implement the policies they choose to support; when these policies are favorable to the claims of movements, the latter will gravitate to conventional forms of protest; but when they are negative, violence or confrontation ensues.[20]

As we saw in the last chapter, differences in the strength of the state underlay Tocqueville's vision of the contrasting nature of collective action in France and the United States. These different degrees of state centralization were probably a major reason for the contrasts in the French and American student movements of the 1960s. The first exploded only in early 1968, was rapidly diffused and soon moved quickly into the political arena, triggering a political convulsion that threatened the Republic. The second produced a much longer, more decentralized series of protest campaigns at campuses around the United States.

Differences in state strength are also related to the causes for the differential pace and timing of the revolutions in Eastern Europe in 1989. Poland, with a state that had never been completely Stalinized, produced the earliest and most vital movement, in the Solidarity strikes of 1980; whereas Czechoslovakia, which was subjected to brutal Stalinist control after 1968, was one of the last to rebel. Polish precociousness and Czechoslovak delay can be seen as the result of the respective strength of state socialism in the two countries.

The seductions of statism

But we should beware of simple structural answers to complex political problems. It would be easy to use state strength as a global predictor of collective action if it was in fact a constant. But "strength" and "weakness" are relational values which vary for different social actors, different sectors of the state and according to how political opportunities evolve. For example, the American state, though it is weak in relation to business, is quite strong when it comes to labor and national security. As a result of this difference, it presents an open door to groups which advance modest goals – what Gamson (1990) calls "the strategy of thinking small" – but sets up a barricade against those who challenge property or security.

Moreover, although some analysts have no hesitation in classifying one state as strong and another as weak, the strength of the state changes as the result of political factors. A state that is strong in the hands of a unified political majority quickly becomes weak when that majority is divided or opposition to it grows. A state that is strong when it enjoys the confidence of business weakens when inflation soars and capital moves abroad. When a new collective actor appears – like Islamic fundamentalism in Iran in the late 1970s or in Algeria in the early 1990s – an apparently strong state can quickly wither away.

Divisions among the political elite are a source of political weakness that is easy to mistake for a structurally weak state. Thus, until the Civil War, the regionally divided American elite limited the strength of the American central state. When that war reduced the South both militarily and politically, the state became a "Yankee Leviathan" (Bensel 1990). Similarly, while the ideologically compact French elite responded swiftly to the Events of May with both educational reform and microeconomic policy,[21] the ideologically divided Italian political class allowed the movements of the late 1960s to stretch into a "sliding May" that lasted well into the 1970s (Tarrow 1989a). In the same period, American Vietnam War protests were effective, not because the state was weak, but because the political elite was divided over the war (Burstein and Freudenberg 1978).

Long-run changes in state strength affect the opportunities of submerged and resource-poor groups. Thus, writes Richard Valelly, after the Civil War, the first American reconstruction failed because the federal government did not have a monopoly of the means of coercion, despite its military occupation of the South. But by the 1950s and 1960s, he continues, "the situation differed, among other things permitting daring movement strategies that captured the attention and support of a national audience" (p. 42).

If variations in movement structure and strategy could be predicted from differences in state structure, then all of a country's movements would resemble one another. But they do not: Even in the same movement sector, there are great differences in movement structure and strategy. One example is the differences in the mobilizing strategies of the Pro-Life and Pro-Choice movements in the United States. In the Pro-Choice movement, according to John McCarthy (1987), a sophisticated leadership and an affluent constituency developed an action repertoire that was centered on direct mail campaigns and channeled contributions into publicity, education and lobbying. In contrast, the Pro-Life movement that was rooted in Catholic Church parishes, drew on a lower middle class Catholic constituency and used direct action campaigns and door-to-door canvassing instead of direct mail. Both movements were equally at home in the political opportunity structure of American public life, yet they chose different strategies and developed different organizational structures.

Was this the result of the weak American state? A weak state certainly provides room for more variation in structure and strategy than a strong one, but the two movements' class and cultural compositions are the major reason for the differences that McCarthy found. Direct mail and lobbying were most effective tools for the secular upper-middle-class constituency of the Pro-Choice movement, while local organization and direct action were more suited to the lower middle class, parish-based supporters of the right to life.

Of course, Pro-Choice and Pro-Life were deeply opposed to one another, so it is not surprising that their strategies and structures differed. But even within the same movement, we find fundamental differences in structure and strategy. For example, Jane Mansbridge shows that, within the state of Illinois, the Equal Rights Amendment campaign lacked a common strategy, structure and culture (1986: ch. 10). Similarly, Dieter Rucht shows that many different forms of collective action and forms of organization were employed by both the French and German antinuclear movements (1990).

The structure of the state is a first and useful dimension in predicting whether and where movements will find opportunities to engage in collective action. But social movements are multidimensional actors, just as the state is a multidimensional target. States deal differently with strong and weak contenders; they show a different face in different sectors and vary in strength over time; and their strength varies as a function of the unity and strength of elites. As a result, it is more useful to specify particular aspects of institutional structure that relate directly to movements than to reify the state as a predictor of collective action.

One of the most important of these aspects is the structure of the party system to which movements accommodate themselves. A strong and monolithic party is less likely to absorb the demands of new social actors, whereas a weaker and more decentralized party system is more easily penetrated by the interests of activated constituencies.[22] Another is the localism of the political process, which, in decentralized states, favors movements with a territorial focus – like the "Not in My Backyard" groups that flourish in the American environmental movement. But the most important comparative difference in how states relate to movements is repression.

Repression and facilitation

In Tilly's definition, "repression is any action by another group which raises the contender's cost of collective action. An action which lowers the group's cost of collective action is a form of facilitation" (1978: 100). The development of modern states produced powerful tools for the repression of popular politics, but some aspects of state development facilitated the rise of movements, as we saw in Chapter 4.

It is easy to see why repression is a more likely fate for movements which demand fundamental changes than for those which merely make ameliorative claims (Gamson 1990: ch. 4). And it is also obvious that while authoritarian states repress social movements, representative ones facilitate them. But there are aspects of repressive states that encourage collective action and characteristics of representative ones that take the sting out of movements. Repression and facilitation are better seen as two separate continua than as polar opposites characteristic of different types of states.

Repression in authoritarian states

That authoritarian states discourage popular politics is implicit in their very definition. In particular, they suppress the sustained interaction of collective actors and authorities that is the hallmark of social movements. But the systematic repression of confrontational protest has perverse and contradictory effects. The very success of repression can produce a radicalization of collective action and a more effective organization of opponents. It was not in democratic Britain or republican France that nineteenth-century anarchists turned to terrorism, but in autocratic Russia and semidemocratic Italy. And we now know how effective the Social Democrats were in organizing workers in Russia – even during the repressive years prior to World War I (Bonnell: ch. 8).

Moreover, not all repressive states are equally effective in closing off opportunities for collective action. For example, in Fascist Italy, groups within Italian Catholic Action organized for resistance under the legitimate umbrella of the Fascist–Vatican Concordat (Webster 1960: chs. 10 and 11). In Communist Poland, books and articles by Solidarity writers continued to be published under the noses of the police and the army during the martial law period of the 1980s (Laba: 155). Even in Stalinist Czechoslovakia, Charter '77 activists were able to continue to meet and maintain a modest presence until 1989.

While it crushes resistance under most conditions, the centralization of power in repressive states offers dissidents a unified field and a centralized target to attack, once the system is weakened. This was one of the contributing reasons for the rapid collapse of state socialism in Eastern Europe after 1989. Where power is centralized and conditions are homogenized, once opportunities are opened – as they were when Gorbachev began his reforms – framing and organizing a social movement are facilitated. The weak have a crucial weapon in such systems, writes Valerie Bunce: They have "a great deal in common" (1990: 6).

The systematic repression of collective action in nonrepresentative systems lends a political coloration to ordinary acts. Listening to Verdi's operas during the period of Austrian control of Italy, or to rock music in the former Soviet Union, took on a symbolic importance that was difficult to repress or even recognize. "V.E.R.D.I.," scrawled on the walls of Milan in 1848, stood not for the name of the nationalist composer, but as an acronym for the slogan *Vittorio Emmanuele Re d'Italia* (Victorio Emmanuel, King of Italy).[23] Graffiti scribbled on the walls of Russian buildings during the 1980s communicated the extent of alienation in Russian society to anyone who could read (Bushnell 1990).

In less determinedly authoritarian states, even how people tip their hats to others or employ forms of address can indicate dissent, as James Scott found in his research in Malaysia (ch. 7). These "hidden transcripts" seldom produce collective action, but they can undermine a consensus in a way that is difficult to repress, because no single instance crosses the line from resentment to opposition. Repressive states depress collective action of a conventional and a confrontational sort, but leave themselves open to unobtrusive mobilization; a signal for solidarity that becomes a resource when opportunities arise.

Repression in nonrepressive states

In representative systems, the constitutional protection of rights has led scholars to regard their states as if they uniformly facilitated popular politics. But representative systems can both disperse and dispatch opposition movements. On the one hand, because they invite criticism and participation, such systems frequently "process" the most challenging elements out of popular politics, as the United States did the race riots of the 1960s (Lipsky and Olson 1976). On the other hand, they can be ruthlessly repressive against those who challenge – or can be made to seem to be challenging – their underlying precepts. The repression of domestic radicals in the 1950s and the suppression of black nationalists in the 1970s should warn Americans against being too complacent about the robustness of their government's respect for civil liberties.

The ease of organizing opinion in representative systems, and of finding legitimate channels for its expression, induces many movements to turn to elections. The dynamic often runs something like this: A movement organizes massive public demonstrations on behalf of its demands; the government permits and even facilitates its continued expression; numerical growth has its most direct effect in electing candidates to office; therefore, the movement turns into a party or enters a party in order to influence its policies. This was the logic that undercut the Italian extreme Left in the mid-1970s, when it turned from confrontation to institutional politics (Tarrow 1989a). It has been used successfully in the American women's movement which has grown increasingly dependent on its alliance with the Democratic Party (Costain and Costain 1987).

The most important impact of such institutionalization is the hardest to measure: how the effect of institutional politics leads to choices not taken. The electoral arena has perverse effects on social movements. Amy Bridges (1986) has shown how the early extension of the right to vote, and the localism of the American political system quickly turned native mechanics and immigrant workers in New York City into Democrats and Republicans.[24] Where civility and compromise count for more than the aggressive assertion of group claims, contingent alliances can turn into strategic understandings, and the practice of institutional politics grow into standing commitments.

Representative states' commitments to pluralism make it easy to marshall support for repressive measures against those who do not share pluralism's values. Liberal systems can be ferociously illiberal when challenged by those who do not share liberalism's values, as American dissenters have repeatedly learned (Hartz 1983: 244–8). Conversely, while authoritarian states systematically repress collective action, the absence of regular channels for the expression of opinion turns even moderate dissenters into opponents of the regime, forcing them to pose the problem of regime overturn as the condition for reform. As Marx wrote in 1843 of the difference between the relatively liberal French monarchy and the repressive Prussian state, "In France partial emancipation is the basis of universal emancipation. In Germany, universal emancipation is the *conditio sine qua non* of any partial emancipation."[25]

Forms of repression and control

Repression can either depress collective action or raise the cost of its two main preconditions – the organization and mobilization of opinion (Tilly 1978: 100–2). This is true in both repressive and nonrepressive regimes. Although nonrepressive states selectively target and isolate challenging groups, their universalistic norms sometimes make this difficult to accomplish. For example, in the 1790s, the fear of Jacobin revolution led the British state to suppress all forms of association, including those – like the antislavery movement – that had little sympathy for republicanism.[26] And in the United States, outlawing the Communist Party during the cold war raised the costs of mobilization across the board, disarming the entire Left until the late 1960s (Tilly 1978: 100–1).

Depressing the preconditions for collective action is a more effective strategy than its direct suppression. For example, when Steven Barkan compared southern cities that used the courts to block civil rights with those who used police violence, he found that the former were able to resist desegregation longer than the latter (1984). But the preconditions of collective action are not always easy to suppress. The first impediment is the cost – both financial and administrative.[27] The second is that nonselective repression silences constructive critics too and blocks information flow upward (Lohmann: 25). Finally, in conditions of depressed organization, when collective action does break out – as it did all over Eastern Europe in 1989 – it turns from a trickle into a torrent as people discover others like themselves in the streets (Kuran 1991; Lohmann 1992).

State structuring of collective action often results from explicit attempts to limit protest by invoking legal penalties – which is why eighteenth-century British magistrates multiplied the number of offenses for which the death penalty was applicable (Tilly 1978: 103). But the effectiveness of such "exemplary punishments" was neutralized by the unwillingness of later magistrates to employ them, and the ability of protesting groups to find ways around them. Exemplary punishments gave way during the nineteenth century to a tendency to prosecute offenders by incarceration.

Jailing protesters and potential protesters remained the major response to collective action until after World War II, when first Gandhi, and then American civil rights leaders discovered that filling the jails to capacity and gaining public sympathy were effective forms of pressure. In response, both in the United States and in Europe, the police and the courts responded to nonviolence by accepting as legitimate forms of collective action that had previously been repressed. Thus the sit–in, which was punished almost universally by incarceration when it was first employed, was increasingly accepted in the 1960s as a form of speech, especially on college campuses.

State toleration for nonviolent direct action is, however, a double-edged sword for movement organizers. On the one hand, it provides a relatively risk-free means of assembling large numbers of people and giving them the sense that they are doing something meaningful for their beliefs; on the other, it deprives organizers of a potent weapon – the image of unreasonable and capricious public authorities throwing sincere young protesters into jail.

Modern states have increasingly substituted less obtrusive forms of regulation for exemplary punishment and incarceration. The requirement that demonstrators apply for a permit gives officials an easy way to keep tabs on their organizations and encourages them to resort to legal means.[28] Substituting the booking and fingerprinting of peaceful resisters for imprisonment can have a chilling effect on protest without filling the jails to capacity or forcing the state to engage in expensive litigation. In Washington, D.C., since the 1960s, organizers even receive free advice on how and where to organize a demonstration. The legitimation and institutionalization of collective action are often the most effective means of social control.

MAKING AND DIFFUSING OPPORTUNITIES

Unlike conventional forms of participation, contentious collective action demonstrates the possibilities of collective action to others, offering even resource-poor groups opportunities that their positions in society would deny them. This occurs when "early risers" make claims on elites that can be used by those with less daring and fewer resources. Moreover, collective action exposes opponents' points of weakness that may not be evident until they are challenged. It can also reveal unsuspected or formerly passive allies, both within and outside the system. Finally, it can pry open institutional barriers through which the demands of others will pour.

Once collective action is launched in part of a system on behalf of one type of goal, and by a particular group, the encounter between that group and its antagonists provides models of collective action, master frames and mobilizing structures that produce new opportunities. These secondary effects take three general forms: in the expansion of a group's own opportunities and those of cognate groups; in the dialectic between movements and countermovements; and, in the creation of opportunities for elites and authorities.

Expanding yours and your friends' opportunities

A movement can experience changes in its opportunity structure as a result of its own actions. For example, protesting groups increase their opportunities by expanding the repertoire of collective action into new forms. Although people normally use the forms of collective action that are known to them, they sometimes innovate, as in the transformation of the private petition into a tool of mass agitation in eighteenth-century England; or the expansion of nonviolence by the American Civil Rights movement. Each new form of collective action finds authorities unprepared; and while they are preparing a response, the protesting group can plan a further escalation of their forms of collective action (McAdam 1983), creating new opportunities and reaching new publics.

One of the most remarkable characteristics of collective action is that it expands the opportunities of others. Protesting groups put issues on the agenda with which other people identify and demonstrate the utility of collective action that others can copy or innovate upon. For example, as we will see in Chapter 7, the American Civil Rights movement expanded the doctrine of rights that became the "master frame" of the 1960s and 1970s (Hamilton 1986). Collective action embodies claims in dramatic ways that show others the way.

Movements and countermovements

This expansion of opportunities not only affects a movement's "alliance system"; it also affects what Bert Klandermans (1989) and Hanspeter Kriesi (1991) call its "conflict system." A movement that offends influential groups can trigger a countermovement. Movements that employ violence invite physical opposition. Movements that make extreme policy demands can be outmaneuvered by groups that pose the same claim in more acceptable form. Movements not only create opportunities for themselves and their allies; they also create opportunities for opponents.

When a movement's success threatens another group in a context of heightened mobilization, it can lead to outbidding and counterprotests. For example, the Italian extreme Left and extreme Right fed upon one another during the late 1960s, producing terrorist campaigns from both extremes (della Porta and Tarrow 1986). Much of the violence that made it seem that Italian society was crumbling was actually made up of leftists' and rightists' attacks on one another. The same was true of the sectarian violence in Northern Ireland, where Irish Republican Army attacks became the pretext for Protestant violence on Catholics.

Violent movements can stimulate peaceful countermovements, too. The lethal attacks on immigrants in Germany in 1991–3 led to the revival of the progressive coalition that had lain dormant since the end of the peace movement of the 1980s. But such protests and counterprotests are a volatile mix; sectarian groups sought to radicalize many of the nonviolent demonstrations against racism. This too can leave the impression that law and order are disintegrating, which in turn helps to justify more repressive policies by the state.

The spiral of conflict between the American Pro-Choice and Pro-Life movements in the 1980s and early 1990s is an example of how movements create opportunities for opponents. The access to abortion rights that was decreed by the Supreme Court in the early 1970s galvanized Catholics and fundamentalist

Protestants to organize against abortion clinics. This Pro-Life movement became so dynamic that it was a major force in the defeat of the Equal Rights Amendment in the 1980s (Mansbridge 1986). Eventually, a radical offshoot of Pro-Life called "Operation Rescue" used such radical direct tactics in the early 1990s that it stimulated a countermobilization campaign by the usually legalistic Pro-Choice forces.[29]

Making opportunities for elites

Finally, protesting groups create political opportunities for elites: Both in a negative sense, when their actions provide grounds for repression; and, in a positive one, when opportunistic politicians seize the opportunity created by challengers to proclaim themselves tribunes of the people. As we will see in Chapter 10, protesters on their own seldom have the power to affect the policy priorities of elites. This is both because their protests often take an expressive form, and because elites are unlikely to be persuaded to make policy changes that are not in their interest. Reform is most likely when challenges from outside the polity provide a political incentive for elites within it to advance their own policies and careers.

When reforms result, they less often embody the policy demands of individual protest movements than a compromise between the interests of reformers, the demands of challengers and the influence of a series of political mediations. It follows that reformist outcomes seldom make either protest movements or their opponents happy, as President Clinton discovered when he tried to mediate between gay and lesbian activists and the American military in 1993.

Political opportunism is not a monopoly of either the Left or the Right, parties of movement or parties of conservation. The conservative Eisenhower administration responded in essentially the same way to the Civil Rights movement as the liberal Kennedy administration – for the simple reason that both were concerned with electoral realignment and wished to minimize the foreign policy damage of American racism (Piven and Cloward 1979: ch. 4). Similarly, it was the conservative French Gaullists who responded to the revolt of May 1968 with a sweeping reform of higher education, as we will see in Chapter 10.

When are parties and interest groups most likely to take advantage of opportunities created by social movements? They appear to do so mainly when a system is challenged by a range of movements, and not when individual movement organizations mount challenges that can be easily repressed or isolated. That is to say, reformist outcomes are most likely when political opportunities have produced general confrontations among challengers, elites and authorities, as in the cycles of protest that will be examined in Chapter 9.

DECLINING OPPORTUNITIES

Political opportunities provide the major incentives for transforming mobilization potentials into action. Stable elements like state strength or weakness, the structure of the party system and forms of repression and facilitation structure the strategies that movements choose. But movements arise as the result of new or expanded opportunities; they signal the vulnerability of the state to collective action, and thereby open up opportunities for others – affecting both alliance and conflict systems. The process leads to state responses that, in one way or another, produce a new structure of opportunity.

The opening of opportunities produces external resources for people who lack internal ones, openings where there were only walls before, alliances that did not previously seem possible and realignments that appear capable of bringing new groups to power. But because these opportunities are external – and because they shift so easily from initial challengers to their allies and opponents, and finally to elites and authorities – opportunity structure is a fickle friend to movements, particularly to those that are based on resource-poor groups.

The result is that openings for reform and reconstruction quickly close, or allow challengers with different aims to march through the gates that the early risers have battered down. Thus, the 1989 revolutions in Eastern Europe that many thought would bring democracy to a part of the world that had long been denied freedom, produced few working democracies, several neo-Communist states and a number of countries that quickly disintegrated into ethnic conflict. Even in East Germany, quickly integrated into a stable Western democracy, the democratic Civic Forum that led the way to unification in 1989 was soon swept aside by the established parties. The most powerful German movement of the early 1990s was a violent racist reaction to economic distress that aimed its fury against immigrants and Jews.

The ephemeral and shifting nature of political opportunities does not mean that movements do not matter. Just as it was a political opportunity that brought the Bolsheviks to power in Russia in 1917, it was the opportunities provided by Gorbachev that broke down the walls of state socialism in 1989. But the shifting nature of political opportunities means that movements must build on more solid resources to prevent opportunities from slipping away. Of these, three are particularly crucial: The repertoire of collective action, the collective action frames that dignify and justify movements, and the organizational structures that link the center to the base of a movement and assure its interaction with powerholders. These are the powers of movement that will be analyzed in the next three chapters.

6

Acting collectively

On the morning of November 23, 1992, the residents of the small German town of Mölln arose to the smell of charred ruins and burnt flesh. During the night, the home of a Turkish immigrant family had been firebombed and three people – a woman and two teenagers – perished in the flames. No messages or press releases were left at the scene. But there was little doubt that it was the work of "Naziskins" – right wing thugs with a vaguely fascist ideology and a hatred of foreigners; a group that had been attacking immigrants, foreigners and Jews since unification three years earlier.[1]

The following weekend there were nationwide remembrances for the victims and massive protests against the outrage all over Germany. In Hamburg, 10,000 people attended the funeral. Most Turkish residents kept their stores closed, and at city halls, memorial gatherings were held. Members of the metalworkers' union put down their tools, and schools all over the country observed minutes of silence. The next Sunday in Berlin, thousands marched against racism and violence in what had been intended as a mass demonstration of peaceful solidarity.[2]

But very soon, a disturbance broke out as a group of "revolutionary Communists," a Maoist organization, fought with "autonomists," left wing militants whose organization dated back to the radical movements of the 1970s. Rocks were thrown, guns appeared and what had begun as a celebration of democratic unity and respect for the rights of immigrants ended in confusion and disillusionment. About ten people were injured in the melée and another ten were roughed up by the police, who made twenty-one arrests.

These incidents illustrate the three major types of publicly mounted collective action that will be analyzed in this chapter. The first, violence against others, is the oldest we know about; the second, the organized public demonstration, represents the main conventional expression of movement activity today; while the third, disruptive direct action, bridges the shifting frontier between convention and contention. Though violence, disruption and convention differ in a number of ways, they share a common thread: All are public expressions of the confrontation between challengers and authorities in the hazy area between institutional politics and individual dissent.

Mounting public actions is not all that movements do; they use different combinations of violence, disruption and convention to run up costs for their opponents, bring out supporters, express their claims and develop strategic relationships with allies. In different ways, they challenge opponents, create uncertainty and build solidarity. Looking at each type separately, and then at the dynamics of their relationships, will help us to chart the power in movement and understand its elusive nature.

CHALLENGE, UNCERTAINTY, SOLIDARITY

The first and most basic aspect of collective action is its capacity to challenge opponents or elites. In Italo Calvino's 1985 novel, *The Baron in the Trees,* there is a fictitious but archetypal example of a challenge when a young nobleman reacts against his father's authority by going up into the trees to live. Calvino's hero's act takes its power from its rupture with convention and its challenge to authority. He does not simply challenge his father's authority rhetorically, but takes an action which *embodies* that challenge and threatens a cost.

Challengers need not occupy public space in order to offer effective challenges. The American abolitionists who transported escaped slaves to Canada on the underground railroad were challenging both the slaveholders and the states' sovereignty; Japanese secretaries who quietly refused to serve tea to their bosses in the 1980s were threatening a deeply inbred structure of Japanese business norms; the Muslim schoolgirls who insisted on wearing headscarves to class in France in 1989 were challenging the secular norms of French public education. Challenges, writes Mary Katzenstein, can take the form of "unobtrusive mobilization" in institutions, in the family or in gender relations (1990).

Scholars of Third World peasants, observing how landlords' authority is often undermined through foot-dragging, petty sabotage, back-biting and tricks, have adopted the locution "resistance" to designate such behavior (Scott 1986; Colburn et al. 1989).[3] But such forms of everyday resistance – far from being in rupture with existing authority – are part of the structure of rural society and are closer to the passive *ressentiment* described by Scheler (1972) than to the collective challenges typical of social movements. The distinction is important, for social movements have two additional characteristics that are missing from everyday resentment: inducing uncertainty and building solidarity.

Returning to Calvino's (1985) story will help to understand the role of uncertainty. The young baron's protest gains its power not only from the drama of his challenge, but from its absence of predictable limits. No one has ever spent the night in the trees before. How can he contemplate such a thing? How long will he stay up there and what will be the cost? The day after he leaves the house, his younger brother ponders on his act:

It wasn't as if I didn't understand that my brother had no intention of coming down. But I made believe I didn't understand in order to get him to say something like: "I'm staying in the trees until snack time . . . or until sunset . . . or until dinnertime . . . or until it gets dark." To get him to say anything that would *signify a limit and put his act of protest in proportion* (emphasis added). (p. 16)

Uncertainty results not only from the uncertain *length* of a protest, as in Calvino's story, but from the indeterminacy of its cost. Nonviolent demonstrations are often more potent than actual violence because they pose the *possibility* of violence without giving police or authorities an excuse for repression. As political scientist Peter Eisinger (pp. 13–14) puts it:

What is implicitly threatening in a protest is not only the socially unconventional display of crowds of people which offends and frightens norm-abiding observers, *but the visions which bystanders and targets conjure up about what such obviously angry behavior could lead to* (emphasis added).

Uncertainty also arises from the possibility that an action will spread to others, thereby increasing its potential costs. This is why movements often claim to represent a broader constituency than those who are present in the protest: it is not antiabortion protesters but "Christians" who oppose abortion; not workers who are hit by layoffs at a particular factory but "the working class" that goes out on strike; not those who suffer from a visible environmental hazard, but "the interests of the planet" that suffer from pollution. To the uncertainty of the limits of a particular action is added the possibility that it will spread to others.

But like the "resistance" of Scott's peasants, the young baron's gesture in Calvino's story is an individual action – the rebellion of a young man against his father. Its impact is limited, not because it is unappealing or undramatic, but because it serves no collective end. Individual acts of defiance may lead to collective action, but in themselves, they are easy to ignore because of the absence of solidarity, which is the third major element in defining collective action.

Collective action not only challenges opponents and confronts them with uncertain limits and indeterminate outcomes; it embodies – or seems to embody – solidarity. A strike only succeeds to the extent that strikers build on preexisting solidarities; a strike that strains this solidarity risks undermining its own effectiveness. Conversely, collective action reinforces – and in some cases creates – solidarity. "Solidarity is founded upon rebellion," writes Camus, "and rebellion, in its turn, can only find its justification in solidarity."[4]

To sum up: The power of collective action results from three possible characteristics – challenge, uncertainty and solidarity. Challenges to authorities threaten costs and erupt in dramatic and often unruly ways. Their power results, in part, from their uncertain outcomes and from the possibility that others will join in. Internal solidarity supports the challenge and hints at the possibility of further disruption. Opponents, allies and bystanders respond, not only as a function of the sharpness of the challenge and the uncertainty it evokes, but from the solidarity they see in the protest.

Organizers therefore try to maximize the challenge and the uncertainty of the actions they organize, draw on the solidarity of participants and imply that they represent broader solidarities. While challenge, uncertainty and solidarity are properties found, to some extent, in all collective actions, some types maximize challenge, others threaten great uncertainty and still others emphasize solidarity. Let us survey the three main types of collective action – violence, convention and disruption – and how they embody these properties, before turning to the dynamics of collective action.

THE CHALLENGE OF VIOLENCE

Violence is not the only form of collective action that poses a challenge, but when most people think of collective action they turn instinctively to the idea of violence. Political scientists have reified this popular assumption by basing their most systematic studies of collective action on the quantitative data on violence that governments collect and disseminate. Violence is the most visible trace of collective action, both in contemporary news coverage and in the historical record. This is not surprising, because violence makes news and concerns those whose job it is to keep order. But it is also because most people have a morbid fascination with violence and are simultaneously repelled by and attracted to it. Finally, violence is the easiest kind of collective action for small groups to initiate without encountering major costs of coordination and control.

Why should violence be the easiest type of collective action to initiate? As I argued in Chapter 1, mass collective action has a high threshold of social transaction costs. The organizers of a peaceful demonstration need a plan of action, bullhorns, banners, a squad of trained parade marshals and a speaker who can hold the crowd's attention. They also must gain the cooperation or tolerance of the authorities. But fomenters of violence need no more than bricks, bats or chains, the sound of breaking windows, the crunch of batons on victims' heads and the solidarity of the gang. Most traditional forms of collective action centered on violence or on the threat of violence because it was the easiest form of collective action for isolated, illiterate and local groups to initiate.

In light of the ease of initiating violence, it is interesting that violence has become more rare in contemporary democracies than the other forms of collective action that we will examine. We already see this change in Charles Tilly's research on British collective action, in the shift from the brawls and rick-burnings of the mid-eighteenth century to the petitions and demonstrations that dominate the historical record by 1834 (1993a). The modern state has increased the amount of concerted collective action but tamed the degree of violence.

Major outbreaks of violence still occur during and after breaks in regimes, when movements lack recourse to legitimate access in their own countries, or at the tail end of movements that have lost their mass base. Violence is also a product of the interaction between protestors and the forces of order. The modern European record, writes Charles Tilly, shows a rough division of labor: "Repressive forces do the largest part of the killing and wounding, while the groups they are seeking to control do most of the damage to objects" (1978: 177).

Although violence frightens people, it has a severe limitation as a political weapon: It reduces uncertainty. As long as violence remains a possibility behind protestors' actions, uncertainty reigns, and collective actors gain psychological leverage vis-à-vis opponents. But where violence occurs or is even likely, this gives authorities a mandate for repression (Eisinger 1973) and turns nonviolent sympathizers away.

In cycles of protest, violence has a polarizing effect on conflict and alliance systems. It transforms the relations between challengers and authorities from a confused, many-sided game into a bipolar one in which people are forced to choose sides, allies defect, bystanders retreat and the state's repressive apparatus swings into action.[5] The threat of violence is a major power of movement, but it turns into a liability as other actors in the polity become frightened, elites regroup in the name of social peace and the forces of order learn to respond. The main reason why organizers of mass demonstrations have learned to keep them under strict control is to limit the costs of violence (Cardon and Heurtin 1990).

It is only in regimes in which order has broken down, or in which citizens are divided by fundamental ethnic, religious or national cleavages, that violence has a greater power than other forms of collective action. In the last thirty years, we have seen major outbreaks of organized violence between sectarian groups in Northern Ireland and Sri Lanka; on the part of Muslim fundamentalists against secular states in the Middle East; and of guerillas against what they regard as illegitimate rule in Afghanistan, Palestine and Latin America. Prevented from dealing with these challenges by legal means, states responded with martial law, political imprisonment and torture and the use of death squads.

The breakup of the former Soviet Union and its dependent states in Eastern Europe after 1989 has increased the amount of violence in the world, mainly on the part of ethnic groups which see in the collapse of Communist control the chance to gain their own states. Both sectarian violence and interethnic rivalries are the outcome of the breakdown of state control when political entrepreneurs see the opportunity to mobilize religion or ethnicity for political purposes. In the concluding chapter, we will ask whether this wave of sectarian and ethnic conflict is leading to a more violent movement society.

The size illusion

In popular memory, the most common fomenters of violence are the mob and the crowd. The image of the "dangerous classes" that developed in nineteenth-century Europe was based on the fear that, once violence erupted, hordes of people would run rampant and social order would be destroyed (Chevalier 1973; McPhail 1991). A whole jurisprudence of crowd control developed around the fear of the mob, and this image of mob violence is still widespread in popular culture.

But violence more commonly occurs at the instigation of small and tightly organized groups than at the hands of unruly mobs. For example, in a study of nearly five thousand protest events in Italy from 1965 to 1975, the vast majority of violent events were found to be the fruit of small groups either clashing with police, destroying property or attacking opposing groups (Tarrow 1989a: ch. 12). Violence by large groups rampaging through a city constituted only one percent of the events in this highly charged period (p. 78). Similarly, most of the violence against people that racked Los Angeles after the Rodney King verdict appears to have been animated by organized gangs rather than rampaging mobs.

As the state has increased its capacity for repression, violent protest has begun to pose extreme risks and high costs. The result is that even in authoritarian systems, opposition movements have become skilled at mounting unobtrusive, symbolic and peaceful forms of collective action that are difficult to repress. Long before state socialism collapsed in Eastern Europe, opponents of the regimes in that part of the world had developed a broad repertoire of actions which avoided violence or even any hint of violence.

The attraction of violence is that it is easy for people without political resources to initiate. But the difficulty of violence is that, once it has begun, it legitimates repression, polarizes the public and ultimately depends on a small core of militants for whom violence has become the main form of politics. When that happens, organizers are trapped in a military confrontation with authorities that it is virtually impossible for them to win. This may be why practically all of the modular forms of collective action that have developed as staples of the contemporary repertoire in democratic states are nonviolent. Or more specifically, they are divided between convention and disruption.

CONVENTIONAL COLLECTIVE ACTION

Mounting a large and nonviolent form of collective action requires organizers to solve a number of problems – problems that I have summarized with the term "the social transaction costs" of collective action. In the nineteenth century, social democratic mass parties attempted to solve these problems by internalizing their base.[6] But most large nonviolent collective actions today are coordinated through a process that more resembles the "contracts by convention" outlined by Hardin (1982) than actual organizational control. Coordinating large and imperfectly integrated groups of people against compact and powerful opponents requires the tacit coordination of participants' expectations (Schelling: 71). This is the major appeal of the conventional forms of collective action for it is easiest for people to employ a form of collective action that they know how to use. One reason for the survival for the *charivari* well into the nineteenth century was that it was a familiar form, easy to employ and with a cultural resonance. The same is true of the major conventional forms of collective action today; although they began as disruptions of established routine, they are by now part of a repertoire that is generally known and understood in the political culture of modern states. Here are two major examples.

The strike

The strike offers a good example of how forms of collective action that begin as disruptive confrontations become modular and ultimately conventional. The first use of the term ''strike'' in English seems to date from the actions of the eighteenth-century sailors who struck the sails of their ships as a sign of their unwillingness to work (Linebaugh and Rediker: 240). But the emergence of the term in many European languages about the same time suggests that it had multiple origins (Tilly 1978: 159).

The strike predates industrialization and often included a variety of social actors, none of whom could really be regarded as ''proletarian.''[7] But unlike the peasant revolt, which was inseparable from the seignorial system, once the strike was invented it was *not* inseparable from any particular occupation. As it became known that strikes could succeed, striking spread from skilled to unskilled workers, from the large factory to smaller firms, from withholding labor to the withholding of produce, from industry to agriculture and from there to the public services. So habitual did the strike become that by now it is a virtual part of the institutions of collective bargaining, with its own jurisprudence, rituals and expectations among both challengers and opponents.

Strikes were not only a means for workers to put pressure on management. In the course of the nineteenth century, they became a source of class solidarity. This was reflected in the increasing exchange of support of workers across occupational and geographic lines (Aminzade 1981: 81–2) and in the ritual of the strike which was designed to enhance solidarity. Moreover, strikes could be employed in combination with other forms: occupations, marches, industrial sabotage, petitions and legal actions. From a spontaneous withdrawal of labor, the strike became the means through which workers built and expressed solidarity, put pressure on opponents, sought external support and negotiated their differences from a position of enhanced, if temporary, power.

The demonstration

Demonstrations also began as disruptive actions that later became institutionalized. They seem to have developed when challengers moved from one target to another, either to attack opponents or to deliver demands.[8] The public meeting that habitually completes a march began when the crowd arrived at its destination, presented its petition or attacked its enemies. It is now more likely to end with the making of speeches and the singing of rock songs.

Public demonstrations were connected to democratization – or at least arose alongside the earliest public campaigns for political and social rights. For example, although there were nearly constant demonstrations outside the Hôtel de Ville in Paris during the first French Revolution, as late as February 1848, parliamentary liberals still had to disguise their demonstrations as "banquets." It was in the democratic phase of the 1848 Revolution that the demonstration appeared in its full modern form,[9] for the leaders of the new Republic could not refuse the people the right to present their petitions (Favre: 16). From then on, the typical form through which all kinds of French movements made themselves known was the peaceful demonstration in a public place.

Unlike strikes, which required some relationship to the withholding of labor or of a product to attract supporters, demonstrations could spread rapidly because they were almost infinitely flexible. They could be employed on behalf of a claim, against an opponent, to express the existence of a group or its solidarity with another group, or celebrate a victory or mourn the passage of a leader. Demonstrations thus became the classical modular form of collective action.

As demonstrations were legalized, they gave rise to both a jurisprudence and a culture (Hubrecht 1990; Champagne 1990). Rather than allowing the police to manhandle demonstrators, organizers began to employ their own parade marshalls (Cardon and Huertin: 199), and developed a repeated sequence of routes, slogans, signs and a regular marching order (Favre 1990). Different movements favored one trajectory or another, so that the political coloration of the group could often be determined from the route of its marchers. Even the role of nonparticipants – the press, the forces of order, bystanders and opponents – eventually became part of the demonstration ritual (Favre: 18–32).

Repressive states almost always regard demonstrations as potential riots which can lead to the savage repression of peaceful protesters and sometimes – as in the events of January 1905 in Russia – to revolution. Constitutional states have come to accept demonstrations as a normal, and even an advantageous practice, as indicated by the fact that demonstrators often receive police protection and even guidance.[10] From the unruly movement of protesters from one place to another – often up to no good – the demonstration became the major modern nonelectoral expression of civil politics.

DISRUPTION AND UNCERTAINTY

Conventional collective action began as disruption. Disruption has taken a variety of historical forms; from the attack on a wrongdoer's house and the assault on a miller's grain store in the eighteenth century, to the barricades of the nineteenth century and the sit–ins and sit-down strikes of our century. In its most direct form, it is no more than a threat of violence: "If you do not produce grain or money," the challenger says, "or do not cease to use the machines that are destroying our livelihood, you may suffer physical harm."

But disruption has a more indirect logic in its contemporary forms. First, it is the concrete expression of a movement's determination. By sitting, standing or moving together aggressively in public space, demonstrators signal their existence and reinforce their solidarity. Second, disruption obstructs the routine activities of opponents, bystanders or authorities. Third, disruption broadens the circle of conflict. By blocking traffic or interrupting public business, protestors inconvenience citizens, pose a risk to law and order and draw the state into a conflict.

Disruption need not take openly threatening public form. First the Civil Rights movement and then the women's movement have taught Americans that if the personal is political, political causes can be advanced through personal means. What would be nondisruptive for one set of social arrangements can be highly disruptive in another; a primary battlefield for American feminism has been the family – even on the part of nonmilitant women bereft of resources.[11]

While the characteristic nineteenth-century form of confrontation was the barricade, the twentieth century has added its own accretions to the repertoire of disruption. When employers found they could lock their workers out of a factory to end a strike, workers invented the sit-down strike and added the factory occupation to their repertoire. To the march ending in a demonstration in a public place were added the tools of nonviolent direct action and the sit-in – perhaps the major contributions of our century to the repertoire of collective action.

Nonviolent direct action

Nonviolent collective action emerged in the twentieth century as the most elaborately theorized form of confrontation. Gene Sharp finds evidence of nonviolence far back in history.[12] But it only received a formal theorization by Gandhi after he and his followers used it against South African discrimination and to overthrow British colonial rule in India.[13] Although the tactics of the movement were peaceful, Gandhi was quite clear about its disruptive aim. In initiating the 1930–1 nonviolence campaign, he wrote to the British viceroy: "It is not a matter of carrying conviction by argument. The matter resolves itself into one of matching forces" (Sharp: 85).

The power of nonviolence lies not only in its challenge to authorities, but in its encouragement of solidarity among people who would hesitate to openly attack them. We see this clearly in its use by the American Civil Rights movement, whose leaders mobilized the conservative, church-going sectors of the African American community for nonviolent direct action. Externally, they counterpoised the well-dressed peaceful marchers of the movement to the thuggery of the police, while turning the religiosity of the southern black middle class into a basis of solidarity.[14]

The power of nonviolent disruption comes mainly from its uncertainty. It is not violent but it threatens violence; its course is planned but its outcome depends on others' reactions to it which cannot be predicted; unless it is kept under strict control, outsiders can free ride on the efforts of the organizers to advance their own goals and tactics. Although Gandhi's campaigns in India are often held up as the model for nonviolent collective action, the massacre of his followers in Amritsar in 1919 – what Gandhi called his "Himalayan blunder" – showed what can happen when the tactic is used against ruthless or uncontrolled opponents.[15]

Although it began as a tool of nationalist agitation in the Third World, nonviolent direct action spread to a variety of movements in the 1960s and 1970s. It was used in the Prague spring, in the student movements of 1968, by the European and American peace and environmental movements, by opponents of the Marcos regime in the Philippines and by opponents of military rule in Thailand and Burma. Its capacity to spread from one kind of movement to very different ones is dramatically demonstrated by its use by antiabortion protesters in the United States.[16]

The power of disruptive collective action lies in its capacity to challenge authorities, foster solidarity and create uncertainty. Such forms as the strike and the demonstration first appeared as disruptive tactics. But eventually, they became as conventional as the petition, the boycott and the tax revolt before them. Other forms, like the barricade and the armed demonstration, fell by the wayside as they proved too easy to repress. The history of collective action is the history of how new and disruptive forms of collective action became part of the conventional repertoire as they were learned, experimented with, reacted to and absorbed by opponents and elites.

In our century, forms like the sit-in, the occupation and civil disobedience have begun to describe a similar path from disruption to convention. Invented by innovative challengers during major cycles of protest, they were theorized and diffused around the world by the mass media and movement evangelists (McAdam and Rucht 1993). They empower movements by their capacity to engage citizens in disruptive confrontations with authorities while offering the latter no valid pretext for repression. When they are repressed despite their peaceful face, the result is often an expansion of conflict to broader publics, empowered by a sense of outrage and indignation.

Such movements have a chance to succeed when they identify consensual issues and frame them in ways that broader publics can identify with; they fail when the regimes they face are more ruthless than they are, or when they fail to control the outcomes of their protests. But they also face a more subtle danger:

Like many of the forms of collective action inherited from the past, they can dissolve into violence or become conventional. This takes us to the dynamics of collective action.

THE DYNAMICS OF COLLECTIVE ACTION

As we look over the panoply of collective action forms in democratic states today, we encounter an apparent paradox: Although disruption of the lives of opponents appears to be the most potent form of collective action, and violence is the easiest form to initiate, the majority of protest forms we see today are conventional; that is, peaceful, orderly routines that break no laws and violate no spaces. Consider the following table of the collective action forms that were found in the Italian press between 1966 and 1973 – a particularly tumultuous period of political and social protest. When these forms were grouped into three broad classes, 56 percent were classed as conventional, 19 percent as

Table 6.1. *Incidence of All Forms of Collective Action as Percentage of Total Forms of Action, Italy, 1966–73*

Action Form	% of All Forms	Incidence
Strike	20.3	1974
March	12.4	1206
Public meeting	9.8	955
Occupation	8.3	812
Obstruction	8.2	797
Assembly	7.3	709
Petition	6.6	639
Violent attack	6.0	589
Attack on property	6.0	584
Violent clash	5.1	497
Clash with police	3.9	382
Forced entry	1.0	100
Hunger strike	.7	70
Rampage	.6	58
Direct action	.4	48
Leafletting	.3	33
Symbolic protest	.3	33
Legal action	.2	18
Random violence	.1	15
Theft	.1	11
Campout in public place	.1	7
Miscellaneous other	1.6	154
Unclassified	.4	48
Total	99.7	9739

Source: Recalculated from Sidney Tarrow, *Democracy and Disorder. Protest and Politics in Italy, 1965–1975* (Oxford and New York: Oxford University Press, 1989), p. 68.

Figure 6.1. *Large Violent Events, Small Group Violence, and Terrorism, Italy, 1966–1983*

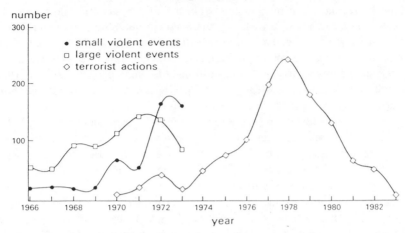

Source: Sidney Tarrow, *Democracy and Disorder. Protest and Politics in Italy, 1965–1975* (Oxford and New York: Oxford University Press, 1989), p. 306.

confrontational and symbolic and 23 percent as violent.[17] Why is convention the numerically dominant form of collective action even during a major cycle of protest?

The data in Table 6.1 expose a second puzzle: While disruption grew rapidly in the first part of the period – as workers used radical forms of action and students occupied universities – by the early 1970s, these disruptive forms had given way to violence. Combining the protest events collected by the author with Donatella della Porta's data on Italian terrorism, we see a sharp increase in, first, small group violence and then in organized terror after the summit of mass protest ended in 1968–9. These data are compared in Figure 6.1:

The two findings seem clear: Even during a period of generalized turbulence, most Italians never went beyond using conventional forms like the strike, the march and the demonstration; and some were even content with petitioning or seeking audiences with authorities. But as in the United States during the same period, the disruptive forms that provided a mass base in 1968 soon gave way to organized and small-group violence. Given the fact that disruption combines challenge, uncertainty and solidarity without incurring the risks of violence or the routines of convention, how can we explain the numerical dominance of convention during such a period of generalized strife, and the shift from disruption to violence within it?

From disruption to violence

Taking the second problem first, we begin from the assumption that collective action – no matter how it arises – is the major resource that organizers use to mobilize followers. Collective action is both cost and benefit (Hirschman 1982). In order to outweigh the costs with benefits, challengers make expressive claims and sweeping demands to gain attention from allies and opponents and to inspire their followers (Gamson and Meyer 1993). The obvious way to gain attention and attract a following is disruption.

When disruptive forms are first employed, they frighten antagonists with their potential cost, shock onlookers and worry elites concerned with public order. But newspapers gradually begin to give less and less space to protests that would have merited a banner headline when they first appeared on the streets. Repeating the same form of collective action over and over reduces uncertainty and is greeted with a smile or a yawn. Participants, at first enthused and invigorated by their solidarity and ability to challenge authorities, become jaded or disillusioned. Authorities, instead of calling out the troops or allowing police to wade into a crowd, infiltrate dissenting groups and separate leaders from followers. Routinization follows hard upon disruption.

Faced by the routinization of protest and the impending defection of supporters, leaders can invent bolder forms of contention or use the same ones in more radical ways. Physical violence and exaggerated rhetoric are used to reinvigorate flagging militants, attract new supporters and retain the notice of the state. But such tactics also chill the blood of bystanders, give pause to prospective allies and cause many who joined the movement in its enthusiastic early phase to defect. As these activists leave the movement, mass, peaceful forms of collective action become harder to mount and the militants at the movement's core become skilled at using their small numbers. The most likely outcome of small numbers and professionalized leaders is violence.

The repressive tactics of the state reinforce this tendency to violence by isolating militants still further. When British authorities turned against Painite and radical groups following the French Revolution, "what remained of English radicalism committed itself to the pursuit of those subversive, clandestine and republican objectives which its more moderate leaders had hitherto consistently repudiated" (Goodwin: 416). The Russian populists who, in the late nineteenth century, built bombs and attacked the aristocracy were, in part, reacting to the repression of the Czarist regime against all forms of open protest.

A similar dynamic could be seen in the late 1960s, as the radical branch of the American New Left split off from its main trunk. When the demonstration against the Vietnam war at the 1968 Chicago Democratic convention led to violent encounters with the police, the movement collapsed. As James Miller writes, "it left behind a congeries of smaller single-issue movements" in some of which "frustrated revolutionists built bombs, turning reveries of freedom into cruel, ineffectual outbursts of terrorism" (p. 317).

No wonder, then, that movements repeatedly divide over the issue of violence. The battle between the Girondins and the Jacobins in the French Revolution was triggered by a dispute about the execution of the king – the Girondins soon following him to the guillotine. Within the British Chartists, there was a long debate about the virtues of physical versus moral action. On the European Left, the Anarchists and Social Democrats argued about the violence of the former and the bureaucratization of the latter.

Movements in recent decades have produced similar bifurcations. In America, even within the largely peaceful Civil Rights movement, the debate between the older, moderate wing of the movement, and the young firebrands who challenged it for leadership, was largely about violence. Each phase of the movement led to increased disputes between the older and the younger branches of the movement. After Martin Luther King, Jr.'s murder and the shift of the movement to the North, his worst fears were realized as violence broke out and was used to justify the "law and order" policies of the Nixon years (Button 1978). In this cycle of protest, as the original forms of disruptive politics were consumed and the movement's center of gravity shifted from the South to the cities of the North, mass movement gave way to the practice of organized violence and thence to movement collapse.

From contention to convention

But the violent turn of radical groups is not the only possible outcome of the problem of sustaining collective action. Alternatively, as the excitement of the disruptive phase of a movement dies, and the police become skilled at controlling it, movements institutionalize their tactics and attempt to gain concrete benefits for their supporters through negotiation and compromise – a route that often succeeds at the cost of transforming the movement into a party or interest group.

At times, the forms of disruption that invite repression are discarded as participants learn to avoid them.[18] At other times the forms of confrontation are themselves institutionalized as authorities begin to tolerate them or facilitate their use.[19] And at times, to win policy successes that supporters demand or authorities proffer, leaders move from confrontation to cooperation. The familiar pattern of goal displacement that observers since Michels have found in social movements results from this shift in tactics.

The impact of this process of institutionalization may be negative, as Frances Fox Piven and Richard Cloward have argued in the case of four movements in the United States (1979). By reducing the uncertainty in their tactics and accepting compromises for their claims, movements may destroy their capacity to inspire supporters and to hold the attention of elites. This was what Piven and Cloward found for the National Welfare Rights Organization. So determined were its leaders to make it into a mass membership organization that the disruptive source of their power was lost (ch. 5).

But there can be compensations for groups that choose the institutional route. Ordinary people are more likely to participate in forms of collective action that they know about than risk the uncertainty and potential violence of radical direct action. Once a movement's chosen form of action crystallizes into convention, it becomes a known part of the repertoire and lowers the social transaction costs of bringing out large numbers of supporters. And given the repertoire's modular nature, these conventional practices can be redeployed, tinkered with and combined with other forms, as we can see from the following examples.

Innovation at the margins

While some parts of the collective action repertoire are rigid (Tilly 1978: 154–5), the core of the modular repertoire is flexible: So much so that, around the skeletons of these major forms, organizers can array a variety of other tactics (Morris 1993: 626–7). Some of these – like petitions, audiences and legal actions – are equally conventional, but their use in combination with strikes or demonstrations increases the marginal power of movements. Others add spontaneity and symbolism to the conventional core, which attracts attention and disconcerts opponents.

Consider first the forms of collective action that can be employed together with the strike. Although strikes are defined as the withdrawal of labor or services, they are often employed in combination with occupations, or together with more conventional marches, petitions and legal actions. Assemblies prepare the workers for strikes and elect strike committees; organizers in an especially militant sector may parade around the factory to attract other workers' support; pickets block the gates of the plant to keep raw materials out.

Even within the fabric of conventional actions, there is room for symbolic innovation and spontaneity. Around the modular skeleton of the demonstration, demonstrators march in uniform or carry pitchforks or monkey wrenches to symbolize their militancy (Lumley: 224). Feminists wear witches' costumes to mock their caricaturing by male opponents (Costain 1992: 49); peace marchers fit themselves out in skeleton outfits to symbolize their fear of nuclear holocaust; lumbermen parade carrying wooden caskets to symbolize the death of the timber industry if environmentalists have their way.

Over the long run, such innovations at the margins may simply enliven a conventional form of collective action by adding to it elements of play and carnival. But they can also change the nature of the repertoire as the innovations themselves become habitual. For example, during the French Revolution, the grisly habit of marching along with victim's heads stuck on pikes was the inverted descendent of the practice of hoisting wax heads of heroes aloft and carrying them around as proxy commanders. It reappeared with each new *journée* of the Revolution.[20] The repertoire of collective action changes through a process of accretion of new elements onto conventional forms. These innovations tend to cluster during periods of social upheaval and political protest, becoming gradually more conventional. As Kafka wrote in one of his most prescient fables:

Leopards break into the temple and drink to the dregs what is in the sacrificial pitchers; this is repeated over and over again; finally it can be calculated in advance, and it becomes a part of the ceremony.[21]

Multiform movements

Some theorists believe that particular actors are drawn inevitably to certain forms of collective action.[22] But this is to misunderstand one of the major powers of the modern movement – its capacity to combine a variety of forms of collective action. Movements are not limited to particular types of action but have access to a variety of forms, either alone or in combination. It is their flexibility that allows them to combine the demands and the participation of broad coalitions of actors in the same campaigns of collective action.

This was beginning to be true in the nineteenth century, when the same movements combined a variety of forms of collective action. For example, as historian Jack Blocker writes of American temperance, its members

conducted surveys, prayed and sang, marched on saloons, marched in parades, marched in demonstrations, and attended meetings and conventions. They destroyed the contents of saloons with axes, hatchets, hammers, rocks, and metal bars. . . . they created pressure groups and political parties, petitioned, circularized candidates, canvassed, voted, and watched the polls. (p. xiv)

Contemporary movements are even more flexible in their available tactics. Consider the environmental movement. Dieter Rucht has compared its tactical repertoire in France and Germany. He found that, at one time or another, antinuclear protestors in these countries used forms of collective action that were expressive or instrumental, confrontational, violent or conventional, and were brought together in campaigns, skirmishes and battles (1990). Although the movement used nonviolent direct action to great effect, it was its capacity to manipulate and combine different elements of the repertoire according to the target, the strategy of opponents and available allies that gave it its flexibility and much of its power.[23]

The same flexibility can be seen in the American women's movement. When the conservative Reagan administration came to power, As Anne Costain notes, "movement groups changed from working inside the institutions of government . . . to more electorally focused events and rising political protest" (1992:

126–7). Activities of the Pro-Choice movement ranged from "teas held at churches to discuss change in the laws and endless trips to the state legislatures" to "counter-hearings" and "speak-outs" (Staggenborg: 29, 44). As the movement took on broader goals, its tactics ranged from education and social gatherings all the way to confronting lawmakers and disrupting public hearings (p. 46). The multiform nature of the women's movement gave it the capacity to use almost every form of collective action but violence.

CONCLUSIONS

The modern movement repertoire offers activists three basic types of collective action – violence, disruption and convention. They combine in different degrees the properties of challenge, uncertainty and solidarity. The first form, violence, is the easiest to initiate, but under normal circumstances it is limited to small groups willing to exact damage and risk repression. The second form, convention, has the advantage of building on routines that people know and that elites will accept or even facilitate. This is the source of its numerical predominance in the repertoire. The third form, disruption, breaks with routine, startles bystanders and leaves elites disoriented, at least for a time. Disruption is the source of much of the innovation in the repertoire; but, for the reasons sketched above, it is unstable and easily degenerates into violence or hardens into convention.

The dynamics of change in collective action are both short term and long term. In the short run, movements pose extreme demands and invent new forms of action to support them. These quickly become habitual, evoke patterned responses and leave militants weary and onlookers bored. Movements that continue to repeat the same actions run the risk of losing support and being ignored. They can respond in one of two basic ways – with radicalization or by moving towards convention. But each of these routes poses risks: While the first narrows their base and invites factionalism and repression, the second leads to compromise and the risk of co-optation that Michels long ago predicted.

In the long run, the repertoire has evolved through the absorption of the innovations that work and the rejection of the ones that do not. Over time, originally disruptive forms like the strike and the demonstration became conventional because they presented effective challenges, maintained and built solidarity and usually avoided repression by controlling violence and uncertainty. In our century, disruptive forms like nonviolent collective action, sit-ins and occupations have begun to produce their conventional equivalents. But when regimes break down and opportunities open for long-repressed minorities – as in the former state socialist regimes – violence resurfaces in more lethal form.

Such movements as ecology, civil rights and feminism have combined challenge, solidarity and uncertainty in their protests. They have maintained support and grown so well over the past three decades, in part because they had available a known, well-understood repertoire of modular forms to build upon. They adapted to change because their leaders innovated on these basic models with skill and creativity. But their success was also based on the capacity to embody politically advantageous and culturally appropriate frames of meaning. In the next chapter, I will turn to how movements mobilize consensus through the framing of collective action.

7

Framing collective action[1]

In Year V of the revolutionary era, the commissioner of the revolutionary executive power in Grenoble wrote:

It is a contravention of the constitutional charter . . . to insult, provoke, or threaten citizens because of their choice of clothing. Let taste and propriety preside over your dress; never turn away from agreeable simplicity. . . . Renounce these signs of rallying, these *costumes of revolt,* which are the uniforms of an enemy army.[2]

The commissioner was in a position to know. In the decade in which he wrote, the French produced the first systematic attempts to reshape a political culture around new forms of dress, holidays, salutations and public works.[3] And as the Revolution spread, so did its symbolism. Supporters would challenge citizens who dared to be seen on the street without the regulation red bonnet; even the king had one stuck on his head when he was brought back from his attempted flight to Varennes (Schama: 603–4).[4]

The myth of the Revolution crystallized into a model of collective action that was transported all over Europe – mainly on the bayonets of the French army. But the attempt to shape it into a consensual model among the French themselves never succeeded. For so divided were they about their Revolution that those who carried its mantle had to wrestle for symbolic legitimacy against those who would push its logic to new extremes and those who wanted to reverse it. It was only by distilling the vivid red of Revolution into the ceremonial purple of Empire that the costume of revolt was transmuted into the cloth of consensus, as Napoleon well understood.[5]

Attempts at symbolic mobilization accompany every modern movement, from the donning of simple military tunics by the Russian and Chinese Communists, to the pagan glitter of the Fascist hierarchs, to the simple khadi of Indian nationalists and the scruffy beards of Latin American *guerrilleros.* Movement leaders wear the costumes and proffer the symbols of revolt to gain support and to mark themselves off from their enemies. But when the dust of revolution settles, the culture of consensus is often more enduring than the costume of revolt.

Finding symbols that will be familiar enough to mobilize people around is one of the major tasks of movement organizations; maintaining the movement's integrity against the claims of inherited culture is the opposite side of that problem. This was hard enough for the French revolutionaries who were dealing with a largely illiterate population through slow and uneven communications. But it has been rendered more complex for today's social movements by the barrage of information that circulates through books, newspapers and especially the mass media. Although slogans, songs and graffiti remain important forms of symbolic communication – especially in authoritarian systems (Bushnell 1990) – in the permanent fair of news and entertainment that suffuses the airwaves today, movements have a harder time "making" news than in the past.

This raises the broader question of the role of beliefs in bringing about political and social change. No serious student of movements any longer believes – if any ever did – that material interests translate straightforwardly into guides to action. Most students think that meanings are "constructed."[6] But we must be wary of turning mass politics into no more than a form of political theatre, a set of "symbol-laden performances whose efficacy lies largely in their power to move specific audiences" (Esherick and Wasserstrom: 839). Movements frame their collective action around cultural symbols that are selectively chosen from a cultural toolchest and creatively converted into collective action frames by political entrepreneurs (Swidler 1986; Laitin 1988).

The distinction is important, for if the struggle between movements and their opponents was primarily symbolic, then a social movement could be understood as no more than a cognitive message center, either reviving old meanings from within a cultural tradition, or spinning new meanings out of leaders' imaginings. In that case, we would be able to "read" the interaction between movements and authorities as a literary critic reads a text – as a contest between competing tropes. But if, as I will argue, meanings are constructed out of social and political interaction by movement entrepreneurs, there is no substitute for relating text to context and asking how movements themselves make that connection. As anthropologist David Kertzer advises, "A view of culture that does not account for interaction between our symbol system and the physical world of human activity is bound to lead to a mystical anthropology" (1988: 175).

How symbolic discourse takes shape and provides power to social movements is the question to be taken up in this chapter. I will first sketch how the concept of political culture has been used by theorists to analyze the symbols that movements employ. I will then argue for a strategic approach to the construction of meaning, based on the concepts of collective action frames, consensus formation and mobilization and political opportunity. The American Civil Rights and the Polish Solidarity movements will be analyzed to show how consensus is mobilized and new meanings constructed in an age when the media do as much or more to control the construction of meaning than states or social actors.

FROM POLITICAL CULTURE TO STRATEGIC FRAMING

Almost thirty years ago, Gabriel Almond and Sidney Verba introduced a new concept – political culture – to connect the structural bases of politics to their institutional outcomes (pp. 1–3). Their argument was that each political system has a greater or a lesser degree of consensus around its legitimating symbols, and that citizens contribute to the maintenance of the system by their knowledge of and support for these symbols. A special kind of culture was the "civic" culture, a mix of subject, citizen and activist orientations that sustains a democratic politics.

Even in its heyday, this concept of culture was never effectively trained on collective action. There were two major problems. First, in the creation and propagation of citizens' attitudes, there was no active agency. The values that Almond and Verba studied – like citizens' sense of political efficacy, support for democracy and mutual trust and cooperation – were generated by history, institutions, habit and outcomes – everything but people making explicit cultural choices. Second, Almond and Verba interpreted dissent in terms of the values they took to be requisite for the maintenance of democratic consensus. To explain values that lay outside that consensus, they resorted to the concept of a "subculture" (pp. 26–9). The result was that the symbols that animated contentious collective action remained residual to the culture of democracy.[7]

Floating culture

Recently, cultural historians and political anthropologists have used the concept of political culture to study revolutionary change. The first to do so – and still the most successful – was George Mosse in his reconstruction of the creation of a German national myth. In his book *The Nationalization of the Masses,* Mosse took his cue from the way the Jacobins manipulated the symbols of the French Revolution. Focusing on the construction of a German national myth, he saw the entire tradition of mass politics growing out of the French Revolution as a species of theatre, steeped in ritual and inherently antiparliamentary to the extent that it posited an unmediated relationship between the people and its leaders (p. 2).

Mona Ozouf took the French revolutionary festival as her subject, showing how changes in the festival reflected the dynamic of the regimes in power (1988). Keith Baker went further, arguing that the symbols generated by the Revolution created a "metanarrative" that later generations would draw upon (1990). Lynn Hunt studied how both public monuments (1984) and pornographic slurs on the Monarchy (1992) reflected the Revolution's need to build a new national myth and destroy the legitimacy of the royal family. Benedict Anderson (1990; 1991) wrote of how nations constructed meanings and – in so doing – invented themselves.

These new approaches to political culture brought to bear a creative mix of history, anthropology, politics and literary analysis. For example, in his study of *Ritual, Politics, and Power,* anthropologist David Kertzer argued that the power of symbols extends from the rituals of consecration to the struggle for power between challengers and the state (1988: chs. 6 and 7). Benedict Anderson combined his knowledge of Southeast Asian politics, the history of nationalism and an encultured Marxism to show how nations "imagine" themselves into existence through the media of print, technology and colonialism (1990; 1991).

But in much of this literature, political culture emerged as oddly disembodied at the same time as it was accorded tremendous power to change people's lives. For example, Baker sees the entire French Revolution as "a script" – "a symbolic ordering of human experience," a "master narrative of time and place." "All this," he continues, "was a rhetorical – *which is to say at once a cultural and a political – act,* part of the competition to fix the meaning of a situation that is inherent in every political moment" (p. 204, emphasis added). But if meanings are "fixed" by such rhetorical renderings, who does the rendering and won't future movements require further agency to be mobilized? Is it enough to establish a discourse in order to continue to shower meanings on the society below?

The same problems of agency and strategy appear in the dramaturgical treatment given to the Chinese student movement of 1989 by two culturally sensitive American scholars, Joseph Esherick and Jeffrey Wasserstrom. They show how the forms of political theatre used by the students had precedents in Chinese political culture (1990). But what of the Statue of Liberty that the same students constructed of papier maché and dragged across Tienanmen Square? One may be forgiven for thinking that its use had more to do with riveting the attention of the international media on the Chinese democracy movement than with evoking the rituals of the Chinese past.

The same problems appear in how the spatial diffusion of nationalism is studied by Benedict Anderson. He is careful to distinguish the diffusion of the *grammar* of nationalism from its texts: The former is inherent in capitalism and technology and travels with them around the world, while the latter is culturally specific and rooted in particular countries. Anderson proposes that modern nationalism was diffused around the world through newspapers, railroads, censuses, maps and museums. But even if we accept his locution that nations are "imagined" – and there is reason to think that conflicts of interest have had a lot to do with the imagining – are we to believe that these imaginings are automatically diffused and unmodified as they move by nationalist movements in places as different from France and America as Beijing and Jakarta, Manila and Singapore?

Even within Europe, the message of the French Revolution was differently read in Italy and Belgium – not to mention Prussia and Austria. Like Mosse and

Baker, Anderson teaches that symbolic construction is an important part of politics; but he so foreshortens the process of diffusion and assimilation of nationalism into the transmission of a universal grammar that political strategy and consensus mobilization – where the practical work of social movements is carried out – is left to his readers' imagining.

We can learn much from these approaches to meaning construction, but the assumption in this chapter will be that the symbols of collective action cannot be read like a "text," independent of the strategies and conflictual relations of the movements which diffuse them over time and across space. Out of a cultural toolkit of possible symbols, movement entrepreneurs choose those that they hope will mediate among the cultural underpinnings of the groups they appeal to, the sources of official culture and the militants of their movements – and still reflect their own beliefs and aspirations. To relate text to context, grammar to semantics, we need a concept more suited to the interactive nature of social movements and their societies. A contemporary group of scholars offers such a concept in their idea of collective action "frames."

Collective action frames

In an important series of papers, sociologist David Snow and his collaborators have adopted Erving Goffman's (1974) concept of "framing" and argue that there is a special category of cognitive understandings – collective action frames – that relate to how social movements construct meaning.[8] A frame, in Snow and Robert Benford's words, is an

interpretive schemata that simplifies and condenses the "world out there" by selectively punctuating and encoding objects, situations, events, experiences, and sequences of actions within one's present or past environment." (1992: 137)

Collective action frames serve as accentuating devices that either "underscore and embellish the seriousness and injustice of a social condition or redefine as unjust and immoral what was previously seen as unfortunate but perhaps tolerable" (p. 137). Social movements are deeply involved in the work of "naming" grievances, connecting them to other grievances and constructing larger frames of meaning that will resonate with a population's cultural predispositions and communicate a uniform message to powerholders and others (p. 136).

A typical movement mode of discourse is built around what William Gamson calls an "injustice frame" (1992: ch. 3). "Any movement against oppression," writes Barrington Moore, "has to develop a new diagnosis and remedy for existing forms of suffering, a diagnosis and remedy by which this suffering stands morally condemned" (p. 88). But it is no simple matter to convince timid people that the indignities of everyday life are not written in the stars and can be attributed to some agent, and that they can change their condition by taking action collectively. Inscribing grievances in overall frames that identify an injustice, attribute the responsibility for it to others and propose solutions to it, is a central activity of social movements. That work is what Snow and his collaborators call, "framing work."

Like Gamson and Moore, Snow and his collaborators believe that frames like injustice are powerful mobilizing resources; but they do not claim that organizers construct them out of whole cloth. On the contrary, in all but the most sectarian movements, organizers relate their goals to the predispositions of their target public. They are thus in a certain sense *consumers* of existing cultural meanings as well as producers of new ones. We will see how this was done in the cases of the Civil Rights and Solidarity movements.

But movement entrepreneurs do not simply adapt frames of meaning from traditional cultural symbols either – if they did, they would be nothing more than reflections of their societies and could not change them. They orient their movements' frames towards action, and fashion them at the intersection between a target population's culture and their own values and goals. This is what Snow and his associates call "frame alignment" (1986).[9]

Such a process is not always easy, clear or uncontested. First, movement leaders compete with other movements, media agents and the state for cultural supremacy. These competitors often have immensely powerful cultural resources at their disposal. Second, movements that adapt too well to their societies' cultures lose the force of opposition and alienate their militant supporters. Third, movement participants often have their own "reading" of events that differ from those of their leaders. In the case of the Civil Rights movement, this led to a serious split in the movement in the latter half of the 1960s; in the case of Solidarity, adversity held the movement together until its leader took power.

In other words, the process of framing is culturally encoded, but it is hardly an automatic reproduction of cultural texts. Inherited symbols – the French Revolution, the rights of freeborn Englishmen, a woman's right to control her reproductive functions – are appropriated by movement leaders, but not unconsciously or unselectively. When a movement organization chooses symbols with which to frame its message, it sets a strategic course between its cultural setting, its political opponents and the militants and ordinary citizens whose support it needs. Only by inscribing our analysis of movement discourse in a structure of power relations can we understand why movements employ particular symbolic practices and not others, and whether they are likely to carry the day.

CONSENSUS AND ACTION MOBILIZATION

Symbols of collective action take hold of a movement through two main processes: over the long run, through a slow capillary process of consensus formation and mobilization; and in the shorter run, through the transformations wrought in popular culture by collective action. The first set of processes can be seen in how movements interact with more autonomous sources of culture, while the second require attention to the process of collective action itself. The sequence of consensus formation and mobilization, and the role of collective action in producing new cultural frames will occupy the remainder of this chapter.

Consensus formation and mobilization

In a 1988 article, social psychologist Bert Klandermans makes the important distinction between consensus formation and consensus mobilization. Consensus formation results from the unplanned convergence of meaning in social networks and subcultures, and takes place outside anyone's direct control. Within these networks and subcultures, writes Klandermans, "processes of social comparison produce collective definitions of a situation" (p. 175). These collective definitions often lie hidden behind official culture, as, for example, the profound alienation of citizens in Eastern Europe being hidden behind their formal acceptance of state socialism until 1989 (Kuran 1991).

Consensus formation produces collective definitions of a situation but it neither produces collective action nor provides clues to action for those who wish to guide people into a social movement. For that to occur, consensus *mobilization* is necessary (Klandermans 1988: 183–91). Consensus mobilization consists of deliberate attempts to spread the views of a social actor among parts of a population (p. 175). Movement organizations are among the actors that attempt to do this. Klandermans lists over thirty means that organizations use to mobilize consensus (p. 184). In so doing, they compete with other organizations, with churches and governments, with the media and with widespread cultural predispositions that go against their goals or are irrelevant to them. The contest is often unequal, as the following examples suggest.

Costumes of consensus

In his ingenious book, *Comrades and Christians,* David Kertzer analyzes the adoption of the institution of the Catholic festival to show how Italian Communists tried to adapt their own celebrations to local practices in the village he studied (1980). Before the Second World War, the high point of Alborio's year had been the *festa* in honor of the Madonna. Four men, clad in white robes, had the honor of carrying a large statue of the Madonna through the streets of the parish. The festivities continued at the church following the procession, when food and drink were served, games played, music performed, and novelties sold (pp. 147–8).

After the war, Communist leaders deliberately drew on this tradition in their own festive occasions, the one difference being that these were "organized to glorify the Party, politicize the masses, and raise money for the Party press" (p. 149). The local church fought back in a competition for ritual supremacy. But given the political strength of Communist local government, only a few stalwarts continued to attend the traditional feast day.

Kertzer's story shows how political entrepreneurs mobilize consensus around the inherited cultural practices of a Catholic society. But it also illustrates the dilemmas of such a strategy. For it was during the years when Kertzer was observing the party's adoption of traditional cultural symbols that it was becoming one of the pillars of a capitalist democracy.[10] The disintegration of its subculture followed soon after. By 1990, it had even given up its name and hidden the hammer and sickle in its flag in a green field.

An alternative is for movements' symbolism to draw upon cultural understandings without adopting their practices. This was the strategy that the majority branch of the American Peace movement adopted in the 1980s. So powerfully influenced was it by America's warfare state that – in contrast to the European movements of the decade – its majority faction called only for a "freeze" in nuclear armaments (Benford 1993). When the Iraqi army invaded Kuwait and the American and other Western governments prepared for a counterattack, flag-waving peace demonstrations were organized in Washington and on the West Coast (*New York Times,* 27 December 1991).

During these rallies, a variety of physical signs drew on the oppositional subculture that had maintained itself since the 1960s. But in a climate of public opinion that was supportive of the president's war policy, the dominant symbolism with which the demonstrators tried to frame their protest was patriotic. As the (*Now National Times,* summed it up for its readers:

There were American flags, there were yellow ribbons, and there were concerned mothers and fathers, wives and husbands, sisters, brothers and friends who understood that the best way to support our troops in the Middle East is to bring them home alive (March–April 1991: p. 1).

What is happening in this protest? Surely not a mechanical aping of the inherited symbols of the American dream, but rather a self-conscious strategy by movement leaders to extend traditional consensual symbols into oppositional meanings. The attempt was ingenious, but in contesting the wave of popular support for a just war waged by a popular president against a Hitlerian villain, the barrage of consensual symbols made not the slightest difference. The costume of consensus cannot mobilize consent against the system that produced it.

Why does it seem so difficult to construct truly oppositional symbols? One reason may be that movement leaders genuinely wish to remain within the boundaries of a political consensus – this was certainly true of most of the American peace protesters. Another is that fear of the state is so great that even messages of rupture are framed in terms of consensus. But a third reason relates more directly to the structure of communication in today's societies: Movements that wish to communicate with a broader public must use the media in order to do so, and the media are not neutral in the symbols that they will receive and transmit.

Media framing and movement strategy[11]

The mass media have transformed political communication since the French Revolution. In the France of the 1790s, the physical images of the Revolution – the red bonnet, the cockade, the carmagnole – served a function of consensus mobilization that is no longer necessary for today's movements, when people can read, distinguish easily among competing groups and can assess the dangers of dissent without physically witnessing heads rolling off the guillotine. Yet the mobilization of symbols is as important in today's movements as it was two centuries ago. For example, what Aldo Marchetti recalls of the demonstrations he witnessed in Milan in the late 1960s is that they had a carnivalesque atmosphere. The workers, he writes,

carried puppets of bosses and government ministers hanging from the gallows, and these were burnt at the factory gates at the end of the march . . . As in a carnival, the demonstration created a sense of the world being turned upside down; for a day or a morning roles were reversed, and the workers became masters of their own time, of the city streets, the business-centre, and of themselves.[12]

What accounts for the continued use of such evocative symbolism? One reason is to afford help in the construction of collective identities; another is to project an image to bystanders and opponents of the movement's ferocity or joy, seriousness or spirit of play (Lumley: 223). But the primary reason is that movements in today's world communicate to a broad public through the mass media, and it is to gain the attention of the media that dramatic, bizarre or foreshortened symbols are arrayed.

Although radio and the press both play an important role in information diffusion,[13] it was television, with its unique capacity to capture complex situations in brief visual images, that brought about a revolution in movement tactics. The extent of this revolution first became evident during the 1960s. The American Civil Rights movement "was television's first recurring news story largely because of its visual elements" (Kielbowicz and Scherer: 83). The coincidence of the movement's appearance with onsite TV newscasting helped it in three ways.

First, it brought long-ignored grievances to the attention of the nation, and particularly to viewers in the North. Second, it visually contrasted the peaceful goals of the movement with the viciousness of the police. Bull Connor's officers not only attacked peaceful young protesters with fire hoses; they were *seen* doing it on national television. Third, television was a medium of communication within the movement too. It helped to diffuse knowledge of what the movement was doing by the visual demonstration of how to sit–in at a lunch counter, how to march peacefully for civil rights and how to respond when attacked by police and fire hoses.

The student movement was the second major testing ground for the impact of television on movements. The co-occurrence of student demonstrations all over the West in 1968 – many of them using the same slogans and forms of action – was, in part, the result of the impact of television. As two students of media's effect on movements conclude, "for members of the audience whose own experiences resemble those of the televised cases, such media attention can serve to cultivate a collective awareness, laying the groundwork for a social movement" (p. 81).

The mass media become an external resource of movements during three stages of their careers. First, the media provide a diffuse vehicle for consensus formation that movements on their own could never acheive. For example, when William Gamson studied the reaction to nuclear accidents in the American press from the 1950s to the 1980s, he found a radical change in how reporters were treating the issue (1988). From the "faith in progress" package that dominated the media in the 1950s, media discourse on nuclear power diversified and sharpened until, by the time of the Three Mile Island near disaster in 1979, the hegemony of "faith in progress" had been severely eroded. By the time of the Chernobyl disaster, a "public accountability" frame, which emphasized the government's responsibility for nuclear safety, was predominant in nuclear discourse (p. 238).

The media help movements to gain initial attention, and this may be the most important stage of their impact. Thus, Edie Goldenberg's research in the United States showed that all four urban groups she studied staged protests early in their careers (1975). Similarly, a left wing student movement studied by the author gained national attention in Italy when it succeeded in blocking the national railway line between Rome and the north of Italy (Tarrow 1989a: ch. 10). In the Netherlands, staging public events was crucial in establishing the public image of the Dutch women's movement (van Zoonen: 13).

Media coverage helps established movements maintain support by bolstering the feeling of status of their members and communicating their activities to their supporters (Molotch 1979). Such media attention relieves leaders of the need to maintain a large full-time staff or a national pyramid of organizers to maintain contact with supporters. When a movement organization wants to signal a change in tactics or policy to its mass base, or strike out towards a new constituency, staging an event that the media will cover is often the easiest way to do so.

But this is the source of a major problem; for the media are far from neutral bystanders at their appropriation for movement purposes. While the media in capitalist democracies may not work directly for the ruling class (p. 75), they certainly do not work for social movements – although occasionally movements take advantage of sympathetic journalists (Gitlin 1980: 26). In a capitalist society, at least, the media are in business to report on the news, and they stay in business only if they report on what will interest readers, or in what editors think will interest them.

How movements are covered by the media and perceived by the public are affected by the structure of the media industry. As Kielbowicz and Sherer write, movements are affected by the media's preference for dramatic, visible events, by journalists' reliance on authoritative sources, by news cycles or rhythms, by the influence of reporters' professional values or orientations; and by how the media environment, mainly the degree of competition, influences the news (pp. 75–6). As a result, the capacity of movement organizations to appropriate the media for their own purposes is limited.

In fact, the influence of the media on movements' perception by the public is double-edged. On the one hand, to gain media attention, organizers can mount dramatic events – "antiroutines" in Molotch's language (p. 77). But such activities lose interest for the media unless there is a change in their routines. One solution is to increase the number of participants in each successive demonstration, as Doug McAdam found to be the case in the civil rights demonstrations he studied (1983). The other solution is to continue to raise the level of drama. When this occurs, the media will continue to offer coverage, but they are quick to give priority to violent or bizarre aspects of a protest – often focusing on the few members of a peaceful demonstration who are bent on disrupting it. Although organizers recognize the danger, dissidents, free riders or simple joyriders are quick to learn how easy it is to capture the attention of the cameras.

The tendency of the media to focus on what "makes" news reinforces the shift from disruption to violence that was described in the last chapter.[14] A single student throwing a rock at a police line makes better copy than any number of marchers peacefully parading down a city street. In this way, the media "accentuate the militant strains found in any collection of activists" (Kielbowicz and Scherer: 86). In their search for novelty, the media can even assign a movement a violent or a juvenile image, especially when television networks allow only as much footage as will fit on the evening news.

Media coverage can also favor one branch of a movement over another in forming its public image. For example, Liesbet van Zoonen found that a series of public events mounted by the Dutch women's movement provided three main issue elements that almost all the media sources featured. These "framing elements" formed the building blocks for the movement's future public identity (p. 13). They set liberal feminist limits to the interpretation of the women's struggle, and described other (radical and socialist) currents in the movement from the standpoint of liberal concerns (pp. 13–14).

When a major campaign or demonstration is organized in Washington or Paris, Amsterdam or Berlin, media coverage reaches millions of people. But contemporary movements are more dependent on consensus formation through the media than the media are on them. To gain a broad following, to communicate with it nationally, and to impress powerholders and third parties with their strength, movements frame issues in ways that the media will broadcast. But the media – which can shift rapidly from one newsworthy item to another – do not depend on movement activities for news. Movements briefly, provisionally and often dramatically "make news"; but they cannot make the media publish news the way they want it to be made.

CONSTRUCTING COLLECTIVE ACTION

Because of the weight of existing cultural frames and the role of the media in transmitting movements' actions, we can begin to see why the framing of a new movement is so difficult. Yet new movements are constructed all the time, and the most successful transcend their societies' cultural frames and, in some cases, lead to revolutions. The cases of the American Civil Rights movement and Polish Solidarity will show how inherited cultural frames can be combined with strategic choices by using political opportunities through the process of collective action.

Framing rights in America

It is striking how naturally Americans frame their demands in terms of rights – whether they be the rights of minorities, women, gay men and lesbians, animals or the unborn. European movements are far less likely to employ a rights discourse, even when their goals and constituencies are similar. But for African Americans, rights have most often been honored in the breach; why then did the Civil Rights movement of the 1960s draw upon them so centrally?

This resulted, first, from the historical fact that the earliest terrain of the movement was the courts, beginning from the concept of equal educational rights. Rights were not an idiom that came automatically to Black Americans convinced of the ingrained racial injustices of the system, but they had proven promising *before* the most conflictual period of the movement developed. Without anyone intending it, the decade of peaceful civil rights adjudication in the 1950s served as an instrument of consensus formation for a generation of future civil rights activists. As Charles Hamilton writes, this context "created a cadre of constitutional lawyers who became in a real sense the focal points of the civil rights struggle" (p. 244).

A second reason why rights became the central frame of the Civil Rights movement was strategic: Equal opportunity rights were a useful bridge, based on traditional American political rhetoric, between the movement's main internal constituency, the southern black middle class, and the white "conscience constituents" whose support was necessary to bolster it from the outside.

Liberals were most easily appealed to by the contradiction between the value that America placed on rights and the denial of equal opportunity to African Americans. Rights had the dual function of building on previous consensus formation and of bridging the white liberals and the black middle class from which the core of the movement came.

But was the Civil Rights movement's concept of "rights" no more than the traditional costume of American consensus? If so, why did the movement have to await the 1960s to emerge and how did it achieve as much as it did? The answer is that the traditional rights frame was expanded and became a collective action frame of the movement only when it was combined with an innovative collective action repertoire. Cultural choices framed the movement around rights at the same time as a tactic was chosen that expanded the meaning of equal opportunity and transformed passivity into activism.

From the late 1950s on, the modest equal opportunity rights frame was accompanied by a highly dramatic and confrontational *practice* – nonviolent direct action. If the doctrine of rights bridged the gap between the traditional subaltern status of southern Blacks and their white liberal supporters rhetorically, nonviolent direct action transformed quietism into activism. Rather than oppose a frame of risky revolt to this quiescent culture, the movement's leaders elaborated a practice of militant quiescence within the most traditional institution they possessed – the black church. It was not the grammar of rights, but the action of peaceful resistance, that turned cultural quiescence into action.

From the beginning, the transformation of the rights frame was interactive. Two key actors played a critical role: a generation of college students who had grown up in the cities where the worst practices of Jim Crow were absent; and the agents of the white power structure whose behavior played into the hands of the movement – and right on television! While the students in their neat suits and demure dresses sat-in, marched, demonstrated, sang and prayed, the police, the sheriff's deputies and the Klan responded to nonviolence with violence, meeting the doves of peace with the police dogs of war. The more violent and unchristian the behavior of white powerholders, the greater the moral superiority of the students' tactic came to seem, and the more reasonable the movement's program. Under the eye of national television, even the hesitant Kennedy administration, because of its razor-thin electoral margin, had to come to the movement's support. It was through the process of struggle that the inherited rhetoric of rights was transformed into a new collective action frame.

The lesson of the American Civil Rights movement is that the symbols of revolt are not drawn off the peg from a cultural closet and arrayed ready-made before the public. Nor are new meanings fabricated out of whole cloth. The costumes of revolt are woven from a blend of inherited and invented fibers into synthetic collective action frames in confrontation with opponents. Once established, they are no longer the sole possession of the movements that produced them, but – like the modular forms of collective action – become available for others to don. This takes us to the concept of "master frames."

Master framing

Once formulated and successfully employed, the collective action frame of one movement campaign is often imported into the messages of other movements. For example, by successfully broadening the meaning of rights, the Civil Rights movement produced a resonance in American society. Snow and Benford point out that once it is enunciated in the context of a period of general turbulence, such a successful collective action frame may even become what they call a "master frame" (1992). Master frames help to animate an entire social movement sector. In the American 1960s and 1970s, "rights" became the touchstone of a number of other movements. As Hamilton writes, "We began to see the heightened politicization of other groups, notably feminists, environmentalists, the elderly, children, the handicapped, and homosexuals organizing and demanding their 'rights' " (p. 246).

Similarly, in Western Europe in the 1960s, the concept of "autonomy," first found among the students and then the working class, became a modular message first applied to autonomy of the students from their bureaucratic universities, then to workers' autonomy from their conservative unions and, finally, to the autonomy of the New Left from its Communist and Socialist party mentors (Tarrow 1989a). In the process, the autonomy frame changed its meaning, serving as what Gamson calls an ideological "package" that could hold a variety of specific claims, some of them conflicting (1988).

What is most important in a "master" collective action frame is that, in a context of general turbulence, permissiveness and social enthusiasm, it is adapted, added to and honed down by the practice of a variety of actors engaged in different struggles against different opponents. In the disillusionment and repression that often follow such periods of mobilization, more confrontational versions of the frame fall into disuse. But beneath the surface, they are still available for future generations of insurgents. What emerges is a flexible and adaptable residue of oppositional framing that may become a permanent feature of the political culture.

Solidarity in Poland

In his fresh treatment of Polish Solidarity, Roman Laba describes the depth of the religious symbolism that he found in the propaganda of the movement that was to become *Solidarnosc* (ch. 7). In a chapter that forms an ironic counterpart to Kertzer's analysis of how the Italian Communists appropriated the symbol of the Catholic *festa,* Laba reproduces a cartoon of Lech Wałęsa with his fist raised in the workers' salute alongside the pope with his hand lifted in a papal greeting (p. 141). He reproduces a poster from the Gdansk shipyard strike showing a crown of thorns to memorialize the martyrs of past industrial conflicts (p. 150). Never did the practice of revolt appear to draw so heavily on the inherited symbols of consensus!

But from its outset, the movement was not so much the expression of a Catholic people as a movement of industrial workers seeking a free trade union (ch. 8). The symbols that guided the Gdansk workers in 1980 were not fundamentally religious, but they drew on religious imagery to recall and draw energy from an earlier wave of strikes. In December 1970, workers had attacked Communist party headquarters in Gdansk and several were killed by the army (Garton Ash 1984: 12–13; Laba: ch. 2).[15] "The myth of the martyrs grew in the fertile subsoil of the national conscience," writes Garton Ash (p. 12), emerging periodically as a resource with which to build solidarity and frame new demands.

As early as December 1970, the fusion of the images of martyred Poland and suffering proletarians appeared in the streets of Gydina and Gdansk. In 1971, workers in the Gdansk May Day parade carried a banner demanding a plaque be erected to commemorate the dead of the preceding year's strikes (Laba: 126). In 1977, the groups that later founded the Free Trade Unions of the Baltic and the Young Poland movement took up the same cry (p. 136). The demand was repeated at a 1979 demonstration outside the Lenin shipyard. During the sixteen months of Solidarity's legal existence, monuments to the martyred workers of 1970 were created at Gdansk, Gdynia and Poznan.

It is significant that the Lenin shipyard electrician who seized the leadership of the Gdansk movement in the summer of 1980 considered it a duty – almost an obsession – to honor the memory of the martyrs of 1970. Lech Wałęsa first gained notoriety at the 1979 demonstration at the Lenin shipyard. Evading arrest to come to the demonstration, he "erupted on the scene" demanding the construction of a monument to honor the dead of 1970. "Everyone should come back the next year, same place, same time," he said, "and *each carrying a stone*." If the authorities refused to build a monument, they would build it themselves out of the stones in their pockets (Garton Ash: 31).

The events that led to the occupation of the Lenin shipyard in July 1980 were also sparked by the issue of the martyrs. When a popular Free Trade Union militant, Anna Walentynowicz, went to a local cemetery to find candle stubs to burn in memory of the victims of 1970, she was fired by the plant management, adding a spark of human outrage to the simmering flames of worker dissatisfaction. "A demand for her reinstatement was bound to win support," writes Garton Ash (p. 38) and the Free Trade Union militants took up her cause along with their wage demands.

At dawn on August 14, militants of the group slipped by plant guards with posters demanding the reinstatement of Walentynowicz and a one thousand zloty pay raise. Plastering them around the shipyard, they set off on an internal march, picking up supporters as they went. Thus began the chain of events that would lead to the establishment of *Solidarnosc* and its temporary triumph over the government. The strike had little to do with religion, but it built a movement for workers' rights within a frame drawn from the cultural toolchest of a Catholic society. When negotiations began to settle the strike in August 1980, high among the workers' demands was the erection of a monument to honor the victims of 1970 (Garton Ash: 39).

Framing within action

The weight of the religious symbols that surrounded the workers' movement when it burst out on the Baltic coast in 1980 can be used to support the notion that symbolism must be culturally resonant to fire people's minds. But these symbols had been culturally available for decades – even in People's Poland. As in the case of the American Civil Rights movement, it was not a symbol inherited from the past that took the movement into its most radical phase, but a new symbol – the symbol of workers' solidarity – that emerged when a new opportunity for collective action emerged. It developed in the course of the struggle and served a strategic purpose for militants locked in combat with powerful opponents.

The crucial success of the Gdansk strikers and of their external supporters was not their ability to call on the traditional symbols of Catholic piety, but to create solidarity between workers in different factories and sectors. This is what defeated the government's strategy of offering wage concessions to some workers and not others. In fact, the very symbol of "Solidarity" was a product of that struggle and not one of its preconditions. As the designer of the Solidarnosc symbol later wrote:

I saw how Solidarity appeared among the people, how a social movement was being born. I chose the word [Solidarnosc] because it best described what was happening to people. The concept came out of the similarity to people in the dense crowds leaning on one another – that was characteristic of the crowds in front of the gate [of the Lenin shipyard]. (Laba: 133)

CONCLUSIONS

What can we learn from the cases of the Civil Rights movement and the Gdansk workers' movement about the power of symbolism in collective action?

First, and most obvious, cultural symbols are not automatically available as mobilizing symbols, but require concrete agency to turn them into collective action frames. Just as nonviolent direct action gained its power from the ability of the NAACP to expand the meaning of rights through a decade of judicial litigation and the practice of nonviolent resistance, the Gdansk movement gained its success when its leaders joined the religious symbol of their slain comrades to their strike demands.

Second, inherited political culture did little in either Poland or America to explain *which* symbols would dignify and energize collective action and which would not. Rights in America and Catholicism in Poland had been available for generations without visibly helping African Americans or Polish workers to throw off their oppression. It is the weaving of new materials into a cultural matrix that produces expanding collective action frames. Combining them depends on the actors in the struggle, on the opponents they face and on their access to a broader public through the forms of collective action they employ and the political opportunities they exploit.

It is in struggle that opponents find out what values they share, as well as what divides them, and fashion new and synthetic frames that they can take to other battles and that evolve into master frames for others. Often they fail, but when they succeed, a movement like Solidarity results. As Laba writes,

Solidarity has usually been assumed to be simply a nationalist movement, its symbolism merely a continuation of nineteenth-century prewar tradition. Such an analysis misses the innovative quality of Solidarity – *the extent to which the dominant symbols were invented during the strikes,* and the degree to which dominant symbols and rituals were lifted from nationalist and socialist tradition and transformed (emphasis added). (p. 128)

8

Mobilizing structures

Ever since social movements became a force for change in the modern world, observers and activists have puzzled over the effects of organization. Some theorists have argued that, without leadership exercised through organizations, rebellion remains "primitive" and soon disintegrates (Hobsbawm 1959). Others, following the lead of Michels in his great work on *Political Parties* (1962), are persuaded that, far from inspiring people to action, leaders can deprive them of their major power – the power to disrupt (Piven and Cloward 1979).[1]

But, as must be obvious, some leaders, working through certain kinds of organizations in particular situations, *do* transform collective action into ongoing movements, while others do not. Equally obvious, movements can emerge without leaders, often producing profound political change. Sometimes organizers are spectators at the birth of movements and take advantage of them to gain a following; but often, they are a product of movements rather than their cause. How are we to explain this diversity of organizational roles?

THREE ELEMENTS OF MOVEMENT ORGANIZATION

Part of the reason for the confusion is that we often fail to distinguish among three different aspects of movement organization. The dominant meaning of the term in contemporary debates is *formal organization* – what Zald and McCarthy call the "SMO," and define as "a complex, or formal, organization that identifies its goals with the preferences of a social movement or a countermovement and attempts to implement those goals" (1987: 20). These are frequently present in movements, but they sometimes compete with other organizations in a broad multiorganizational field and with *non*organized actors, attempting to become the focal points for contention (Schelling 1978: 57 ff.).

A second meaning of organization, not to be confused with the first, is *the organization of collective action,* which is the form by which confrontations with antagonists are carried out. The organization of collective action ranges from temporary formations of challengers all the way to formal cells, branches and militias. It is either controlled by formal movement organizations in loose contact with such formations or completely autonomous of them. In any given movement, there may be a variety of forms of organization of collective action, some autonomous, others under leadership control and still others in some loose relationship to formal organizations. The most effective organization of collective action draws on social networks in which people normally live and work, because their mutual trust and interdependence can easily be turned into solidarity.

The third element is the one that is most often ignored: These are the connective *mobilizing structures* that link leaders with the organization of collective action – center with periphery – permitting movement coordination and allowing movements to persist over time. When a formal organization appears in a movement, its leaders attempt to develop mobilizing structures to take charge of the activities at the base. But mobilizing structures can exist prior to, and autonomous of, movement leadership and, in some cases, operate through other organizations or within institutions.

It is only when mobilizing structures are internalized and the organization of collective action is controlled by higher-level leaders that a movement comes under the domination of a single organization. This is the kind of movement organization that Michels condemned. But it is far less common than is often supposed, and the power of centralized movements is often an illusion. On the other hand, decentralized movements lack coordination and are easily dissolved and repressed. It is only when mobilizing structures provide coordination among the elements of a movement that the coordination problem is solved and enough autonomy remains at the base to provide incentives for autonomy. The problem for movement organizers is to create organizational models that are sufficiently robust to stand up to opponents, but flexible enough to change with new circumstances and draw on energies at the base.

In this chapter, a failed nineteenth-century example – the 1851 insurrection in France – will show how all three elements – formal organizations, mobilizing structures and the organization of collective action – must come together. Two alternative solutions to the problem of organization – social democracy and anarchism – follow, showing how polarized are the organizational types in social movements. Between the two extremes are a variety of intermediate solutions, mostly unstable and often ending up in formal organizations. In the second half of the chapter, the organizational innovations that have appeared since the 1960s will be discussed. The argument of the chapter is that the most effective forms of organization are based on autonomous and interdependent social networks linked by loosely coordinated mobilizing structures.

A FAILURE AND TWO SOLUTIONS

In the early morning hours of December 2, 1851, troops loyal to President Louis Napoleon occupied the French National Assembly, launching the coup d'état that history has remembered as the Eighteenth Brumaire.[2] In Paris, where hundreds of Republicans were rounded up, resistance was quickly overcome. But the story in France's South and West, where a loose network of Montagnard Republicans had grown up, was very different.

In the days following the coup, an armed insurrection broke out throughout southern and central France. "These provincial rebels," writes Ted Margadant, "proclaimed revolutionary commissions in over one hundred communes; they seized control of an entire department as well as a dozen *arrondissement* capitals; and they clashed violently with troops or gendarmes in thirty different localities" (p. vii). But by December 10, the army had the rebels on the run, especially in the cities. Their organizations crumbled rapidly, and when the form of collective action they favored – the armed demonstration – fell apart before armed force, they were unable to coordinate their resistance in different parts of the country.

In many of its particulars, the 1851 insurrection seems like one of Hobs-bawm's "primitive rebellions." The pattern is familiar: News of some outrage, real or imagined, arrives in a village. Suffering economic distress and aggrieved at abuses of their rights, the villagers gather at the sound of the tocsin, arms at the ready. Primitive signs mark their solidarity: bits of red cloth, portraits of the Virgin, pitchforks and hunting rifles. Emboldened by their numbers and their leaders' rhetoric, they confront authorities at some central place, are mown down by superior force and the survivors return to their farms. As a result of such images, the largest provincial uprising in nineteenth-century France was long remembered as "a *Jacquerie,* a mindless outburst of lower-class hatred against the rich and the well-educated."[3]

But the insurrection had a number of features that should give us pause before filing it away as an expression of traditional rural rage. For one thing, it was not "rural" in the strict sense, for it combined Republicans from the cities and towns with rural peasants and workers (p. 29). For another, its themes were national and political, and not local and parochial.[4] Finally, the revolt made manifest a substantial interdependence of action and belief among a variety of social groups, urban and rural, peasants and craftsmen, leaders and followers who were united in confronting powerholders. It was a modern social movement.

Two striking signs of the revolt's resemblance to modern movements were the rapidity of its diffusion and the similarity of its forms of action. Reaching almost instantaneously over broad areas of southern and central France, according to Margadant's estimates it involved nearly 100,000 men from about 900 municipalities, nearly 70,000 of them in arms by the time it was suppressed. As we follow the pattern of diffusion, we also see that, rather than spreading through a jungle telegraph along the back lanes of rural France, it spread outward from the towns and large bourgs to the villages (pp. 5–8).

Was the movement organized? That depends upon what one means by move-ment organization. At some minimum level, the 1851 insurrection possessed all three of the elements of organization outlined above. At the summit, there was a scattering of tight Republican organizations led by the men of 1848. Most of these were middle class, many were intellectuals and they diffused the Republican ideas, administered the oaths and gave the orders in some places to unleash resistance against the coup. The police – unable to believe that ordinary peasants could organize armed bands – exaggerated the power of these Republican groups, but they were focal points in the larger movement.

At the base of the movement were the centers of collective action that attacked *mairies,* fought with troops and roused other villages to action. These were not random collections of rural hooligans; they came from stable village social and family networks – many of them incubated in *chambrées* and drinking clubs. Their interpersonal trust and ties of family and locality provided them with the solidarity necessary to support collective action. That they were insufficient to organize an armed resistance was evident in their brutal suppression.

It was the links between center and periphery – what I call here "mobilizing structures" – that connected the Republican Montagnards to the local networks that organized collective action. These ties were neither internalized in an organization, nor were they spontaneously formed. First developed on the basis of commercial links between the towns and villages, after the declaration of the Republic in 1848 they took political shape in Republican election organizations (pp. 115–16).

These mobilizing structures were effective enough to launch collective action and diffuse word of the uprising to other regions. But the links between the urban Montagnards and the local networks in the villages were personal and intermittent, and in the war that soon developed, they quickly broke down. As Margadant writes, once the local armed bands appeared in public, "poor communications and administrative countermeasures limited the extent of concerted regional action" (pp. 232–3). Local groups were more likely to respond to word of a successful uprising elsewhere than to orders that came down from unseen bourgeois Republicans. The lack of stable and trust-creating vertical structures to link center and periphery of the movement was its major disability. It was to the solution of this problem that the next phase of European social movements turned.

The social democratic solution

At the end of the 1848 Revolution, the remnants of the Republicans, socialists and liberals who had lost to the forces of reaction retreated into emigration, intellectual activities and "abeyance structures" that kept the flame of revolution flickering (Rupp and Taylor 1987). In the next few decades a new social actor appeared – the industrial proletariat – naturally forming a new organization of collective action at the base and giving rise to a new set of organizations at the summit, the Social democratic and labor movement.

Between the organizations of European social democracy and the workers at the base, however, there was at first no natural or consistent set of mobilizing structures. In some countries, in fact, the distance between syndicalist workers and parliamentary socialists was so great that competing organizations were formed. But the German Social Democratic Party (SPD), with characteristic determination, undertook to formalize the relations between summit and base and make them permanent. The result was to vitiate the movement of its spontaneity and its energy and leave it incapable of facing the threat that arose in the 1920s.

The Social Democrats encapsulated their members into permanent federal structures that arose from local branches through provincial and regional federations, to central committees and national executives at the top. Short-term and maximum programs were proclaimed and debated at national congresses. Discipline was expected of those who joined, and collective actions were periodically organized to advance the movement's goals. From a scattered network of insurgent groups and secret societies, the workers' movement grew into a vast formal organization.

The circumstances of semi-authoritarian Germany reinforced the Social Democrats' incentive to internalize. Bismarck's ideas of empire, and his attitude towards the working class, developed directly out of the harsh reaction to the 1848 Revolution. In such an environment, Social Democracy needed discipline and mass support to survive. With legalization, an interlocking structure of parties, unions and health and recreational organizations was developed to link party and base.[5]

Such was the international prestige of the SPD that its organizational model was imitated throughout Central, Northern and Eastern Europe.[6] The less disciplined British Labour Party model had influence as well, but even the SPD's ideological opponents were inspired by its example. Alarmed by the danger of collectivism that they saw in social democracy, Catholic leaders developed competing social and political movements, adopting as a model the cooperatives and mutual benefit societies that the Social Democrats had invented, and eventually forming denominational parties along similar lines.[7]

Where Catholics, Protestants and socialists struggled for supremacy, as in the Netherlands, this process of organizational mimesis made political life appear as a pitched battle between bureaucratic armies, each with its own "pillar" of schools, cooperatives, newspapers and party branches.[8] By the late nineteenth century, European political life was polarized into opposing political monoliths, each with its central leadership, permanent staff, cadres of grassroots militants and reserve armies of card-carrying members.

This was the model of organization – the Central European working-class movement, with its panoply of unions, cooperatives and popular services – that Michels had in mind when he formulated his Iron Law. It was never a universal model, but the result of the particular political configuration of semi-authoritarian Germany and its diffusion to other settings. To face a hostile environment, protect the workers from repercussions and use the vote effectively, the Social Democrats turned the movements' networks at the base into permanent branches and controlled the organization of collective action. If militancy melted away once representation for the lower classes was achieved, no one should have been surprised. One group of competitors were anything but surprised.

The anarchist countermodel

Even as German Social Democrats were building a "state within a state," in other parts of Europe and in America, some were organizing around different organizational models. The most serious challenge came from the anarchists – whose political theory and political practice were opposed to social democracy in every respect. Where the Social Democratic parties were led by politicians and intellectuals and aimed at taking over the bourgeois state in the name of workers in formal organizations, the anarchists distrusted politics and sought to destroy the state through the workers' natural energy and combativeness. Social democracy they dismissed as "authoritarian," and castigated the intellectuals who led it as traitors to the cause.

The anarchists resisted the tendency to become a party. Their instinctive organizational model was provided by Proudhon, who had theorized that a network of workers' associations, democratically organized and loosely linked in a voluntary federation, could eventually replace both the state and capitalism.[9] But lacking an organizational template like that of their opponents, they developed in different forms in different parts of Europe in close approximation to local economic and political conditions.

In England, where revolutionary impulses were pretty much dead by the 1870s, the major tendency was toward a sturdy form of "guild" socialism. Where anarchism gave way to syndicalism, as it did in France, the result was a mentality of sterile *ouvrièrisme* – the conviction that revolution would emerge from the healthy instincts of the working class. It was in Eastern and Southern Europe, where economic conditions were backward and political organization less developed, that anarchism remained a mass movement into the twentieth century.

Isolated from the popular masses by the millenarian character of their message, the Russian *narodniki* hurled themselves at the power structure, imagining that their courage and bravery would unleash the rebellious potential that they thought lay hidden in the peasants. The latter responded with indifference, if not with hostility, and long prison terms and doleful memoirs were the lot of many populists. Similarly, hounded by the police and the authorities, the Italian anarchists encapsulated themselves into tight cells in which they hatched utopias and plotted the overthrow of the state. As Daniel Guérin writes;

Free rein was given to utopian doctrines, combining premature anticipations and nostalgic evocations of a golden age. . . . The anarchists turned in on themselves, organized themselves for direct action in small clandestine groups which were easily infiltrated by police informers. (p. 74)

Just as the dream of the general strike inspired their French counterparts, the illusion that the state was bound up in the person of its rulers led the Italian and Russian anarchists to engage in acts of violence – and produced a wave of bombings that cast suspicion on the entire Left and isolated them still further. Where the hierarchy of social democracy helped to turn a movement into a party, the anarchists' obsession with collective action and their allergy to organization transformed them into a sect.

New polarizations

The polarization between institutionalization and disruption that we saw in social democracy and anarchism was replicated to some extent in the movements of the 1960s. For example, by the early 1960s, most of the American Civil Rights movement was institutionalized (Piven and Cloward: ch. 4). From the streets of Selma, the battle for civil rights gravitated to the lobbies of Congress and to neighborhood community organizations subsidized by government. Most of the major Civil Rights organizations were soon constrained by the rules of the game of ordinary politics.

The same shift into institutions could be seen in most of the New Left, both in Europe and America. In the United States, from the sit–ins and draft-card burnings of the mid-1960s, many anti–Vietnam War activists moved into the public interest groups and peace lobbies that flourished in the 1970s and 1980s. And from battling the police and organizing the urban poor, French and Italian student organizers formed political organizations and entered the trade unions and the Communist Party.

But at the same time, more determined militants, who were critical of the "long march through the institutions," split off into radical organizations to carry the fight to the heart of organized capitalism. Just as the anarchists had opposed the Social Democrats' moderation with extremist appeals and bombings, fractions of the Civil Rights movement and parts of the New Left tried to outbid their competitors by drawing sharp lines between their own militancy and the moderation of their opponents.

In parts of the Civil Rights movement, respected black leaders were castigated as "Uncle Toms" and white activists were read out of organizations like SNCC and CORE in the name of black self-development. The New Left, born in 1961 at Port Huron on a platform of unity, gave rise to breakaway terrorist groups like the Weather Underground.[10] In Western Europe, factions of the movements of 1968 became more radical and produced underground offshoots. Every shift of the main trunk of the New Left towards institutional politics pushed these militant groups further into sectarianism and violence.

Italy provides us with the most notorious example. Just as the bulk of the

New Left was moving from disruption into the political process, a second generation of militants broke away and sought to disrupt the capitalist state with exemplary acts of violence. Each new generation outbid the one before and sought political space with more outrageous actions: first in the form of "extra-parliamentary groups" extolling mass violence; and then as underground cells using "vanguard violence" and "proletarian expropriation." And once violence had marked them as enemies of the state, there was no other way to survive than by going underground, where their ideological and organizational isolation led them to the only kind of action that small and sectarian groups can produce – organized terror.[11] The nineteenth-century polarity between anarchism and so-cial democracy was replayed in the shadow of the New Left.

BETWEEN HIERARCHY AND DISRUPTION

Social democracy and anarchism were not the only models of movement organi-zation available. Elsewhere, there were movements whose leaders sought inter-mediate solutions. Where the Social Democrats attempted to internalize move-ment within organization and the anarchists foreshortened all organization into collective action, the nineteenth-century American civic movements that fought slavery and alcohol, and advanced the causes of women's suffrage and agrarian populism, built flexible organizations within larger movements. These were loose umbrella organizations that coordinated – rather than internalized – com-ponents at the base. This allowed the movement to reside in the structures of everyday life and religion, and to mobilize and demobilize according to the issues on the agenda.

The organization of collective action of these movements ranged from infor-mal social networks of public-spirited women and men, to local churches and fraternal orders. The mobilizing structures that coordinated center and periphery varied from episodic communications between militants, lecture tours and prayer meetings, to state federations and political parties. Most were informal and required only a minimum of resources to maintain.

These organizations rose and fell with cyclical frequency, along with the waves of movement whose enthusiasm they reflected. At the height of each cycle, when they could draw upon existing social networks and local churches, they were highly effective in mobilizing people against opponents and putting pressure on the state. When reforms were accomplished or mobilization de-clined, militants disappeared into private life or into "abeyance structures" like churches or lodges. When a new cycle of protest appeared, these interorganiza-tional contacts served them in good stead (Buechler 1986; Blocker 1989).

Although Europeans thought of movement organization in terms of the polari-ties of social democracy and anarchism, intermediate models based on enthusi-astic, semiformal and episodic organization rooted in informal social networks were also common in Europe – for example, in the Chartists in Britain and in the Republicans who reemerged in France in the 1860s. In the 1871 Paris Commune, for example, Roger Gould found that the enlistment groups in the Paris National Guard were most effective when they were based on informal social ties rooted in the neighborhoods.[12]

The same informal, unstable and enthusiastic model of organization reappeared in the "new" social movements of the 1970s and 1980s, which replayed many of the organizational themes of their nineteenth-century predecessors (d'Anieri, Ernst, and Kier 1990; Calhoun 1993). Both at the summit and the base, their leaders fashioned a variety of organizational variants and innovations. But, as in 1851, the most difficult problems would arise in linking summit and base.

Innovations at the summit

As in many other ways, the 1960s were a watershed for organizational innovation. This was not only because that decade produced a tidal wave of movements – from the Third World nationalist and Civil Rights movements of the early part of the decade, to the New Left, antiwar and feminist movements of the years that followed. These movements arose amid technological and social changes that gave them a new set of resources and connections with which movement organizers could work.

First in importance was the discovery that by drawing upon the "external" resources provided by their environments, movement leaders could create an implicit structure out of proportion to their internal strength. The expansion of the mass media from print to electronics – and especially the advent of television – was the most important of these developments. From civil rights marchers braving police dogs and hoses to the New Left's publicized draft card burnings, to the public spectacle of gay or lesbian soldiers "coming out," television's appetite for dramatic visual images was a tool that was nurtured and exploited by movement organizers.

The implications for movement organization were profound: If movements could transmit their messages to millions of people across the airwaves, encouraging some to follow their example and larger numbers to take sympathetic notice of their claims, it was possible to create a movement without incurring the cost of building a mass organization. This had been true in the past with the advent of cheap newspapers. But where the press only described what movements wanted, television showed graphically how they behaved, and how their opponents responded, in a form of public spectacle that required little in the way of formal mobilizing structures and could be copied.

A second set of changes revolved around the increased amount of money, free time and expertise that young people had available in the postwar boom years (McCarthy and Zald 1973; 1977). Not only did disposable family income rise substantially all over the West after World War II; by the 1960s, young people had become a targeted market for consumer goods and the center of a new youth culture (McAdam 1988: 13–19). Both in Europe and America, they were entering universities in much larger numbers, where they had more free time and were exposed to broader currents of ideas than young people in the past. If nothing else, they provided many more conscience constituents to lend their numbers and their skills to minority movements (Marx and Useem 1971).

Affluent conscience constituents are nothing new in the world of social movements; the members of the Russian intelligentsia who threw themselves into radical activity, and the genteel New Englanders who led the American abolitionist movement were no more self-interested than the white civil rights workers who joined black CORE and SNCC activists in the South, or of the intellectuals who fought for the rights of untouchables in India. If there is a difference, it is found in the greater mobility of recent activists and their increased capacity to use their resources on behalf of others.

Organizers have not been passive beneficiaries of these changes. They have been quick to take advantage of the same advances in communication and fundraising that more conventional political and interest groups use – first through the mimeograph machine, then through computerized direct mailing lists, and more recently with the fax, the E-mail network and the video camcorder.[13] As a result of these and other changes, organizers can mount and coordinate collective action across a broad sweep of territory without the need for formal mobilizing structures. Although there were precedents for this in the nineteenth century, the first modern examples of this new organizational lightness, flexibility, and versatility date from the 1960s when "transitory teams" of organizers formed, disbanded and reformed around particular issues and campaigns, first in the Civil Rights movement and then in the New Left.

Other movements took advantage of the external resources of foundation grants and government largesse to form professional movement organizations around issues like neighborhood improvement, the environment, drunk driving, gender issues and gay rights. Their activities ranged from educational efforts and lobbying to occasional participation in confrontational protest, but centered around set piece demonstrations like Earth Day and marches on Washington.[14] Like the public interest groups that they increasingly came to resemble, they mastered the art of direct mail campaigns and – like the transitory teams of movement activists – built a public image without creating large mobilizing structures.

Professional movement organizations also drew on professionals in the traditional sense; for example, the scientists and technical experts who lent their authority as well as their expertise to the ecological and antiwar movements. The same was true of the women's movement, which increasingly depended on the services of the feminist lawyers who lent a legalistic framework to much of the movement's activities (Mansbridge 1986). The trend to professionalization has also affected more controversial movements like gay rights. As John d'Emilio writes, "the gay movement, especially its male sector, has increasingly narrowed its focus towards court cases and legislative lobbying efforts" (p. 192). Professionalization is by no means only a tool of mainstream "consensus movements" (McCarthy and Wolfson 1992; Schwartz and Paul 1992).

Campaigns and coalitions

If the new lighter, "externalized" movement organizations have a weakness, it is their lack of a permanent cadre of grassroots activists. It is, in part, for this reason that they cultivate ties with like-minded groups, attempting to compensate for the weakness of their constituency base by assembling concentrated numbers at strategic places and times. Such groups seldom organize major demonstrations on their own, but do so through coalitions that come together from time to time around particular issues. The antiwar coalitions of the late 1960s, the pro-abortion movements and the peace movement of the 1980s developed this technique of collaboration to a high level – in some cases forming quasi-permanent peak organizations to coordinate their efforts.

The American peace movement, because of its weakness, perfected the technique of organizing through coordinated campaigns even before the 1960s (Kleidman 1992). In the 1930s, the postwar period and the 1960s, peace activists experimented with different forms and degrees of cooperation. By the 1970s, writes Tom Rochon, in both Europe and the United States "many of these were federations of existing organizations, pulled together to take advantage of the new possibilities for mobilization" (p. 79).[15] So common has the practice of joint campaigning by coalitions of organizations become that Jürgen Gerhards and Dieter Rucht have coined a new word to describe it – they call it "mesomobilization" (1992).

Gerhards and Rucht describe two Berlin mobilization campaigns in the late 1980s in which such alliances played a key role. One was a campaign to protest Ronald Reagan's visit to the city in 1987; and another an anti-IMF campaign in 1988. In both, an enormous number of semi-coordinated but autonomously mounted actions were carried out by a large number of support groups – 140 groups in the anti-Reagan campaign and 133 against the IMF. The committees that were formed to coordinate the campaign dissolved when each campaign was over. When, in 1991–2, racist attacks began on immigrants, the same technique of forming a temporary coordinating committee from among many disparate organizations was employed.

In contrast to the more inclusive organizations of their social democratic predecessors, these Berlin campaigns possessed organizational flexibility that allowed ideological, social and political pluralism to flourish. They mounted a variety of activities, giving each group the chance to stress its particular interests and not to feel lost in the crowd. In contrast to the centralized movement organizations of the past, they possessed an organizational flexibility and ideo-

logical plurality that probably increased the overall rate of activism. But when
the campaign was over, there was no permanent organization in place to put
pressure on lawmakers or to protect immigrants from assault.

Innovations at the base

If the spread of affluence and mass communications has given organizers at the
summit new resources, it has also deprived movements of the steady participation at the base that prewar movements could count on through party branches
and union locals. People who watch television in the evening and go away for
long weekends are less interested in attending meetings and marching in Sunday
demonstrations than their parents were in the 1930s and 1940s (Allardt 1962).
While some movements, like the French and Italian Communists, attempted to
maintain these structures well into the 1980s, participation became more and
more indifferent and was soon more expensive to maintain than to abandon
(Hellman 1988).

Contemporary movements draw upon other mobilizing structures – not primarily created for collective action – to recruit followers and gain allies without
having to create permanent branch organizations. For the discipline and uniformity of the social-democratic model, they substitute autonomy and democracy
at the base as incentives for participation. The strategy of drawing on existing
structures of solidarity may weaken the ties between center and base, but,
when it succeeds, the resulting heterogeneity and interdependence produce more
dynamic movements than the homogeneity and discipline that were aimed at in
the old social-democratic model.

Some of the mobilizing structures within which movements recruit are surprising. Much of social movement theory conceives of movements as if they
always develop through "rupture" against institutions (Melucci 1980; Touraine
1988). But Mayer Zald and Michael Berger have shown that movements often
emerge *within* institutions, using them to develop contacts among networks of
dissidents and employing their ideologies, literally conceived, against their
official bearers (1978). In fact, given the weak resources of new movements, a
position within a "host" institution provides such movements with opportunities for communication and consensus mobilization that they would otherwise
lack (Katzenstein 1990; Tarrow 1988).

With its centralized structure and official dogma, the Catholic Church has
long provided a home for emergent heterodox movements. More recently, a
similar insurgency has developed within the historically most passive sector of
the American church, its female monastic orders.[16] In the Middle East, the
flexible structures of Islam have permitted fundamentalism to thrive within it.
In Iran, Algeria and most recently the Sudan and Egypt, radical clerics inspire
unemployed young men to levels of militancy that have not been seen in the
West since the 1930s. When pursued by police, they find refuge in the mosques.

Movements in democratic systems are more likely to recruit activists through friendly organizations – what sociologists Fernandez and McAdam call the use of "multiorganizational fields."[17] Through either bloc or individual recruitment, movements use the good offices, the publications and even the premises of associations with which they have affinities to recruit supporters and spread the word of impending campaigns. For example, much of the recruitment for the European peace movement was done through friendly religious, union and party organizations.[18] The same was true of the majority of participants in the Mississippi Freedom Summer campaign. Fernandez and McAdam found that participants in Freedom Summer were more likely to have been active in its "multiorganizational field" than people who originally applied for the project and then withdrew (p. 337).

Recruitment into movements from existing organizations is scarcely a new phenomenon. As we have seen, many of the participants in the French 1851 insurrection were recruited from the *chambrées* and friendly societies of their villages (Agulhon 1982). A large proportion of the recruits to the early American women's movement came out of churches and voluntary associations (Rosenthal et al. 1985). What is unusual in contemporary movements is the density of the organizational matrix from which movements can recruit. When more organizations are more readily available as reservoirs for recruitment into a wide spectrum of movements, we may be witnessing the foundation for a movement society.

Free spaces and permanent places

Internal democracy is a recurring preoccupation of the political culture of movement organizations (Rosenthal and Schwartz 1990). Building their ideas from movements ranging from the Knights of Labor of the nineteenth century to the Civil Rights and women's movements of the 1960s, Sara Evans and Harry Boyte argue that, at the heart of successful democratic movements there are "environments in which people are able to learn a new self-respect, a deeper and more assertive group identity, public skills, and values of cooperation and civic virtue" (1992: 17–18). Where European social democracy solved the problem of coordination by encapsulating the working class into permanent organizations, and the anarchists tried to inspire mass revolt by mounting dramatic attacks on authority, community-based movements build strength by involving people in democratic decision making at the base of their movements.

Theorists of the "new" social movements of the 1970s and 1980s tried to link them to the technological issues and Keynesian welfare states that developed in postwar capitalist democracies. But long before there was a welfare state, "new" movements were already based on similar forms of face-to-face identity building as sociologist Craig Calhoun writes (1993). In early nineteenth-century industrial movements, religious communities and feminist movements, primary social networks had internal processes that were as participatory as the internal lives of the new social movements of today (d'Anieri, Ernst, and Kier 1990). And in Third World movements like the Mexican teachers' movement studied by Maria Cook (1990), extensive membership participation helped to defend the movement against repression.

What is "new" about the "free spaces" in contemporary movements is that organizers have understood the power that lies in face-to-face communities and tried to fashion techniques designed to embed them in larger movements without encapsulating them into rigid hierarchies. The "consciousness raising" phase of the women's movement is an example of such deliberate techniques (Evans 1980); the participatory style of many peace and ecology groups is another (Rochon: 83). As sociologists Naomi Rosenthal and Michael Schwartz observe; "primary movement groups constitute the growth sector of social movements" (p. 54).

In Berlin and Amsterdam, Berkeley and Ann Arbor, networks of potential activists thrive within a loose counterculture, providing a recruitment base – but also obstacles to permanent incorporation – for intermittent movement campaigns. The problem is that – as the rapid decline of the peace movement of the 1980s shows – organizers have not been very good at turning such "free spaces" into permanent places – that is, sustained movement activity. Between the small professional cadres at the summit of these movements and their heterogeneous sources of mobilization at the base, the problem of center–periphery linkages requires a permanent solution that goes against the grain of the grassroots political culture of many of these movements.

LINKING SUMMIT AND BASE

European Social Democrats linked summit and base through a formal hierarchy of branches, committees and organizations. The anarchists responded by denying the distinction between summit and base, ultimately denuding themselves of the latter. The new movements of today link summit and base through a variety of both formal mechanisms and informal connections that draw on people's social ties, on their habits of working and living together and on their zest for planning and carrying out collective action.

Some of these connections are the results of the new resources and capacities described above. When a movement can publicize its program and actions through the media, to some extent, it externalizes the costs of collective action. But the opposite side of the coin is also true; for the media have a logic which only occasionally coincides with the aims of the movement. Professional movements' dependence on the financial contributions of affluent subscribers also has a cost – especially when facing opponents who have the commitment and the free time to go into the streets (McCarthy 1987).

Movement organizers have learned that the need to link summit and base does not require the vast bureaucratic networks of the old social democratic model. But it does require looser linkages in order to retain contact with supporters and mobilize them when campaigns of collective action are organized. To put this more analytically, organizations must fulfill the function of coordination required for effective collective action while maintaining the autonomy at the base needed to provide participatory incentives for supporters. To be effective, a movement need not create a permanent organization so much as assure their contact with autonomous social networks through what we may call, with Thomas Ohlemacher, a set of "social relays."[19]

Two anthropologists, Luther Gerlach and Virginia Hine, identified such center–periphery linkages in the movements they studied in the United States in the 1960s (1970). Neither the Pentacostal or the Black Power movements were spontaneous eruptions of collective action or centralized bureaucracies, but were what Gerlach and Hine call "decentralized, segmented and reticulated."[20] As they observe, "these very characteristics are highly adaptive in that they promote the growth of the movement, prevent effective suppression of it, and promote the desired personal and social changes" (pp. 64–5).

National movements sometimes institutionalize this decentralized model of center–periphery relations by "enfranchising" local affiliates (McCarthy and Wolfson 1993:4–6). Such organizational franchises allow a small national umbrella organization to coordinate the activities of a broad base without expending scarce resources on internalization. A spectacularly successful case of this was the Committee for Nuclear Disarmament (CND) in Britain in the 1980s. After almost two decades of living on the margins of British politics, CND had few members and a skeletal national organization (Maguire 1990). But it was able to quickly capitalize on growing antiwar sentiment in Britain by forming a loose alliance of local groups and special focus groups that did not take their orders from above. It was enough for national CND to inform its branches and affiliate groups of an impending campaign to elicit collective action as long as the cycle of peace protest continued.

The tyranny of decentralization

But such loose mobilizing structures have the defects of their virtues. While encouraging base autonomy and allowing activists free spaces of democracy and participation, they permit – and indeed encourage – a lack of coordination and discontinuity. For example, while the women of the Greenham Common peace camp kept the British army at bay for months, their devotion to internal democracy led to bitter fights over the issue of whether to allow male comrades to spend the night there (Rochon: 82). Similarly, in the womens' groups that Judith Hellman studied in Italy, personalism became a kind of "tyranny" that made formal decisions impossible and, on occasion, left noninitiates feeling excluded (pp. 195–6).

The best that organizers can hope for in the long run is to construct or utilize loose links between networks of activists who have ties of solidarity and are interdependent. Such networks are most natural when they emerge from occupational, neighborhood or familial ties. Social networks are sometimes created in the course of collective action. But they endure longer and are more likely to produce an ongoing social movement when they are rooted in preexisting social ties, habits of collaboration and the zest for planning and carrying out collective action that comes from a common life.

CONCLUSION

There is no single model of movement organization. As Marwell and Oliver argue, heterogeneity and interdependence are greater spurs to collective action than homogeneity and discipline (1993). The encapsulation of the European working class into mass parties and unions was a solution for the long term that left the workers unprepared for collective action when crisis struck. The anarchist countermodel was an organizational weapon for the short term that left its proponents isolated from their purported mass base. Contemporary models – transitory teams, professional movement groups, decentralized organizations and free spaces – are variations on, and combinations of, these experiences. What underlies the most successful of them – from the 1851 insurrection to the 1980s peace movement to the democratization movements in Eastern Europe in 1989 – is the mobilization of preexisting solidarities through autonomous movement networks which stimulate larger publics into collective action.

Such movements cannot be artificially formed; nor can they be maintained in a permanent state of readiness. The dilemma of movement organizations is that when they permanently internalize their base, they lose their capacity for disruption; but when they move in the opposite direction, they fail to maintain a sustained interaction with allies, authorities and potential supporters. The ''solution'' is not an internal resource or structure at all, but the opening up of political opportunities that is usually outside organizers' control.

Collective action can occur under a variety of circumstances, and isolated movements crop up all through modern society. But the major power of movement is exerted when opportunities are widening, elites are divided and realignments are occurring. On such occasions, even movements that are poorly organized can take advantage of generalized opportunities. Organizers often imagine that they have the power to create social movements; but the frequent collapse of movement mobilization that *seemed* well organized and brilliantly led suggests that both the sources of movements' power, and their limits, are the results of political opportunities. Both the openings and the shifts in opportunities are most clearly manifested in the cycles of protest that recur in modern history and that we will turn to in the next chapter.

PART III

Movement dynamics

9

Cycles of protest

The powers of social movements are a mix of internal and external resources. If movement organizers succeed in mobilizing the base of their movements, this depends not on formal organization, but on the social networks in which supporters are found, and on the mobilizing structures that link them to one another. If leaders frame collective action with their demands and ideologies, their proposals are woven into a cultural matrix and, in modern societies, depend on the mass media to be communicated to allies and enemies. If movements innovate in the forms of collective action that they use, most innovations are marginal changes in the conventional repertoire that they use to reach a broader audience. And finally, it is the political opportunities created by modern states and the changing opportunities in their environments that give movements the incentives to mobilize and diffuse collective action to broader movements. It is to an understanding of these broader movements and the cycles of protest in which they arise that this chapter is devoted.

When I use the phrase, cycle of protest, I am referring to a phase of heightened conflict and contention across the social system that includes: a rapid diffusion of collective action from more mobilized to less mobilized sectors; a quickened pace of innovation in the forms of contention; new or transformed collective action frames; a combination of organized and unorganized participation; and sequences of intensified interaction between challengers and authorities which can end in reform, repression and sometimes revolution.

When we turn to social scientists' research on waves of collective action, we find an odd paradox. Although recognizing their importance for social movements, they are more apt to pay attention to individuals, movements and especially to social movement organizations. Even students of revolution have often ignored the relationship between cycles and revolutionary situations, as Charles Tilly has noted in his recent *European Revolutions* (1933b: 13–14). If protest cycles are such major watersheds of social and political change as I have claimed, why do we have so few studies of such periods?

One reason is that movement organizations are easier to fix in place and time than broader protest cycles and are more accessible to investigators – many of whom come from within their ranks. Protest cycles, in contrast, often begin within institutions, spread into confrontations among ordinary people and bring the scholar face-to-face with some of the less edifying aspects of collective action – the crowd, the mob, the armed insurrection. When they end in repression and disillusionment, as the revolutions of 1848 did, they make depressing reading for movement sympathizers.

A second reason for the neglect of cycles is that they occupy no clearly demarcated space with respect to institutional politics. Students of "collective behavior," for example, distinguish it from behavior in institutions. But a brief reflection on 1848 and other cycles will show that insurgencies often begin within institutions, and that even organized movements become rapidly involved in the political process where they interact with interest groups, unions, parties and the forces of order. To encompass cycles, our account must link social movements to struggles for power both in institutions and outside of institutions, and this requires us to adopt a degree of methodological syncretism that runs across the grain of the division of labor of contemporary social science.

The idea that entire systems go through cyclical change has been found among three main groups of scholars: Cultural theorists who see changes in culture as the source of political and social change (Brand 1990; Swidler 1986); political historians and historical economists who look for regular cycles of political or economic change (Schlesinger 1986; Hirschman 1982); and social theorists who see changes in collective action resulting from changes in states and capitalism (Tilly 1984: ch. 1).

The first school emphasizes the global nature of cycles, the second, their regularity, and the third, their derivation from configurations of structural change. All three can prove useful, but they all focus on macropolitical and macrosociological relations *between* cycles; none examines the structure of the cycle itself. What is most important about this structure is the broadening of political opportunities by early risers in the cycle, the externalities that lower the social transaction costs of contention for even weak actors, the high degree of interdependence among the actors in the cycle and the closure of political opportunities at its end.

Organizations and authorities, movements and interest groups, members of the polity and challengers interact, experience conflict and cooperate in such periods, and the dynamic of the cycle is the outcome of their interaction. "Actions," as sociologist Pam Oliver writes, "can affect the likelihood of other actions by creating occasions for action, by altering material conditions, by changing a group's social organization, by altering beliefs, or by adding knowledge" (1989: 2). These actions create uncertainty and undermine the calculations on which existing commitments and alliances are based, leading supporters of the regime to trim their sails and opponents to make new calculations of interest and alliance. The outcome of such many-sided interactions depends less on the balance of power and the resources of any pair of actors, than on the generalized nature of contention and its multipolar nature. This is why, as we will see, although the beginnings of protest cycles are similar, their endings are far more disparate.

In what follows, I will sketch the main elements within a protest cycle to help us to understand how cycles unfold and how they end. The key concept is the opening, diffusion and the closure of political opportunities. I will then trace the main lineament of the first major international cycle of protest – the 1848 Revolution – before comparing three cycles in recent history, the 1930s, the 1960s and the liberation movements in Eastern Europe in the last decade.

OPPORTUNITIES AND CYCLES

The generalization of conflict into a cycle of protest occurs when political opportunities are opened up for well-placed "early risers," when they make claims that resonate with those of others, and when these give rise to objective or explicit coalitions among disparate actors and create or reinforce instability in the elite. The early demands that appear in a cycle do two things: First, they demonstrate the vulnerability of authorities to such demands, which signals to other contenders that the time may be ripe for their own demands. And, second, "they inevitably challenge the interests of other contenders, either because the distribution of benefits to one group will diminish the rewards available for another, or because the demands directly attack the interests of an established group" (Tilly 1993b: 13).

Although cycles do not have a uniform frequency or extend equally to entire populations, a number of features characterize such periods in recent history.[1] These include heightened conflict, broad sectoral and geographic diffusion, the expansion of the repertoire of contention, the appearance of new movement organizations and the empowerment of old ones, the creation of new "master frames" linking the actions of disparate groups to one another and intensified interaction between challengers and the state.

Conflict and diffusion

Protest cycles are characterized by heightened conflict: not only in industrial relations, but in the streets; not only there, but in villages and schools. In such periods, the magnitude of conflictual collective action of many kinds rises appreciably above what is typical both before and after. Particular groups recur with regularity in the vanguard of waves of social protest (for example, miners, students); but they are frequently joined during the peak of the cycle by groups that are not generally known for their insurgent tendencies (for example, peasants, workers in small industry, white-collar workers).

Cycles of protest also have some traceable paths of diffusion from large cities to the rural periphery, or – as is often the case – from periphery to center. They often spread from heavy industrial areas to adjacent areas of light industry and farming, along river valleys or through other major routes of communication. They appear among members of the same ethnic or national group whose identities are activated by new opportunities and threats. The uncertainty created by widespread contention increases the importance of ethnicity or other communal characteristics in people's mutual recognition, trust and cooperation (Bunce 1991).

What is most distinctive about such periods is not that entire societies "rise" in the same direction at the same time (they seldom do); or that particular population groups act in the same way over and over, but that the demonstration effect of collective action on the part of a small group of "early risers" triggers a variety of processes of diffusion, extension, imitation and reaction among groups that are normally quiescent.

Diffusion is misspecified if it is seen only as a contagion of collective action to similar groups that are making the same claims against equivalent opponents. A key characteristic of protest cycles is the diffusion of a propensity for collective action from its initiators to both unrelated groups and to antagonists. The former respond to the demonstration effect of a collective action that succeeds or at least is not suppressed, while the latter produce the countermovements that are a frequent reaction to the onset of collective action.

Repertoires and frames

Protest cycles are the crucibles out of which new weapons of social protest are fashioned. The barricades in the French revolutions of the nineteenth century; the factory councils of 1919–20; the sitdown strikes of the French Popular Front and the American New Deal; the "direct actions" of the 1968–72 period in Italy: In the uncertainty and experimentation of a cycle of protest, innovation accelerates and new forms of collective action have space to develop and be refined.

Of course, not all of the collective action innovations that appear in these periods of generalized contention survive past the end of the cycle. Some are directly linked to the peak of contention, when it seems to some that anything is possible and the world will be transformed (Zolberg 1972); others are the result of the very high levels of participation characteristic of cycles and cannot be sustained when mobilization declines. As participation declines and utopia recedes, more conventional forms come to dominate, and those who thought a brave new world was coming either retreat into private life or engage in increasingly desperate acts of violence. The most successful new forms become part of the future repertoire of collective action.

With a similar logic, protest cycles produce new or transformed symbols, frames of meaning and ideologies to justify and dignify collective action and help movements to mobilize a following. These typically arise among insurgent groups – which is how the traditional concept of "rights" expanded in the United States in the 1960s – and then spread elsewhere in the system – for example, as the American "rights" frame spread to women, gay men and lesbians, Native Americans and to campaigns for the rights of the unborn and even animals in the 1970s and 1980s. Waves of mobilization are the crucibles within which new cultural constructs are born, tested, and refined. These may then enter the political culture in more diffuse and less militant form and can serve as a source for the symbols around which future movement entrepreneurs mobilize a following.

Movement organizations

The increase in collective action towards the peak of a cycle creates incentives for new organizations to form and for old ones to radicalize their tactics. Protest cycles almost never fall under the control of a single movement organization. The high point of the wave is marked by the appearance of "spontaneous" collective action; but in fact, both previous traditions of organization and new organized movements structure their strategies and outcomes. Nor is it the case that "old" organizations necessarily give way to new ones in the course of the cycle – many of them adopt the radical tactics of their competitors and adjust their discourse to reflect a broader, more aggressive public stance.

To the extent that organizations become the major carriers of a protest wave, contention will not cease just because a particular group has been satisfied, repressed or becomes tired of life in the streets. Organizations born in collective action continue to use it. Once formed, movement organizations compete for support through collective action. The common spiral of radicalization observed in many protest cycles is the outcome of such competition for support. A key element in the decline of movements are disputes over tactics, as some militants insist on radicalizing their strategy while others try to consolidate their organizations and deliver concrete benefits to supporters.

Increased interaction

Finally, during periods of increased contention, interactions between groups of challengers and authorities increase in frequency and intensity and become multipolar rather than bipolar. Conflicts between elites widen into deep cleavages between social groups; new centers of power develop – however temporary and ephemeral – convincing insurgents that the old system is collapsing and producing new and sometimes bizarre alliances between challengers and supporters of the regime. These coalitions sometimes form the bases of new governing coalitions. More often, they split apart as some branches of the movement seek more radical change and others try to institutionalize their gains.

These characteristics can be found in many modern protest cycles, beginning with the revolutions of 1848 which we will examine. That conflict produced major watersheds of turbulence, collective action and political conflict almost everywhere in Europe. In each country grassroots insurgency was encouraged by opportunities at the summit, expanded by conflicts within the elite and mobilized by organized groups that took advantage of these opportunities to threaten order, challenge opponents and in some cases attack the regime. But like twentieth-century cycles, the revolutions also contained elements of political mediation, reform and adaptation. Out of them, later movements were formed, new collective action frames were fashioned and future political cleavages were etched.

THE FIRST MODERN CYCLE

In the winter and spring of 1848, rebellions were breaking out all over Europe.[2] On parts of the continent, the bad crop yields of the past few years appeared to be the main cause of the uprisings, but in other areas, harvests had been improving since the disastrous one of 1846.[3] In some countries, disputes over the suffrage were the trigger for the agitations of issue; but in others, the suffrage had already been expanded and in still others it only became an issue after the revolution. Finally, religious and ethnic cleavages were the source of important struggles in some countries, but in others there was no visible communal conflict.[4]

Although they sprang from a variety of sources, the uprisings of early 1848 struck observers as a single event of continental importance. Engels devoted considerable resources to raising insurrections in Germany just as Bismarck's career as an opponent of democracy was being launched. Mazzini made his way to Rome where he helped to hasten the end of the Roman Republic, while Garibaldi returned from Latin America to raise insurrections in the Italian states. Tocqueville saw the revolution as the last chance for France to combine popular representation with limited government (1987: 61 ff.). In his 1847 program for the moderate opposition, he had foreseen the vast nature of the imminent conflagration. "The time is coming when the country will again be divided between two great parties," he prophesied; "Soon the political struggle will be between the haves and the have-nots; property will be the great battlefield." (pp. 12–13).

By the middle of 1848 in every major European country, regimes were threatened or overturned. People marched, met, organized assemblies and com-

Figure 9.1. *1848 Events by Month, March 1847–August 1849*

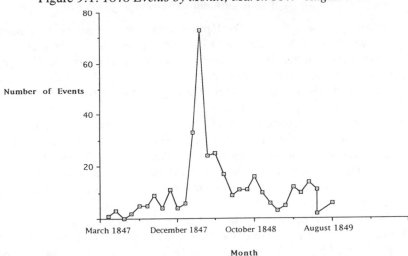

Source: Sarah Soule and Sidney Tarrow, ''Acting Collectively, 1847–1849: How the Repertoire of Collective Action Changed and Where It Happened,'' paper presented to the annual conference of Social Science History Association, New Orleans, Louisiana. 1991.

mittees and erected barricades. Rulers either scurried to places of safety or rushed through reforms to forestall further rebellion. Figure 9.1 demonstrates the dramatic rise and fall in conflict and response by combining the number of public events from Jacques Godechot's chronology for all the major European states for which he provides information on collective action in the 1848 revolutions.[5]

Godechot's series begins in March 1847, when the first major events occurred, and continues for thirty months through the end of August 1849. He includes a detailed outline of events of national importance for Austria–Hungary, Belgium, Britain, France, the German and Italian states, the Netherlands, Poland, Spain and Switzerland. Some of these events were contentious and violent; others were routine electoral and legislative acts; others were the actions of public authorities; still others, the interventions of foreign powers. His chronology allows us to record only the *number* of events and not their duration or the number of participants, but it provides us with a graphic picture of the rapid spread of contention and the political and military responses to it across Europe in the revolutions of 1848, and will help us to introduce the dynamics of protest cycles.

A transnational movement

By aggregating these events across Europe, Figure 9.1 disguises the transnational nature of the 1848 revolutions. I will focus, here, only on the four major continental units – Italy, France, Germany and the regions of the Hapsburg Empire. The time–series of events in each country from Godechot's chronology are represented for France and Italy in Figure 9.2 and for Germany and Austria in Figure 9.3.

The national data reported in Figures 9.2 and 9.3 show a fitful rise in contention prior to February 1848 in most of the countries – with the exception of Italy – a near-simultaneous explosion of conflict in the spring of 1848, and a variety of national patterns for the remaining period. The pattern of similar beginnings and different endings of the cycle depended, in part, on the incidence of foreign intervention late in the period; but it will remain a salient characteristic of the twentieth century cycles we will turn to later in this chapter.

Although France has received the lion's share of attention, the events of February 1848 in Paris were presaged in three less central areas – Switzerland, Belgium and Italy. Not for the first time in history, a revolution that attacked the core of the European power system began in its periphery. In Switzerland, divisions among Catholics, liberals and radicals gave the more liberal Protestant

Figure 9.2. *1848 Events by Month, 1847–1849; France and Italy*

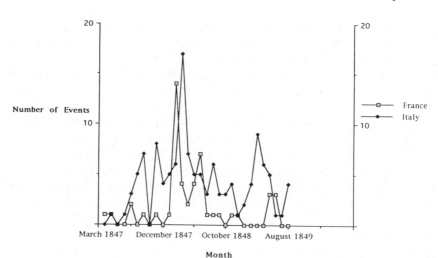

Source: Sarah Soule and Sidney Tarrow, "Acting Collectively, 1847–1849: How the Repertoire of Collective Action Changed and Where It Happened," paper presented to the annual conference of Social Science History Association, New Orleans, Louisiana. 1991.

Figure 9.3. *1848 Events by Month, 1847–1849; Germany and Austria*

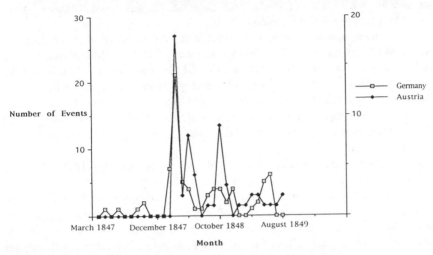

Month

Source: Sarah Soule and Sidney Tarrow, "Acting Collectively, 1847–1849: How the Repertoire of Collective Action Changed and Where it Happened," paper presented to the annual conference of Social Science History Association, New Orleans, Louisiana. 1991.

cantons unusual margins for maneuver over their Catholic opponents. Their military successes in November of 1847, the support they enjoyed from the British, and the inability of the Austrians to intervene encouraged the party of change throughout Europe. No less French a historian than Halèvy would later assert that "the revolution of 1848 did not arise from the Parisian barricades but from the Swiss civil war" (Sigmann: 193).

Events in Brussels – so recently linked to Paris by rail – were another source of encouragement to the French opposition. If the king of the Belgians could appoint a liberal government, liberal parlementarians in France were challenged to press the French government for expansion of France's limited suffrage. Though a "Belgian legion" made a futile attempt to cross into Belgium from France in March, this time it was Belgium that influenced France, rather than vice versa.[6]

The Italian events of 1847 were even more remarkable, given that they began in benighted Rome, where an apparently liberal pope had just been chosen, and reached their peak in Sicily which was ruled from Naples by an anything-but-liberal Bourbon dynasty. From April to July 1847, Pope Pius conceded reforms to the papal states, triggering agitations both in Rome and in the Po valley towns, leading the rattled Austrians to occupy Ferrara. This was followed in the southern kingdom by an insurrection in Messina, riots in Naples and the concession of a liberal ministry in the South by a frightened King Ferdinand.[7] Even in the peasant backwaters of Puglia and Calabria, "clubs" and "circles" were formed along French lines (Soldani 1973).

Communications moved in both directions. As word of the agitations in Rome and Messina spread northward, they were studied in Milan and Venice, and were covered in detail in the French and German press. Agitations broke out in the Austrian-occupied parts of Northern Italy; and in the Kindgom of Sardinia, King Carlo Alberto was pressured to accord his people a constitution. The peace of Europe established at the Congress of Vienna was breaking down at the periphery where its vulnerability was demonstrated to reformers and radicals at its core.

Politically that core had always been Paris, and in February 1848, Paris did not disappoint the radicals. Although France was outpaced by Italy in the early sequence of events, Figures 9.2 and 9.3 suggest its importance in touching off rebellions in the other major areas of Europe. The most dramatic sign that an international protest wave was afoot was the rise in contentious events outside of France following the collapse of the July Monarchy. Paris was not the trigger for all the European revolts of these years, but it was a catalyst for its most intensive phase.

Creating opportunities

Narrative histories of revolutions often concentrate on either their structural preconditions or their enthusiastic heights. But the immediate conditions of such explosions are found in the opening of opportunities within the polity – not only in the sense that the system is shown to be "ripe" for change, but in the more dynamic sense that alignments within it shift, access opens, elites divide and allies appear for challengers outside the system – the elements of political opportunity that were examined in Chapter 5.

In the revolutions of 1848, conflicts at the summit provided opportunities first to moderates, then to organizations outside the elite and eventually to ordinary people. These changes were not begun by the downtrodden masses but by institutional and social elites whose conflicts provided opportunities for others to organize and mobilize. Incentives spread from elites to masses through the press, through legal and illegal political organizations, and increasingly, through collective actions that demonstrated the boldness of the opposition and the vulnerability of the regimes.

On the eve of the "springtime of peoples," such struggles were opening up in many of the countries of Europe. Of the major capitals, only Vienna doesn't appear in Godechot's chronology until 1848 – except for the defeats it suffered in Switzerland and Italy.[8] In Paris, Berlin, and Rome, popular insurrection was presaged by realignments in the political class that opened opportunities for others. The French developments of 1847–8 can be used to illustrate this process.

By the early 1840s, most Central and Western European regimes, including France's, had semiconstitutional governments which provided a good deal of scope for elite debate, focusing increasingly on the issue of the suffrage (Anderson and Anderson: 307–17). French reformers were not so foolhardy as to wish to extend the vote universally, but the agitation around the suffrage revealed cracks in the elite and uncertainty in the government that were key factors in triggering contention among the poor.

The first stage in the unraveling of the Regime was its response to the parlementary opposition's demand for reform. Rejection of its modest proposals threw the moderates into the arms of the Republicans, launching the campaign of "banquets" that were thinly disguised demonstrations for reform that took the debate from the Chamber to the streets, and from Paris to the provinces. Because these banquets were sponsored by the legitimate opposition and were entirely peaceable, the government hesitated to repress them. But because they bridged the tactical interests of parlementary and extra-parlementary groups, the campaign passed rapidly from the parliamentary opposition into the hands of a coalition of extra-parlementary agitators and journalists who suddenly published a program calling for the National Guard to attend the final banquet as a body (Tocqueville 1987: 26–7). The liberals tried to pull back, but by the day scheduled for the biggest banquet of all – in Paris on February 22 – it was too late, and the initiative passed into the hands of the Guard and the urban poor (p. 20).

The first stage of the revolution was centered on the Chamber, but before it had gone very far, barricades were raised on the streets of Paris, diligence drivers were taking advantage of the tumult to destroy the railway lines, Jews were attacked in the eastern provinces and forest preserves were invaded. But the walls of the July Monarchy had been sapped from within before they were attacked from without. As Ronald Aminzade writes, "as soon as we look even a little deeply into the historical context of the 1848 events, the continuities between institutionalized and movement politics become more evident" (1994: 4).

The peak of the cycle

As in many of the protest cycles that followed, the peak of contention in the spring of 1848 was marked by an expansion of the forms of collective action. In 1848, these were the public meeting, the demonstration, the barricade and violence against others. Although the 1848 Revolution has been remembered for its most confrontational movements, the co-occurrence of these collective action forms tells us just how broad participation was. As liberal and conservative gentlemen were holding sober meetings and learned conferences, radicals were organizing demonstrations, workers and artisans were building barricades and peasants were attacking landlords and taking over forest reserves.

The barricades were the disruptive centerpieces of the various Parisian *journées* (Traugott 1990; 1993). They were mounted in the February days when the Monarchy was overthrown; in April in Rouen, when workers took to them after the defeat of the Republican candidates they had supported in the elections; during the June days, after the Assembly dissolved the national workshops; and again in June 1849, when a French army landed at Civitavecchia to reinstate the pope. Barricades spread rapidly across Europe wherever the Revolution took on a radical character.

But the peaks of protest cycles are also marked by an increase in violence. The attacks on Jews in the spring of 1848 were a presentiment of the ethnic conflicts that marked the passage of the revolution eastward. In Germany the first months of the revolution were marked by scores of such attacks. When Hungarian landowners shook off the rule of Vienna, they quickly put their boot on the necks of subject Serbs. As in Yugoslavia after the 1989 revolution, in Eastern Europe, the breakdown of order in 1848 opened a Pandora's box of opportunities for interethnic violence.

But the revolutions also produced endless public meetings and learned conferences and parliamentary gatherings. What did the Sicilian rebels do when they took over Palermo in January 1848? They formed committees for restoring order, ensuring provisions, securing finance and controlling information (Tilly, Tilly, and Tilly: 130). How did German liberals respond when the king of Prussia dissolved the *landtag* in June 1847? They met in Offenberg in September and in Oppenheim in October to discuss future actions (Godechot: 199–200). Even in Austrian-ruled Serbia, Croatia and Transylvania, the revolutionary events of February and March 1848 produced meetings and committees. The most long-lasting, and the least productive, was the "professors' parliament" in Frankfurt that was at first tolerated and then broken up.

Mass demonstrations were a third important part of the repertoire of 1848 – in fact, the demonstration came into its own in France in that year. If we can assume a resemblance between Godechot's *"manifestation"* and our term "demonstration,"[9] we will find in his chronology thirty-one major demonstrations in the twelve months from July 1947 to June 1848. But it was from February through April 1848 that we find the greatest density of demonstrations. In France and Italy, Germany and Austria there were mass demonstrations by liberals and democrats, students and workers. The peaceful occupation of public space, the public meeting and the barricade, as well as traditional attacks on others were a hallmark of the intensive peak of the cycle.

Cyclical decline

As the revolutions progressed beyond the effervescence of the spring of 1848, the peaceful demonstration and the public meeting begin to disappear from Godechot's chronology, to be replaced by terms like "attack," "clash," "dissolve," "intervene" and "defeat." The last public demonstration he lists was a demand for work in Berlin on October 31, followed soon after by the retraction of the reforms that the Kaiser conceded in the previous spring. People stopped demonstrating when armed force began to be employed against them.

Increasingly, armed clashes took on an international dimension. Austrian armies attacked the liberals in Northern Italy, the French intervened in Rome, and Russian troops moved against the Hungarians in aid of the Hapsburgs. By the end of 1849, Godechot's chronology provides a picture of almost unrelieved armed strife, foreign intervention and a collapse of popular collective action. In France, the cycle dragged on through the Second Republic and ended only with Louis Napoleon's coup in 1851.

Like many other protest cycles, the 1848 Revolution left the most bitter memories where the hopes it had generated were highest. At first welcomed by radicals and democrats across Europe, the revolutionaries of 1848 were soon denounced for their "hollow rhetoric, their mystical idealism . . . and their generous illusions" (Sigmann: 10). In Germany, the year was soon labeled *"das tolle Jahr,* while the British ambassador to Paris, Lord Normanby, wrote that 1848 left "almost every individual less happy, every country less prosperous, every people not only less free but less hopeful of freedom hereafter" (Postgate: 266). The memory it left in Italy was of confusion and chaos; even today, the expression to *"fare un quarantotto"* means to create confusion. "What we remember most" after the intoxication of a "moment of madness", writes Aristide Zolberg, "is that moments of political enthusiasm are followed by bourgeois repression or by charismatic authoritarianism, sometimes by horror but always by the restoration of boredom" (1972: 205).

THREE MODERN CYCLES

The same characteristics found in the revolution of 1848 can be found in three cycles in recent history for which we have significant information: the period of the Popular Front in France and the American New Deal; the movements of the 1960s in Western Europe and the United States; and the Eastern European democratization wave that began in Poland in 1980 and ended in the collapse of the USSR in 1991. The first was centered in organized labor, although other occupational groups, like farmers and the unemployed, also appeared in it; the second was centered among students, although workers and urban movements were also present in Western Europe; and the third, though it began among workers and intellectuals, rapidly spread to entire populations.

Popular Front and New Deal

From 1934 to 1936, a wave of protests swept across France, leading democrats to fear an assault on the Republic from the right, and propertied interests to fear anarchy from the Left. While peasant leagues threatened order in the provinces, right wing formations reminiscent of the German brownshirts filled the squares of Paris. Faced by these pressures, the government fell, new elections were called, and a Popular Front headed by socialist Léon Blum came to power. As if by prearranged signal, workers all over France occupied their factories and brought the economy to a halt.[10]

Spain had a Popular Front in the mid-1930s too. As the result of a strike wave in Asturias and Catalonia, the center–right wing government fell and a left wing coalition came to power. Strikes were legalized, participation was extended to the workplace and the separatist claims of Basques and Catalans received support from the government. As in France, the Popular Front gave the Spanish Communist Party the first government it could support since its creation in the early 1920s.

About the same time, factory workers in Flint, Michigan and Akron, Ohio were employing sit-down tactics like those of French workers, paralyzing production and occupying the premises of Fisher Body and Goodyear Rubber (Piven and Cloward 1979: ch. 3). Their grievances were different and their ideologies less articulated than those of their European counterparts, but they too acted in the midst of a political reform movement of national scope – the New Deal of Franklin Roosevelt.

The European and American student movements''[11]

From 1968 to 1972, a wave of student and labor unrest arose in Europe that would eventually envelop almost every area of society. Two movements in particular reached historic proportions: in France, the short but explosive "movement of May" nearly toppled the self-assured Gaullist regime while, in Czechoslovakia, a short spring of reform was followed by a brutal military crackdown. At about the same time, an Italian *maggio strisciante* (sliding May) shut down schools, universities and factories, while in Germany, a wave of protest jarred that country's complacent political class. Even in Poland, the dramatization of Adam Mickiewicz's play, *Forefathers,* touched off a series of events that led to a movement of university students (Wejnert 1994).

In the United States, the years of hope began earlier, in the Civil Rights movement of the early 1960s and in the anti–Vietnam War agitations that culminated in the "Days of Rage" at the Chicago Democratic Party convention. As in Europe, university students were in the vanguard of the American movements, but the workers who played a central role in France and Italy were largely absent.

What is most striking in thinking back to the movements of the sixties is the common frames of collective action in what Doug McAdam and Dieter Rucht call "the cross-national diffusion of movement ideas" (1993). Not only ideas, but movement tactics crossed the Atlantic in the 1960s. Although – also in retrospect – movements of the 1960s were far from revolutionary, they aptly illustrate what Tilly writes about the cross-national diffusion of revolutionary situations; "The demonstration that one important state is vulnerable . . . signals the possibility of making similar demands elsewhere" and makes available transferable expertise and doctrine (1993b: 14). This was spectacularly the case in Eastern Europe in 1989 and after.

The collapse of state socialism

In Poland in the summer of 1980, a workers' protest exploded in the shipyards along the Baltic coast. It began in workplace disputes and – as in earlier Polish strikes – was triggered by the government's announcement of price increases. But this time, an interfactory committee born of working class solidarity made it no longer possible for the authorities to divide and conquer. Before it was over, the wave of protest had spread through the country, to farmers and students, creating an institution unique to the Communist world – an independent union called *Solidarnosc*.[12]

Nine years divided the early strikes on the Baltic coast from the collapse of state socialism in Eastern Europe, so we cannot really talk about an integrated cycle. But Poland's "self-limiting revolution" was not so much different from, as it was a prefiguration of, the patterns that emerged elsewhere in the region. That workers in the heart of the Lenin shipyard could organize resistance with other workers and intellectuals, maintaining an underground life under martial law, told dissidents throughout Eastern Europe that their turn would eventually come. When it did, it was triggered from the source of authority in Moscow with the promise of Gorbachev's reforms and his warning that his East European allies were on their own.

VARIATIONS IN MOVEMENT DYNAMICS

Though each of these protest waves took a different form, they appear, in retrospect, to be international waves of mobilization and reform. France's 1934–6 agitations were a response to the 1933 victory of fascism in Germany; the student protests of the 1960s were an expression of a movement that began at Berkeley and spread through the common opposition to the Vietnam War; the Polish strikes, though unprecedented in scope, capped five years of labor unrest and, in retrospect, were the first signs of the impending collapse of the Soviet Union's Eastern European empire.

At the peak of each wave, citizens developed particular forms of collective action. The factory occupations that marked the French 1936 strikes were similar to the sitdown strikes of Flint and Akron; while the university occupations of Berlin, Turin and Paris in 1968 linked European students to their American homologues. As for Solidarity, its most striking feature would prove to be the roundtable discussions between Solidarity leaders and the government that foreshadowed the form of negotiation that swept Eastern Europe in 1989.

In each of the cases, a spiral of demands spun outward from conflicts that began within the elite and produced political opportunities for outsiders. Early claims grew out of concrete conflicts of interest. But as the protests spread, coalitions of challengers formed organizations and broadened their claims, often radicalizing them into general challenges to authority. The breadth of these movements and their rapid diffusion seemed to threaten the established order, giving rise to countermovements, demands for law and order, and sometimes to reform. In the end, what began as conflicts over claims became interlaced with struggles for power.

Diverse endings

Viewed from a distance, each wave of collective action described a parabola; from institutional conflict to enthusiastic peak to ultimate collapse. After gaining national attention and state response, they reached peaks of conflict that were marked by the presence of movement organizers who tried to diffuse the insurgencies to broader publics. As participation was channeled into organizations, the movements, or parts of them, took on a more political logic – engaging in implicit bargaining with authorities. In each case, as the cycle wound down, the initiative shifted to elites and parties.

But the multipolarity of the interactions in these cycles made their endings far less similar than their beginnings. The diffusion of collective action from early risers to latecomers, and the shift of political opportunities from challengers to their allies and then to elites, increased the number of interactions and sent the cycles off in divergent directions. Especially the involvement of foreign powers turned the ends of these cycles into different directions.

The French Popular Front responded to the 1936 strikes by increasing minimum wages, limiting working hours and ending the tradition of settling strikes with police truncheons, while in Spain it ended in civil war. The reforms that accompanied the 1968 student protests in Europe were carried out by different governmental coalitions and each ended differently. In France, this was a conservative coalition; in Germany, a Social Democratic one; and in Italy a shifting sequence of center–left and center–right wing governments. Some of the same differences were reflected in the "new" social movements of the 1970s and 1980s (Koopmans 1993). In Poland, the Jaruzelski government declared martial law in 1981, clapping Solidarity leaders into jail and attempting to put the stopper on dissent. Its greatest success was negative – it avoided the threat of Soviet military intervention.

Nor did the differential paths of these mobilization waves end with their collapse. In France, the Popular Front was soon defeated. But after the war, the Fourth Republic turned to its reforms for the model of its welfare state. In Italy, France and Germany, the movements of 1968 split into a number of strands, with some elements entering the political parties and unions, others flowing into cultural and religious movements and the most extreme turning to armed violence. The outcomes of protest cycles are found in political struggle. It is the nature of that struggle and the strategies of the actors in each country that determine the outcome of the cycle, as we will see in the next chapter.

10

Struggling to reform

"Struggling to reform": What a strange phrase to use in introducing a discussion of the outcomes of social movements! For most movements seek much more than reform, and many reject reformism altogether. Movement activists demand fundamental social change, the recognition of new identities, entry into the polity, the destruction of their enemies or the overthrow of a social order – but seldom reform. When, as we saw in the last chapter, movements cumulate in a general cycle of protest, claims become so broad and elites so besieged that profound changes are forced onto the agenda. Nevertheless, as I will argue in this chapter, the structure of politics through which movement demands are processed forces them into a common crucible from which modest reforms are the most likely outcome of struggle.

THE AMBIGUITY OF MOVEMENT OUTCOMES

There are almost as many taxonomies of the outcomes of social movements as there are studies of the subject. The best-known typology is the simplest – that of William Gamson. In *The Strategy of Social Protest,* Gamson distinguished between two kinds of outcomes: receiving new advantages and gaining acceptance (1990: ch. 1). A fourfold typology is suggested by Dieter Rucht, who focuses on both the internal and external, and the intended and unintended effects of movements (1992). Paul Schumaker identified five kinds of system responsiveness, ranging all the way from "access responsiveness" to "impact responsiveness" (1975). Paul Burstein and his collaborators added "structural impacts" to Schumaker's list of five (1991).[1]

To complicate matters still more, it is not easy to identify a particular movement cause for a specific policy outcome, since, to movements' voices, we must add the impact of interest groups, parties and executives and the length and corrosiveness of the political process. Particularly in the context of protest cycles, elites do not respond to the demands of any single movement, but both to the generalized confrontation they face from challengers, and to competition from inside the polity. Elites mediate among the demands placed on them, looking for solutions that will defeat their enemies, impose social control and satisfy allies and supporters.

It is in part for this reason that challengers are almost always disillusioned with reformist outcomes. It is also why there can be no one-to-one equilibrium between the efforts and resources of a single protesting group on the one hand, and its success on the other. "Success" is the outcome of a parallelogram of forces from which even a weak challenger may emerge in a better position than a strong one when the former is well placed to take advantage of political opportunities. The political process is not quite a lottery, but it actively intervenes between the resources and goals of a movement and its success or failure.

What helps a movement to succeed? Most students agree that it is its challenging or disruptive power that brings about success. For example, reviewing the recurring waves of welfare reform in the United States, Piven and Cloward write: "Relief arrangements are initiated or expanded during the occasional outbreaks of civil disorder produced by mass unemployment" (1972: xiii). Similarly, the Tillys concluded from their study of a century of conflict in Europe that "no major political rights came into being without readiness of some portions of those [protesting] groups to overcome the resistance of the government and other groups" (1975: 184). Students of the collapse of Communism are more circumspect, but few would deny that popular pressure helped to convince elites in Eastern Europe to give up the ghost.

But if challenge and disruption are what trigger the outcomes of movement, does the impetus for change disappear when movement challenges recede – as they invariably do when activists tire, supporters gain satisfaction or movements are suppressed? Scholars of movements have sometimes argued that once the threat of disruption declines, their leaders are co-opted and their organizations are institutionalized (Lowi 1971; Piven and Cloward 1979). The end of a cycle of protest, it would follow, brings a return to the status quo.

Viewed from a distance, the generalization seems to be valid. For example, as collective action was repressed and radicals split off from liberals, the outcomes of the revolutions of 1848 were almost uniformly repressive. In Berlin and Vienna, constitutions that were conceded in the heat of the movement were withdrawn; the French Republic of 1848 was overthrown by its own President less than three years after being installed; the national minorities that liberated themselves from Hapsburg rule were returned to Austrian control; the pope took up his throne and the king of the Two Sicilies returned to Naples. As for the German states, 1848 showed the political weakness of liberalism and began the process of unification under imperial auspices. Even in Britain, the last great Chartist demonstration was repressed in 1848, and the movement soon disappeared.

But in the long run, the effects of 1848 were not nearly so regressive. The constitutional settlements of Piedmont and Switzerland not only endured, but prospered, the first forming the basis for the unified Italian state that emerged in 1861, and the second becoming a middle class democracy that was a haven for exiles for years to come. Although Hungary fell back under Hapsburg control, by the 1860s it had gained equality in the empire. As for France, by the mid-1860s, the Republicans who had been defeated in 1851 were openly running candidates in local elections; by 1871 the Republic was in power. The more ambitious schemes of the men and women of 1848 were nowhere realized, and many relapsed into alienated pessimism or went into exile. *"Post coitum omnia animal triste"*, writes Aristide Zolberg, quoting the old adage to reflect how disillusionment follows the end of a "moment of madness" (1972: 205–6).

But protest cycles do not simply end and leave nothing but lassitude or repression in their wake; they have indirect and long-term effects that emerge when the initial excitement is over and disillusionment passes. Especially when movements transform their initial challenges into permanent access to power and leave lasting networks of activists behind, they can reappear after the cycle is over and new opportunities appear (Amenta, Carruthers, and Zylan 1992). Three kinds of long-term and indirect effects are important – and increasingly indirect. The first is the effect of protest cycles on the political socialization of people who participate in them, the second the effects of struggle on political institutions and practices and the third the contribution of protest cycles to changes in political culture. All three are initially shaped and mediated by the structure of political opportunity.

THE POLITICAL IS PERSONAL

"What we remember most" after the intoxication of a protest cycle, writes Zolberg, "is that moments of political enthusiasm are followed by bourgeois repression or by charismatic authoritarianism, sometimes by horror but always by the restoration of boredom" (1972: 205). Economist Albert Hirschman goes even further; he cites a "rebound effect," in which individuals who have thrown themselves into public life with enthusiasm, return to private life with a degree of disgust proportional to the effort they have expended (p. 80).

Hirschman and Zolberg are both struck by the disillusionment and backlash that follow the ends of movements. But disillusionment results, not from activism itself, but from the gap between the goal of a movement and its actual outcomes. Moreover, disillusionment may only be short term – the result of immediate disappointments and exhaustion; in the long run, activism may beget more activism, radicalization more polarized attitudes and movement activism leaves behind attitudes more favorable to movement. What do we find in the literature on these three kinds of outcome?

Memories and generations

Jack Nelson, a successful New Orleans attorney, who had taken on a series of civil rights cases for the movement in the early 1960s, used the following terms to describe the personal impact of his activity to oral historian Kim Rogers:

I changed *my* life. And, rather than trying to change the world by using this person, that organization, I probably started to change my life. . . . And, you know, I said, wait a minute, I gotta change. And I changed, and then everything just came naturally (p. 172).

But everything *did not* come naturally to all of Rogers's respondents. The younger generation of CORE and SNCC activists she interviewed found their postmovement years disappointing. "Disillusioned with and cynical about the political process," she writes, they "despaired of meaningful change through the political process," remaining "highly interested but ambivalent about politics, and often yearned for the collective intensity of their pasts" (p. 174). Their determined assault on the white power structure, their involvement with poor rural Blacks and their subsequent failures left the CORE and SNCC activists more deeply disappointed with the results of the movement than integrationists like Nelson.

The contrast between Nelson and his generation, and the CORE and SNCC activists of the protest generation, embodies a fundamental dichotomy in the impact of movement experience on the lives of participants: between personal empowerment and disillusionment. Both are common correlates of movement participation, but they are opposed in their implications. How can we account for the differences?

One hypothesis is that the more risky and costly the involvement, the more likely is the former activist to emerge from it disillusioned and alienated. The problem we have in assessing this hypothesis is the difficulty of finding comparable information for high-risk and low-risk activists who have enough in common to give us confidence that it was their experiences – and not other factors – that were responsible for their later attitudes. But one remarkable study gives us a privileged outlook on the problem: Doug McAdam's book on the Mississippi Freedom Summer project (1988), along with fragments of information from other countries, can help us answer the question.

White heat[2]

In describing his hopes for Freedom Summer, SNCC organizer Bob Moses had called in 1964 for an "annealing process" in Mississippi. Whatever this meant for Mississippi's white power structure, "in the 'white heat' of that Mississippi summer, volunteers who went there experienced their own annealing process," writes McAdam (p. 186). For many Freedom Summer volunteers, "politics became the central organizing force in their lives.'' From that time forward, ''everything else – relationships, work, etc. – got organized around their politics'' (p. 187).

The politicizing effects of the 1960s movements were by no means limited to Americans. In Italy, a high proportion of the new cadres recruited into the parties of the Left came from the movements of that decade. For example, forty percent of those who were recruited into the Italian Communist Party as active militants during the 1970s came to the party from the student, women's and labor movements of the previous decade, compared to less than twenty percent who had entered the party earlier.[3] Other movement cycles around the world led to similar accretions of militancy and politicization. In Indonesia, for those who joined the radical Socialist Youth after World War II,

> the tidal-wave rage for politics roared on out of control. Each person felt as though he, she, could not be truly alive without being political, without debating over politics. . . . Politics! politics! No different than rice under the Japanese Occupation. (B. Anderson 1990: 38)

Movement participation is not only politicizing – it is empowering, both in the psychological sense of increasing the willingness to take risks, and the political one of gaining new skills and broadened perspectives. Returning from Freedom Summer in Mississippi to the University of California in the fall of 1964, a Freedom Summer volunteer told McAdam: ''Freedom Summer tended to boost you; you felt like you had been there and you knew what you were talking about'' (p. 166). Another put it this way: ''Everybody knew about the summer project and everybody wanted to ask me what is was like and . . . I was an authority, an instant authority on the civil rights movement'' (1988: 170).

As a result of their politicization in the Civil Rights movement in Mississippi, many former activists played key roles in the Free Speech Movement in Berkeley and, later on, in the national student, antiwar and women's movements (p. 203). The latter was particularly affected; women who participated in civil rights activities learned from their experience that their male counterparts were often no less sexist and dismissive of women than their opponents. Their resentment, added to the confidence they had gained in the South, was a key ingredient in the new women's movement that grew out of the New Left (Evans 1980: chs. 4 and 5). Interviewed twenty years later, former women volunteers were more often involved in contemporary social movements than their male counterparts, and were more likely to belong to political organizations (p. 222).

Movement involvement not only politicizes people; it can radicalize them. Jack Blocker records this for the temperance movements of nineteenth-century America; they began with attempts at moral suasion, turned to more aggressive tactics when others failed and posed more ambitious demands of policymakers (Blocker: xvi). The same is true of more recent movements; when McAdam compared the political attitudes of returning Freedom Summer volunteers to those of applicants who did not participate, he found that the first group had moved leftward ideologically while the others remained more moderate. And when Carol Mershon compared the attitudes of Italian factory organizers recruited during the "Hot Autumn" to those of their peers, she found the former group to be more egalitarian and more likely to see industrial relations in stark class terms (pp. 311–15).

A myth has grown up – mainly generated from Hollywood movie scripts – that former activists sell out their radical ideas and turn their talents to exploiting the mainstream. But the evidence for this is based on the biographies of a few well-placed figures, and there is a good deal of contrary evidence. For example, activism during their student years was the best predictor of radical attitudes among adults interviewed in Fendrich and Krauss's study of former Japanese and American student radicals (p. 248). The same was true in Italy; when the attitudes of Communist activists recruited from the movements of the late 1960s were compared to those of their comrades who had no independent movement experience, the former were more tolerant of protest and less punitive towards violence (Lange, Irvin and Tarrow: 34–6).

The most convincing findings on the effects of movement participation were analyzed by French political scientist Annick Percheron for former participants in the conflicts surrounding the Algerian war and the Events of May 1968 (1991). Percheron's analysis involves two major improvements over other studies: First, by studying national samples, she was able to compare former participants to population groups who were not involved in either set of conflicts; second, by dividing the results by political party identification, she could compare the attitudes of former "student radicals" to corresponding groups of nonparticipants within the three major political families of France.

Percheron found that, among the supporters of these three major political groups, participation in Algerian war protests or in the Events of May did not produce distinct attitudes, but did reinforce the attitudes that were most characteristic of their respective political groups. More politically active than their peers, she writes, "they expressed in more extreme form the opinions that marked their respective party identities" (pp. 56–7). If these differences can be ascribed to the effects of May 1968 or the Algerian conflict – and not to prior or to later experiences – then we can infer that the effect of movement participation is polarization within political families along the lines of movement/nonmovement experience.

Isolation and regret

In the aftermath of the movements of the 1960s, there was a good deal of the metaphysical angst that Zolberg and Hirschman predicted, both in the United States and in Europe. As the activist culture of the sixties gave way to the disappointments of the seventies, and to personalism in the eighties, many activists were isolated in a movement subculture. During the 1970s, writes McAdam, "the activist subculture was slowly disintegrating, leaving the volunteers who remained active more and more isolated as the decade wore on" (1988: 205).

Past activism also had an effect on activists' personal lives. For example, McAdam calculates that forty-seven percent of the Freedom Summer volunteers who married after that summer went through a divorce between 1970 and 1979. Among the applicants who didn't go to Mississippi, the comparable figure was under thirty percent (p. 208). The personal costs of activism were disproportionately high for women volunteers (pp. 220–1) – not because they preferred a celibate life, but because they were isolated by their independence and leftism from a political culture that was moving to the right.

Both in the United States and in Italy, former activists suffered occupational instability too; changing jobs and suffering unemployment more than nonparticipants. Many of those interviewed by McAdam in America delayed entry into the job market in order to continue their activism, entering it only during the stagnant seventies and never making up for the time lost (pp. 109–212). The same was true of the former leaders of the Italian movement *Lotta continua,* many of whom were still working on the margins of the job market when they were interviewed in the mid-1980s.[4]

Western Europe was different than the United States in one important way: Many members of the generation of the 1960s had a professional outlet that was lacking for American activists who kept the faith – they could move into mass parties of the Left or into the militant trade unions. In contrast, former activists in the United States found little outlet for their activism in the party system, especially after the devastating defeat of George McGovern in 1972. As for the unions, although a few activists became grassroots organizers, the innate conservatism and secular decline of the American labor movement made them poor outlets for activism.

Keeping the faith by keeping in touch[5]

But neither apathy nor professionalization were the most typical outcomes for the generation of the 1960s; most entered private life but continued to be active in one or another form of social movement or political activity. These findings have been replicated in a number of studies. In the United States, nearly half of the former Freedom Summer volunteers that McAdam interviewed were still active in at least one social movement twenty years later. Former Italian activists interviewed by the author were likely to be active in one of the country's traditional left wing parties, in the Green Party or in a social movement. Fendrich and Krauss found that former Japanese activists were frequently active in a left wing political party or movement (p. 245). And among the participants in Algerian war protests and in the Events of 1968 in France, Percheron found a much higher level of political involvement than among other supporters of the same parties (pp. 54–5).

No doubt personal commitment counts for much in the maintenance of activism, but those sixties activists who were still active in Western Europe or the United States during the 1980s were often embedded in networks of former activists. The British peace movement of the 1980s was rooted in the unilateral disarmament activists of the 1960s who kept a presence alive during the lean years of the 1970s (Maguire 1990). In Italy and the United States, it was still possible in the 1980s to track down former activists by following a network trail from one respondent to another.[6] Activists who lacked such networks were less likely to survive the doldrums of the 1970s (Gelb: 281).

The fierce politicization and radicalization at the height of a protest cycle leaves disillusionment behind, and produces defection among some members of a protest generation. Others – embittered by the failures of mass activism – spin off into utopianism or violence, like the militants who ended up in the Weather Underground in the United States or in the Red Brigades in Italy. But a high proportion of the former activists from the 1960s emerged empowered, radicalized and connected to informal networks of future activists.

OPPORTUNITY BETWEEN STRUGGLE AND REFORM

But there is a paradox: The struggles of these activists from the 1960s seldom led to little more than incremental reform. Why did this happen? My answer follows from the general theoretical assumption that underlies this study: Since movements are born, diffused and processed through the logic of political opportunities, it is the changing structure of opportunity emerging from a protest cycle that determines who wins and who loses, and when struggle will lead to reform.

To illustrate this thesis, I will compare two different movements. The first – the French student movement of 1968 – was considered the wonder of the Western world when it broke out and, together with its allies, paralyzed the Fifth Republic. The second – the American women's movement – was slow-starting, appeared only as an offshoot of the Civil Rights movement and worked, for the most part, within the institutions of American politics. But because of their radically different opportunity structures, the first was an instant marvel yet a long-term failure; whereas the second, although seeming to go from disappointment to disappointment, has brought about profound change in American politics and society.

French students[7]

May 1968 in France is a near-laboratory case for studying the political impact of a major wave of protest. As two of its most acute historians observe:

despite the retreat of the movement and its rejection in the ballot box, the Events were the carriers of potentialities that, by one means or another, durably mortgaged the French political scene in a way that had to be immediately faced. (Capdevielle and Mouriaux: 219, author's translation)

The protest wave of May 1968 was followed by a major educational reform, the Orientation Law for Higher Education, which attacked the sclerotic structures of French higher education against which the students of May had first struck. But as the initiative shifted from the students to reformers and educational interest groups, and then to the conservative political class, the reform was scaled down and ultimately emasculated. A brief review of how this happened will silhouette how opportunities narrow and reforms are reshaped as disruption collapses and elites reconstitute their power.

In the early spring of 1968, left wing students in the newly created University of Nanterre demonstrated on a variety of grounds against arbitrary administrative authority as well as against more global targets. Their demonstration in the courtyard of the Sorbonne in early May was met by a combination of police thuggery and governmental uncertainty. When a group of demonstrating students were roughly hauled off in police vans, middle-class Parisians were incensed. And when news of the outrage was diffused to other areas, every university in the country and a number of secondary schools were shut down by strikes and occupations.

The May protests were rapidly diffused across the country: groups as different as cadres, white collar workers, public employees, farmers, Catholics, parents' associations and even football players were rapidly swept into them. As the movement broadened, to the natural self-intoxication of students engaged in collective action was added their leaders' desires to broaden their appeal to a wider public. As a result, the concrete issues of university governance that triggered the movement were displaced by the broader claims – even by the demand that the system of capitalist domination be replaced and the imagination released.

Surrounded by contestation on so many sides, the authorities were placed on the defensive. When the movement spread to the working class – the undigested reservoir of Fourth Republic politics – the government understood that it was facing a potential revolution. Joint action with the students was sporadic at best, but the objective coalition among students, workers and an array of other groups gave each part of the movement a force it could not have had on its own.

Separating the working class from its newfound allies was the first task of the government. In a reversal of his neoliberal policies, Prime Minister Pompidou negotiated dramatic wage increases with the unions (Bridgford 1989). Frightening the middle class with the fear of revolution was the second, accomplished both by President de Gaulle's threatening gesture to use the army, and by a massive counterdemonstration by his supporters. When the parties of the Left announced their readiness to form a government, de Gaulle had the opportunity he needed. The opposition was soundly defeated in the elections of June, and the Gaullists and their allies were returned to power with an overwhelming majority.

In the months following the June elections, the government – not without opposition – boiled down the jumble of demands for educational change that had erupted in May into a major reform law – the *loi d'orientation*. A new, left-leaning education minister, Edgar Faure, was given *carte blanche* to remake higher education around the goals of participation, multidisciplinarity and autonomy of the universities. Of these three goals, only the first responded to the students' demands and to de Gaulle's mandate. But Faure needed to create a coalition of support from amongst students, academics, educational interest groups and advocates of administrative centralization, so he broadened the agenda to include the creation of multidisciplinary universities autonomous from the ministry.

By September, the *grandes lignes* of a fundamental reform were announced. By September, it was put before Parliament (Fomerand 1974: ch. 5).[8] It would be difficult to imagine that so major a change could have been introduced into the hidebound structure of French education without the impulse of a major political earthquake. But was the *loi d'orientation* a success for the student movement? Most students, and their supporters on the Left, saw it as a failure. Movements do not produce their major effects directly, but through their interaction with more conventional forces and the elite, as opportunities shift to the political system. The students had no plan for university reform, and by September, their influence was weakened, both by the satisfaction of working class wage demands and by the breakdown of their own solidarity (Tarrow 1993c: 589–92). And as the center of gravity shifted from the streets to the political arena and the threat of disorder receded, the reformers' leverage was reduced. By the spring of 1969, with the defeat of de Gaulle's referendum, his sudden retirement and Faure's replacement in the Education Ministry, there was a greater gain for the conservative professorate and for the preservation of order than for the dissatisfied students.

What can we conclude from this sequence of events in France's most revolutionary upsurge since the Popular Front? Although the window of opportunity opened up by the May movement was the major cause of the willingness of a conservative government to contemplate reform, it did not stay open sufficiently long to allow its impulse for liberation to be transformed into success. The reform's weakness was due, in part, to the rapid collapse of the movement; in part, to the students' divisions and demoralization after the failure of the previous June; and, in part, to the defection of their working class allies. Like the "processing" of racial crisis in America (Lipsky and Olson 1976), a major struggle had been politically processed into a modest reform.

American women[9]

Students were the "early risers" in the French cycle of 1968; in contrast, if there was ever a movement that seemed dependent on gates of opportunity that were opened by others, it was the American women's movement of the 1960s. Many of its founders gained their first political exposure in the Civil Rights movement and in the New Left (Evans 1980: chs. 3–7); while others were the heirs of moderate older women's lobbies (Rupp and Taylor 1987). When the new women's movement appeared on the scene in the mid-1960s, "many observers," writes Anne Costain, regarded it as "a transitory phenomenon, imitating the black civil rights movement, but without that movement's capacity to endure" (1987: 1).

But the women's movement *did* endure, and prospered into the 1990s as much of the original élan of the Civil Rights movement was consumed. The signs of growth in the womens' movement were both attitudinal – as more and more women declared themselves sympathetic to feminism – and organizational – with membership in major feminist organizations growing to about 250,000 by the early 1980s (Klein 1987; Mueller 1987). Even during the 1970s – when the American activist culture declined – the women's movement grew stronger, affording women "a vehicle to sustain their activism as well as a community to support a more general feminist lifestyle" (McAdam 1988: 202). The results were gains in the legislative arena and a spectacular growth in the number of women elected to office (Mueller 1987: 96–7). To provide one quantitative indicator of success: The number of bills on women's issues introduced in Congress nearly doubled between the early 1960s and 1973–4 (Costain 1992: 10–11).

The American women's movement never made the dramatic entry of the French students or other confrontational movements of the 1960s. Many of its early advocates were polite, middle-class women who worked quietly in the background of conventional politics and interest groups; others were feminist lawyers who carried out their movement work on the sidelines of busy careers; most were not organizationally active at all – or worked in organizations whose primary purpose was labor, civil rights, family issues or public health. Moreover, the movement's progress was marked by significant defeats: in the failure of the Equal Rights Amendment in 1983; in the whittling down of the right to an abortion during the Reagan and Bush administrations; and in the Senate's approval of the Clarence Thomas nomination to the Supreme Court in 1991.

But the public signs of a dynamic movement were everywhere present. Between 1965 and 1975, there was a tremendous increase in press coverage of both women's events in general (Costain 1987: 9); and of protest actions in particular (p. 19). With the appearance of a "gender gap" in the electorate in the 1970s, politicians were quick to begin to respond to women's issues (Freeman: 206–8). The movement's apotheosis came with the election of 1992, when a large number of women were elected to Congress while a number of others were appointed to high levels of the Clinton administration. This was a movement that began slowly, in the shadow of civil rights and the New Left, but steadily grew in strength and importance.

What explains the dramatic differences between the success of the American women's movement and the failure of the French students? In terms of all four powers in movement that we have examined – repertoires of contention, collective action frames, movement structures and especially political opportunity structure, although American women had a slow start, they were far better favored. The following comparisons, of course, leave out the nuances and diversity of each movement, but they show how movements are, in part, the products of resources outside their control.

Contentious and noncontentious repertoires

While the French students used a contentious repertoire that was highly disruptive and potentially violent – recalling the most conflictual moments of French history – the American women's movement used a variety of forms of collective action – public and private – that leaned heavily toward the conventional and the symbolic.

The French student movement was remarkably peaceful through the spring of 1968, turning violent only rarely during the winter and spring of the following year. That there were remarkably few casualties in the Events of May was partly the result of a restrained policy on the part of the police, and partly the result of the movement's rapid rise and fall – the longer, "sliding May" of Italy showed how easily violence could break out when confrontation was protracted and the police were out of control. But the dramatic confrontations, barricades and occupations mounted by the French students alarmed middle-class opinion – an attitude that was deepened by the strikes that deprived the French of basic services. By the time of the June elections, distaste for student "enragés" was widespread, even in the working class.

In contrast, although occasional boycotts, civil disobedience and sit–ins marked high points of the American women's movement, its reliance on symbolic and cultural challenges, conventional marches and demonstrations, and educational and lobbying activity placed it in the mainstream of American collective action. In addition, in the interstices of American family and work groups, feminists acted out the slogan "the personal is political" (Evans 1980: ch. 9). Even in that bastion of male dominance, the armed forces, and in closed institutions like the Catholic Church, women acted collectively by means of what one observer calls "unobtrusive mobilization" (Katzenstein 1990).

Framing collective action

There were also major differences in the two movements' discourses and symbolism. French students employed a language and a symbolic discourse that isolated them from the language of ordinary French citizens. "Power to the imagination!" and "The struggle continues!" were slogans that could engage student enthusiasm but had little resonance among people waiting on line for gasoline or unable to collect their paychecks. The permanent assembly at the Odéon theatre in May 1968 produced lively debates and built up a spirit of comradeship, but the dirt and anarchy of the occupied Sorbonne seemed no more than a *chien–lit* to those who read about it in the newspapers.[10] When the police cleared it out, the French heaved a collective sigh of relief.

In contrast, an important aspect of the American women's movement, and one of its major successes, was its attention to signification. "Women" rather than "girls"; "gender" rather than "sex"; "partner" rather than "girlfriend": Such changes in common language have become widespread in American popular culture as the result of women's realization that "naming" subjects goes a long way towards changing them. The American women's movement is the best example we have of social psychologist Bert Klandermans' observation that public discourse can have a profound impact on collective identities, and that the latter become a resource in collective action (1992: 87–9).

Mobilizing structures

Organizational networks are a third area of contrast between the two movements. Each had in common with many of the movements born in the 1960s a dedication to autonomy, decentralization and spontaneity. But the French student movement spread by instant diffusion, and rapidly collapsed as the students went off to their vacations in June. When they returned the next academic year, only the most militant remained to contest the university elections provided for under the Faure plan. Their militancy, their small numbers and their isolation led these groups to use violent methods to block the elections, leading the government to send police to the campus, dismaying more moderate students and turning former faculty allies into opponents.

In the long run, the fundamental organizational problem of the French student movement was that it was no more long standing than student generations; when the students graduated and dispersed into the wider society, so did their movement. By the next cycle of opportunity for student mobilization, which did not come until the mid-1970s, an entire new student generation was in place and the networks that had been formed in 1968 were long gone.

In contrast, the American women's movement developed a broad, varied and growing network structure ranging from informal women's collectives, to women's studies programs in universities to formal organizations like NOW, WEAL and NWPC.[11] A substantial "women's rights" network was already in place when the "new" movement of the 1960s appeared (Rupp and Taylor 1987). The new branch of the movement added an emphasis on informality and personalism that is still evident in the style of the movement today. The focus on personal experience in small group networks "within which women could share the intimate details of their lives" has often cost the movement dearly, but it does provide free spaces in which consensus could be maintained and new activists recruited within the bonds of friendship (Evans 1980: 215). Even a major defeat like the ERA was not enough to shatter the networks at the base which remained to fight again another day.

Seizing and making opportunities

Collective action repertoires, frames and organizations are important powers, but they can galvanize movements into action only when they are activated by specific incentives. Incentives can be personal and organizational, but the major incentives to activation are the structures and changes in political opportunity. It is through the changes in their respective opportunity structures that the failure of the French student movement and the success of the American women's movement can best be explained.

We saw earlier how the routine of parliamentary politics was first used by French reformers in attempting to reform the educational system after May and then wore down their initiative as the threat of disorder declined. With its reinforced electoral majority and control of the parliamentary agenda, the French government was able to take university reform in hand and guide it to a politically safe conclusion in a way that less centralized regimes, like the Italian or the American ones, were unable to do.

Far less based on the threat of disorder than on the promise of realignment, the American women's movement took longer to bear fruit, but it eventually emerged as a major factor in American politics. The structure of the American party system – and especially of the Democratic Party – has been crucial to the movement's strategy and its success (Costain, 1992; Freeman 1987). In Freeman's view, the Democratic Party recognizes groups as a function of "whom they represent", and not "who they know" (p. 236). This factor has given women a weight in the party's councils that they lacked in the Republican Party, making the Democratic platform a useful sounding board for feminist concerns.

While French and Italian women have become important constituencies in the left wing parties of these countries, the American women's movement has developed an uneasy and shifting alliance with the party system. But it is electoral opportunities that have produced the greatest incentives for change in gender politics. "We have gotten a lot of mileage out of this gender gap," said

one lobbyist for a women's organization; "Hell, we don't want to close it . . .
We want to widen it" (Costain and Costain 1987: 206).

In summary, French students erupted on the scene far more dramatically than
American women. But the uncontrolled repertoire of the French students, their
obscure and abstract discourse, their lack of consistent mobilizing structures and
permanent networks and, especially, the migration of political opportunities
from the movements of May to the government converged to reduce the power
of their movement. American women, who first mobilized in the shadow of the
Civil Rights movement, combined a rich and varied repertoire, a meaningful
discursive politics, a network structure embedded in society and institutions and
an electoral advantage that have made the women's movement among the most
successful in American social history, effecting – among other things – a
profound shift in political culture.

CHANGING POLITICAL CULTURE[12]

Political culture, as I argued in Chapter 7, is an elusive concept that is difficult
to capture empirically. But it is hard to avoid the impression – even if it is
difficult to demonstrate – that the most far-reaching impacts of cycles of protest
are found in slow and incremental changes in political culture. We can see these
changes in three ways: in the impact of movements on collective action frames,
on repertoires and on policy agendas.

In his evocative article, Aristide Zolberg (1972) concluded of "moments of
madness" that they bring about significant transformations in three ways. First,
a "torrent of words" and ideas that involves an intensive learning experience
whereby new ideas, formulated initially in coteries, sects, etc., will emerge as
widely shared beliefs among much larger publics. Second, these new beliefs
become anchored in new networks of relationships that are rapidly constituted
during periods of intense activity. Third, from the point of view of policy,
instant formulations arising from the peak of a protest cycle become irreversible
goals that are often institutionalized (p. 206). Each of these themes implies an
indirect and a mediated – rather than a direct and immediate – effect of protest
cycles on political culture. This is why we need to look well past the end of the
cycle to observe its effects.

Turning to the first of Zolberg's hypothesized changes – the appearance of
new beliefs among a broader public – just as new ideas filter down from their
originators to those who "vulgarize" and domesticate them, new forms of
collective action invented in the enthusiasm of the peak of the cycle become
modular. It is not simply that the same people continue to use the same forms of
action; as their uses become known and they are learned throughout society,
they become conventional forms of activity for others to use – even for some
who do not share their originators' goals or preferences.

For example, in the United States the sit–in was used by and developed during the Civil Rights and antiwar movements of the 1960s; it spread from there to the environmental and peace movements in the 1970s; and it was ultimately appropriated by movements antagonistic to liberal causes like the antiabortion movement. Not the new invention itself, but its distilled, refined and routinized products became part of the collective action repertoire. If it continues to be absorbed into the political culture, it may ultimately affect the definition of citizenship.

Second, just as networks of activists form at the peak of a movement cycle and diffuse new ideas and tactics to others, they maintain movements during periods of inertia and reaction. What Doug McAdam found with his former Freedom Summer participants was also true of the Czech signers of Charter '77 who emerged again at the heart of the movement to overthrow communism in 1989. To the extent that former activists remain embedded in a political community, McAdam concludes, "they are likely to feel some pressure to be active and also to feel more optimistic about the effectiveness of their activism" (1988: 218).

Even during long periods of political stagnation – like the 1950s – personal networks keep alive the idea of movement among small groups of activists. "Feminism in the fifties?" Leila Rupp and Verta Taylor rhetorically ask: "Presumably these were years of domesticity and conformity for American women, not years of discontent and protest" (p. vii). But Rupp and Taylor found evidence that feminism was surviving among women whose activism – however restrained – assured the continuity of the movement in a climate of antifeminism (pp. 110–11). The same was true of women's networks in the conservative years of the Reagan administration, when the movement was visibly stagnating and some of its policy achievements were rolled back. In personal networks and secondary associations, these women kept the flame of feminism alive by keeping in touch.

Finally, although movements do not collapse the distance between the present and the future, as the enthusiasts of the "moment of madness" at the peak of the cycle wish, they sometimes "drastically shorten the distance, and in that sense they are successful miracles" (Zolberg 1972: 206). Merely placing a new issue on the agenda in an expressive and challenging way – at least in liberal democratic states – enables coalitions to form around them, and for them to be aligned within general cultural frames.

But this does not happen directly or even in a linear fashion. In fact, as their ideas are vulgarized and domesticated, the early risers in a protest cycle often disappear from the scene. But a portion of their message is distilled into common frameworks of public or private culture while the rest is ignored. Thus, the women of the first American suffrage movement disappeared rapidly from the political scene as the country was caught up in a great civil war and then in a rapid process of industrialization. But the goals they left on the agenda – and even some of their ideological justifications – remained for those who fought for them under more propitious circumstances.

The early risers in a protest cycle and those most responsible for its success often anguish when they see it spin off in directions they never imagined. When two of the founders of the American Republic, John Adams and Thomas Jefferson, looked back at what their generation had wrought, they were horrified. Instead of a republic of virtue, writes Gordon Wood, "America had created a huge, sprawling society that was more egalitarian, more middling, and more dominated by the interests of ordinary people than any that had ever existed" (p. 348). Hating the business culture that was sweeping the country, Jefferson too never appreciated "how much his democratic and egalitarian principles had contributed to its rise" (p. 367). "All, all dead," he wrote to a friend near the end of his life, "and ourselves left alone amidst a new generation whom we know not, and who knows not us" (p. 368).

The effects of social movement cycles are indirect and to a large extent unpredictable. They work through capillary processes beneath the surface of politics, connecting the utopian dreams, the intoxicating solidarities and the enthusiastic rhetoric of the cycle's peak to the glacially changing, culturally constrained and socially resisted pace of social change. Few people dare to break the crust of convention. When they do, they create opportunities and provide models of thought and action for others who use them to seek more conventional goals in more institutionalized ways. What remains after the enthusiasm of the cycle is a residue of reform.

Such cycles have risen and fallen periodically over the last two centuries. Each time they appear, critics and enthusiasts think the world is turning upside down. But just as regularly, the erosion of mobilization, the conflicts that arise between sectors of the movement and the opportunities it creates for opponents and elites bring the cycle to an end. For two hundred years the power of movement has been briefly electric and seems irresistible at the time, but is eroded and integrated by the political process.

But much has changed in the contemporary world. Movements arise more easily and spread more rapidly than they used to do. The violent conflagrations of the last decade from Iran to the Soviet Union and Eastern Europe have led some to suspect that the cyclical rhythm of the past has been broken; that we are moving into a stage of history in which movements will arise continuously, escape the pull of the political process and be increasingly violent. Are we living in such a "movement society?" Or is the dynamic of protest cycles traced in this and the last chapter simply taking new forms and being integrated in new ways into the political process? This is the question I will turn to in the final chapter.

11

A movement society?

In 1789, as word of France's revolution reached England, abolitionist Thomas Clarkson crossed the Channel to urge his French colleagues to join his country's antislavery agitation. Clarkson took the same route again in 1814, following a second wave of agitation in Britain. But "twice," writes the leading American student of antislavery, "he failed utterly." (Drescher 1994). Although the French abolished slavery in their colonies in 1794, this was no more than "a desperate response to wartime contingencies," writes Drescher (1991: 712), and was reversed when Napoleon came to power. Only when it coincided with greater political earthquakes did antislavery cross the channel (pp. 719–20).

Two hundred years later, diffused by word of mouth, printed page and television, collective action spread rapidly across the internal boundaries of the Soviet bloc. As the French were commemorating – and burying! – the bicentennial of their Revolution,[1] a new wave of revolution swept over the Communist world. Centered on Eastern and Central Europe, enjoying a brief, tragic echo in China, the movement eventually gave way to savage confrontations in Romania, in the Caucasus and ultimately in Yugoslavia. Not only in semi-Stalinized Poland and in the restive Baltic states, but in ironfisted East Germany and subjugated Czechoslovakia, within a year communism was gone. By 1991, even the Soviet Union, heartland of proletarian internationalism, had collapsed, giving way to a galaxy of semi-democratic, semi-market, deeply conflicted societies.

When we compare the rapid diffusion of the movements of 1989 to Clarkson's inability to bring abolitionism across 30 miles of water, we can begin to understand the progress of the social movement over the past two hundred years. For not only did Eastern Europeans rebel *en masse* in 1989: They did so against similar targets, at virtually the same time and in the name of goals that varied only in their details. In 1789 antislavery advocates had difficulty crossing the English Channel. But in 1989 the democracy movement spread from Berlin to Beijing in a matter of weeks.

The significance of this change is still emerging, and its implications for democracy are mixed – to say the least. But its implications for the nature of social movements were profound. For not only did these changes close the door on the most important revolutionary movement of the twentieth century; by the end of 1989, not only in Eastern Europe, but all over the Communist bloc, the movement against state socialism had become general and its modalities modular. Even in Italy, so far from the periphery of world communism that its Communist Party was barely recognizable by 1989, party leaders rejected their historic identity and changed their flag (Ignazi 1992).

But the heart of the movement was in Eastern Europe. There, with little prior organization, people who had never met (or who knew each other in the apolitical networks of what Eastern Europeans were calling "civil society"), were employing similar forms of organization and action, and in the name of similar frames of meaning, rose up against authorities. If the Communist Party elites gave in practically without a fight, it was not only because they had lost heart, but because they could see what forces were arrayed against them and knew what it would take to suppress them. Not only this movement, but *the* social movement triumphed in 1989.

The rapid spread and dramatic success of the movement of 1989 was a reflection of the powers of movement that I have described in this book. But it also raises some troubling questions for social movement theory and about the emerging world order; about the increase of violence, the recrudescence of ethnic conflicts, the possible transcendence of the national state and the internationalization of conflict. In this chapter, I will first review what I have argued here about the power in movement before turning to the questions raised by the cataclysm of 1989 and its violent aftermath.

TWO HUNDRED YEARS OF MOVEMENT

Since collective action is the common denominator of all kinds of social movements, we began with the theory of collective action. Twenty years ago, political scientists and sociologists interested in social movements began to look at their subject not from the standpoint of actions taken, but as a puzzle; based on the assumption that collective action is difficult to bring about. I argued in Chapter 1 that this puzzle *is* only a puzzle (and not a sociological law), because in so many situations and against so many odds, collective action *does* occur, often instigated by people with few resources and little inherent power.

The "solution" to that puzzle was first sought by collective action theorists building on economist Mancur Olson's theory that "large groups" mobilize members through selective incentives and constraints. While the Olsonian theory worked well for interest groups, it was inadequate for social movements for the simple reason that they are multipolar actors in sustained conflict with opponents and have few incentives or constraints to deploy. Unlike voluntary associations, movements are not organizations, and those who try to lead them have little or no control over those they hope will follow them.

The central task for movement organizers is to resolve what I called the "social transaction costs of collective action"; creating focal points for people who have no sources of compulsory coordination, who often lack direct connections with one another and have few, if any, internal resources. While large firms and interest groups solve their transaction cost problem by internalizing their assets, movements seldom have this option. Indeed, organizers who try to turn their "base" into disciplined cadres squander much of their energy on achieving internal control. How movements become the focal points for collective action and sustain it against opponents and the state was the central question of the book.

I argued, in response to this question, that the main incentives for movement creation and diffusion are found in the structure of political opportunities. Increasing access to power, realignments in the political system, conflicts among elites and the availability of allies give early challengers the incentives to assault the power structure and create opportunities for others. The diffusion of movements takes place by many mechanisms and draws on a variety of resources; but the major incentive for new groups to join a movement are the political opportunities that are exposed by the actions of "early risers" and exploited by others.

In response to political opportunities, movements use different forms of collective action singly and in combination to link people to one another and with opponents, supporters and third parties. They take advantage of both the familiarity of these forms of action – by a kind of "contract by convention," in Russell Hardin's term (1981) – innovating around their edges to inspire the imagination of supporters and create fear and uncertainty among opponents. Collective action is best seen not as a simple cost, but as both a cost and a benefit for social movements.

The balance between the costs and benefits helps determine the dynamics of the movement. As the benefits of a particular form of collective action decline, organizers have incentives to develop new actions, increase the numbers of participants or radicalize their interaction with opponents. The conflicts and defections within social movements, as well as their confrontations with the state, are, in part, the result of the attempt to maintain the movement's momentum through the use of new and more daring collective actions.

But in the formation of a social movement, there is more than a "pull" toward particular forms of action; there must also be a "push" from solidarity and collective identity. Solidarity has much to do with interest, but it produces a sustained movement only when consensus is built around common meanings and values. These meanings and values are partly inherited and partly constructed in the act of confronting opponents. They are also constituted by the

interactions within movements. One of the main factors distinguishing successful movements from failures is their capacity to link inherited understandings to
the imperative for activism.

Collective action is often led by movement organizations, but these are
sometimes beneficiaries, sometimes inciters and at other times destroyers of
popular politics. The recurring controversy about whether organizations produce
movements or suppress them can be resolved only if we examine the less formal
structures that they draw upon – the social networks at the base of society, and
the mobilizing structures that link them to the focal points of conflict. Sustaining
a movement is the result of a delicate balance between suffocating the power in
movement by providing too much organization and leaving it to spin off use-
lessly away through the tyranny of decentralization (J. Hellman 1987).

Opportunities, cycles and the consumption of movement

But collective action repertoires, cultural frames and organization are only the
potential sources of power; they can be employed just as easily for social control
as for insurgency. The recurring protest cycles that were described in Chapter 9
are the products of the diffusion of political opportunities that transform the
potential for mobilization into action. In these crucibles of conflict and innovation, movements not only take advantage of available opportunities; they create
them for others by producing new forms of action, hammering out new "master
frames", activating social networks and making coalitions that force the state to
respond to the disorder around it.

That response is often repressive, but even repression is often mixed with
reform. Particularly when counterelites within the system see the opportunity to
aggrandize themselves in alliance with challengers, rulers are placed in a vulnerable position to which reform is a frequent response. As conflict collapses and
militants retire to lick their wounds, many of their advances are reversed, but
they leave behind incremental expansions in participation, changes in popular
culture and residual movement networks. Movement cycles are a season for
sowing, but the reaping is often done during the periods of demobilization that
follow, by latecomers to the cause.

If cycles of protest are opened up by expanding opportunities, how do they
decline as they inevitably do? Is it simply because people tire of agitation,
because enervating factional struggles develop within their movements, because
organizations become oppressive or because elites repress and placate challengers? All of these are contributory causes of cyclical decline, but there is a
more systemic cause as well: Since the power in movement depends on the
mobilization of external opportunities, when opportunities expand from challengers to other groups and shift to elites and authorities, movements lose their
primary source of power. For brief periods of history the power in movement
seems irresistible; but it disperses rapidly and passes inexorably into more

institutional forms of politics. Let us turn to how the power in movement has changed.

1789/1989

If each new social movement had to create anew its forms of collective action, its frames of meaning and its mobilizing structures, then the collective action problem would be insuperable and the world would be a much quieter place than it has become. If there is a central message in this book, it is that the power in movement is cumulative. Social theorists are forever discovering waves of "new" social movements; but the claim of "the new" fades when we contemplate the larger historical picture. For new movements not only repeat many of the themes of their predecessors, like identity, autonomy and injustice (Calhoun 1993), but build on the practices and institutions of the past.

It was the consolidation of the national state in the eighteenth century that created the framework in which national social movements developed. They resulted both from statebuilders' penetration of society and from their creation of common frameworks for citizenship. Although expanding states sought to repress opposition and reduce the periphery to obedience, they also created national categories of identity, standard relationships and offered a fulcrum on which people could fight out their social conflicts with others.

This creation of a central state target and fulcrum for conflict transformed how people made claims. Using the central state to seek a benefit or attack an opponent meant using the repertoire of collective action that state elites recognized. In democratic states, the mass, modular and largely peaceful repertoire of the twentieth century was the result. The novelty of this new repertoire was not that it existed, but that it had the capacity to bring broad coalitions of challengers together in sustained interactions with national states, and to mount general claims against them.

Why did this capacity develop when it did in the West? It was the rise of modern states and an international capitalist economy that provided the targets and the resources that helped movements to flourish and that laid the bases for today's social movements. Movements began in the West because that was where the consolidated national state first appeared. When western states and expanding capitalism moved outward to colonize the rest of the world, they brought the preconditions and the practices of the social movement with them.

In the process of movement development, two major structural changes were critical: regular associations which provided legal and conventional forms that more contentious actors could employ; and new and expanded means of communication which diffused models of collective action and new cognitive frames from one sector or country to another. Though early analysts insisted on the importance of class in galvanizing these movements, it was through the interclass and translocal coalitions created through print and association that the first successful movements took shape. The nationalist movements that spread across Europe and America and throughout the world had the capacity to cross class lines and form such interclass coalitions.

These were not random processes. Repeated confrontations linked specific social actors with their antagonists through forms of collective action that became recurring routines: the strike between workers and employers; the demonstration between protesters and opponents; the insurrection between insurgents and the state. The national social movement developed as a sequence of sustained challenges to elites, authorities or opponents by people with collective purposes and solidarity, or by those who claimed to represent them.

Once these opportunities, conventions and resources became available to ordinary people, the problem of social transaction costs could be solved and movements could spread to entire societies, producing the periods of turbulence and realignment that I have called cycles of protest. Such periods had repercussions that sometimes resulted in repression, sometimes in reform, often in both. They were the major watersheds for the innovations in collective action we see today, for changes in political culture, for increased political involvements and for the creation of future networks of militants and supporters.

The first major cycle of protest occurred in 1789, but its diffusion across the borders of France was carried mainly on the tips of French bayonets. The first major international cycle occurred during the 1848 Revolution. The most recent ones before 1989 were the anticolonial movements of the post–World War II period, and the 1960s movements in Europe and the United States. These latter movements were, in the main, nonviolent. While 1848 ended in armed strife and foreign intervention, both anticolonial nationalism and the movements of the 1960s brought the tools of nonviolent direct action to new heights of refinement and effectiveness.

The movements of Eastern Europe in 1989 were in many ways the culmination of these trends. Like these earlier movements, they were not class movements; they were, at first, remarkably nonviolent; and they spread rapidly across the region. Both new and old forms of collective action were employed; new frames of meaning like anticorruption and participation joined the themes of injustice and liberation; the organizations used were weak but collective action and consent spread through social networks at the base. As in the past, the major incentives that turned underlying discontents into movements were political opportunities.

Of these opportunities, the most important were transnational: the openings, the realignments, the splits between reform and orthodox Communists and the encouragement to dissidents produced by Gorbachev's domestic reforms and by his policies towards Eastern Europe. As each country in the region experienced the weakening of its elites and the crumbling of their resistance, newer and wider opportunities were created. The movement spread much as the 1848 Revolution had done, by a process of imitation, diffusion, reaction and transformation of scattered movements, culminating in elite negotiations and the attempt to build new institutions out of struggle.

But like 1848, as the movement wound through Eastern Europe, the mood shifted from liberalism and representative government to ethnic particularism and national assertiveness. If crowds of Czechs and Slovaks turned out to demonstrate for freedom in Prague and Bratislava in 1989, by 1992 these cities had become the capitals of a country split in two; if thousands of Hungarians demonstrated at the tomb of Imre Najy in 1988, by the early 1990s, the parties that liberated their country from communism were having difficulty attracting a plurality of voters. If West and East Germans joined in an ode to freedom on the Berlin Wall in 1989, by 1991 "Ossies" and "Wessies" were watching each other with suspicion, In Poland, the Solidarity leaders who had started the process a decade earlier split into rival political parties. And in Russia the democratic movement of the late 1980s gave way to a range of semi-parties, some of them holdovers from the recent regime and others reviving forms of xenophobia from the Czarist past.

Immediately after the ebullience of 1989, some observers foresaw old elites being rapidly swept off the public scene, state-run economies rapidly privatized and a new democratic politics emerging in the image of the West. But by the early 1990s, not only were old elites still active in many parts of the former Communist world – some of them transformed from *apparachniks* into *entrepreneurniks* – but the privatization of their economies was making heavy weather. Under the strain, the opportunities and the uncertainties of the post-1989 years provided space for a variety of players, not all of whom had democracy or the market as their goals. Just as the Springtime of Freedom of 1848 was closed by Napoleon's coup of 1851, the Ode to Freedom at the Berlin Wall was the prelude to the ethnic conflicts of the 1990s and the carnage at Sarajevo.

A MOVEMENT SOCIETY: TRANSNATIONAL AND VIOLENT?

How representative was the movement of 1989? It certainly had peculiarities due to the nearly unique nature of the Soviet bloc. For example, it was the first movement in history to destroy a powerful multistate empire in one blow. It was also – at least at first – predominantly handled through peaceful negotiation, with the menace of mass violence held in abeyance in almost every country of the region until state socialism was gone. But despite its particularity, the 1989 cycle can help us to see some of the ways in which the national social movement has changed in its two-hundred-year history. If these changes are substantial and cumulative, then the world may be moving from a logic of alternation between periods of movement and periods of quiescence into a permanent movement society. At this stage, all we can do is guess at the possibilities and speculate about their implications.

Transnational movements

When we return to the comparison between Clarkson's failure in 1789 and the success of 1989, we see one major difference; that movements spread far more rapidly now than they did in the past – even in the absence of formal organizations. This is, in part, an expression of the universality of the repertoire of collective action, in part, due to the rapidity of global communication, and, in part, because of the appearance of transnational movements. The contrast between antislavery in 1789 and the movements of 1989 will illustrate all three points.

In contrast to Clarkson's inability to bring abolitionism across a mere thirty miles of water in 1789, the knowledge of how to mount a social movement had become so general by 1989 that the liberation from state socialism took remarkably similar form across a continent and a half. For example, the human chain that protestors stretched across the Baltics in 1989 was the same tactic that had been used a few years earlier by the European peace movement. The "round table" that was used to outline the future division of power in Poland was adopted in many other countries of the region. "What is remarkable," write Valerie Bunce and Dennis Chong, "is the speed with which the masses in each country converged on particular strategies, coordinated its actions, and successfully executed its plans" (1990: 3).

Second, the appearance of global television had a great influence in the diffusion of the movement, and this is not limited to Eastern Europe in 1989. In the eighteenth century, movements were still diffused by word of mouth, by print and association or by people like Clarkson who acted as missionaries of movement. But in 1989, the spread of the democratic movement in Eastern Europe – not to mention its tragic echo in China – left little doubt that collective action can spread by global communication. Not only do potential protestors learn about political opportunities through the mass media; when they see people not very different from themselves acting in contentious ways succeeding, it is easy for them to imagine themselves doing the same. And just as they learn *from* television, they have become skilled at using it to project word of their movements to international centers of power.

Third, because of the centrality of the national state, movements like antislavery spread slowly and took different forms in different parts of Europe (Drescher 1987: 199); so did the democratic movement of the late eighteenth century. In the nineteenth century, both radical democracy and socialism were diffused more quickly, but it still took fifty years for social democracy to reach Russia – and it arrived in very different form than in the West.

The most recent cycles of protest have been inherently – and perhaps increasingly – transnational and thus have diffused more rapidly. The decolonization movements in the former British and French empires; the European and American New Left of the 1960s; the peace movements of the 1980s; global environmental movements like Greenpeace: These are no longer cases of simple imitation and diffusion, but expressions of the same movement acting against similar targets. The movements of 1989 in Eastern Europe were extreme in this respect, but in their interdependence and mutual dependence on international trends, they were not so different than these other recent movements.

The archetypical case of a transnational movement in recent years has been militant, fundamentalist Islam. Its spread from Iran to Afghanistan, to the Bekaa Valley and the Gaza Strip, and more recently to North Africa bridges institutional religion and guerilla warfare. In between these extremes of violence and institutionalization, its organizers have employed an array of similar tactics everywhere: the mobilization of slum dwellers, the intimidation of women, the extortion of funds from small businessmen – even elections, when this has been convenient. One deeply rooted secular movement – the Palestinian Liberation Organization – has been severely challenged by Islamic competition; the Soviet army was forced out of Afghanistan by another; while the Sudanese government was overthrown by a third. The Algerian government was only saved from Islamic domination by a military takeover. And by 1992, even secular Egypt was under attack from internationally supported fundamentalists.

The spread of such transnational movements as militant Islam leads to a larger and more portentous question. Since we seem to be living in an increasingly interdependent world, are we becoming a single movement society? And if we are, will movements lose the cyclical and national rhythms of the past and take on the character of continual turbulence spreading across national boundaries out of the control of national states? A movement society may be an increasingly violent society. What is the evidence for such a claim?

Ex-prisoners of the state?[2]

In his book *Turbulence in World Politics*, James Rosenau argues that we are becoming a single, more turbulent world. Rosenau sees the entire period since the end of World War II as the beginning of a new era of "global turbulence." Among the factors that convince him that ours is an era of turbulence is "a marked increase in the number of spontaneous collective actions" and their rapid spread around the world (1990: 369). If Rosenau is right, then the implications for the future of civil politics is troubling.

The national social movement grew out of the efforts of states to consolidate power, integrate their peripheries and standardize discourse among groups of citizens and between them and their rulers. Many of the characteristics of the social movements we have seen in this book grew out of that relationship – including the conventionalization of collective action, the channeling of movements into national opportunity structures and the institution of citizenship itself. If movements are becoming transnational, they may be freeing themselves of state structures and thence of the constraining influence of state-mediated contention.

Three kinds of arguments can be made on behalf of this thesis. First, the dominant economic trends of the late twentieth century have been towards greater international interdependence. "The increasing fluidity of capital, labor, commodities, money, and cultural practices," argues Charles Tilly in a recent paper, "undermines the capacity of any particular state to control events within its boundaries" (1991a: 1). One result is that strikes that used to be mounted against domestic capitalists must now be risked against multinational corporations whose capital can be moved elsewhere. The interdependent global economy may be producing transnational collective action.[3]

Second, the economic growth of the 1970s and 1980s increased the imbalance of wealth and poverty between the North and West and the East and South, while bringing their citizens cognitively and physically closer to one another. This is not only the result of faster communication and cheaper transportation, but because, since the end of World War II, Third World countries have attempted to mimic the economic success of the West. The result is that the East and South have internalized elements of the social structure of the West and North but have not internalized their wealth" (Arrighi 1991: 40).

Interdependence and the international gap in income both contribute to a third factor: a continued stream of migration that takes different forms than in the past. In the nineteenth century, much of the international movement of population went from core to periphery, with migrants permanently leaving their homes behind. The current wave of migration overwhelmingly favors the industrial countries of the West and immigrants seldom lose touch with their country of origin. "The Filipino maid in Milan and the Tamil busdriver in Toronto," observes Benedict Anderson, "are only a few sky hours away" from their homeland and seconds away by satellite telephone communication (1992: 8).

While mass population movements have become one of the major sources of domestic conflict in the contemporary world (Zolberg 1989), citizenship – the expected outcome of immigration in the nineteenth century – has become an impossible dream for most immigrants. A major cultural cleavage pits immigrant groups with restricted citizenship rights against increasingly restive indigenous populations in states whose governments, from Paris to California, are under pressure to reduce the rights of resident immigrants and to cut them off from further entry. All over the West, from the eastern border of Germany to the southern border of the United States, doors are being shut to immigrants, and – just as important – earlier arrivals are being sealed off into immigrant ghettos.

One result – the rise of racist movements in Western Europe – we have already seen. But another is the rise of what Anderson calls "long-distance nationalism" (1992). For every nineteenth-century Mazzini and Garibaldi who fomented revolution at a great distance from their home country, there are thousands of Palestinians in New York, Punjabis in Toronto, Croats in Australia, Tamils in Britain, Irish in Massachusetts, Algerians in France and Cubans in Miami whose ties to their countries of origin are kept alive through transnational social networks (Anderson 1992: 12).

Most of these meekly accept their subaltern status and hope for an affluent return to their homelands. But others use the ease of international communication and transportation to support movements at home. By more-or-less covert financial contributions, by fax and E-mail, by letter bombs and discrete arms purchases, these long-distance nationalists are disturbing the neat symmetry between national states and national social movements that the world has inherited from the last century.

Not only nationalist migrants, but transnational ecologists, developmentalists and fighters for the rights of minorities increasingly aim their actions at other people's governments. We live in an age when rubber tappers in Brazil can enjoy the assistance of American nongovernmental organizations; when U.N.-supported technical teams teach Indian ecologists to use video cameras that they can employ to mobilize peasants; and when racist propaganda produced in the United States finds it way to the apartments of European skinheads. The modern state, which began its consolidation in opposition to its territorial enemies, is becoming increasingly permeable to nonterritorial movements. As a result, the social movement may be becoming an ex-prisoner of the state.

If this is true, what are the implications for the character of social movements and for social conflict in general? If nothing else, the characteristic pattern whereby political cycles result from the processing of challenges within national states may be extended over time and space by crossnational extension. Fundamentalist Islam is the most successful example: When the expansion of the Iranian revolution failed in the Iran–Iraq war, Afghanistan became the major field of action; when the Red Army left Kabul, fundamentalist militants moved on from Peshawar to Cairo, to Algiers and eventually to New York.[4] Where movements respond to political opportunities across state boundaries, they can escape the mediation and control of any single state.

As long as these expressions of integral religious nationalism were bounded within the Third World, Western governments and their citizens remained relatively indifferent. But with the attack by Islamic militants on the World Trade Center in New York in 1993, long-distance nationalism moved to the West. The diffusion of militant fundamentalism to the heart of world capitalism showed that, in the interdependent contemporary world, modernization does not equal secularization and that international trends deeply affect the internal order of states.

This leads to an even more worrying concern. Over the past two hundred years, there has been a slow, ragged but inexorable civilizing trend in the nature of collective action and in the state's means of controlling it. We saw in Chapter

Six, as modular repertoires linked social movements to the state, violent and direct forms of attack were increasingly replaced by the power of numbers, by solidarity and an informal dialogue between states and movements. The cycle of the 1960s, with its remarkably low level of violence and employment of nonviolent direct action, was the apotheosis of this trend. But the guerilla wars, the hostage takings and the ethnic conflicts of the past two decades must make us wonder whether the trend to a peaceful repertoire was no more than a historical parenthesis and is now being reversed.

The integralist beliefs – if not the violent methods – of militant Islam bear a striking resemblance to trends in Western culture: to politicized ministers who preach intolerance on Sunday morning television; to the "rescuers" of unborn fetuses who refuse to recognize womens' rights to reproductive freedom; to orthodox attacks on secular values in education and personal life; and to xenophobic political parties that claim their nations' natural superiority. The methods are different, but how different are the French *Front National* or the Hungarian Way, from the zealots of Gush Emunim or the fanatics of the Party of God?

Citizens of modern states have lived through such "moments of madness" before. It is enough to remember that severed heads were paraded around the streets of Paris on pikes during the great democratic French Revolution, or that Jews were attacked in France and Germany during the Springtime of Freedom in 1848, to find parallels for the violence and intolerance that have emerged in the West since the 1980s. The concern raised by these more recent outbreaks is that – if, in fact a "movement society" *is* developing out of the social, economic and cultural changes of the late twentieth century – it will have a different cultural valence than the movements that broke out in Boston in 1765, in Paris in 1848 and in the nonviolent movements of the 1960s.

Is the New World Order that was supposed to result from the liberation of 1989 turning instead into a permanent state of violence and disorder? Have the resources for violent collective action become so widely accessible, integralist identities so widespread, and militants so freed of the national state that a permanent and violent movement society is resulting? Or will the current plethora of ethnic and religious movements be partially outgrown, partially domesticated and partially mediated by the political process, as in previous cycles of protest?

The violence and intolerance of the 1990s constitute a truly alarming trend. But this is not the first great wave of movement in history, nor will it be the last. If its dynamic comes to resemble the social movements that we have encountered in this book, then its power will at first be ferocious, uncontrolled and widely diffused, but later ephemeral. If so, then like previous waves of movement, it will ultimately disperse "like a flood tide which loosens up much of the soil but leaves alluvial deposits in its wake."[5]

References

Accornero, Aris, Renato Mannheimer, and Chiara Sebastiani (1983). *L'identità comunista. I militanti, le strutture, la cultura del Pci.* Rome: Editori Riuniti.

Agulhon, Maurice (1982). *The Republic in the Village. The People of the Var from the French Revolution to the Second Republic.* Translated by Janet Lloyd. Cambridge and New York: Cambridge University Press.

Allardt, Erik (1962). "Community Activity, Leisure Use and Social Structure," *Acta Sociologica* 6:67–82.

Almond, Gabriel, and Sidney Verba (1989). *The Civic Culture. Political Attitudes and Democracy in Five Nations.* Newbury Park and London: Sage Publications.

Amenta, Edwin, Bruce G. Caruthers, and Yvonne Zylan (1992). "A Hero for the Aged? The Townsend Movement, the Political Mediation Model, and U.S. Old-Age Policy, 1934–1950," *American Journal of Sociology* 98:308–39.

Aminzade, Ronald (1981). *Class, Politics, and Early Industrial Capitalism: A Study of Mid-Nineteenth-Century Toulouse, France.* Albany: State University of New York.

(1993). "Capitalist Development, Class Formation, and the Consequences of Political Repression," *Political Power and Social Theory* 8:79–106.

(1994). "Between Movement and Party: The Transformation of Mid-Nineteenth Century French Republicanism," in J. Craig Jenkins and Bert Klandermans, eds., *The Politics of Social Protest: Comparative Perspectives on States and Social Movements, in press.*

Anderson, Benedict (1990). "Language, Fantasy, Revolution: Java, 1900–1945," *Prisma* 50:25–39.

(1991). *Imagined Communities. Reflections on the Origin and Spread of Nationalism,* 2d ed., rev. London: Verso.

(1992). "Long-Distance Nationalism. World Capitalism and the Rise of Identity Politics," Center for Asian Studies, Amsterdam Netherlands.

Anderson, Eugene N., and Pauline R. Anderson (1967). *Political Institutions and Social Change in Continental Europe in the Nineteenth Century.* Berkeley and Los Angeles: University of California Press.

Apter, David E., ed. (1964). *Ideology and Discontent.* Glencoe, Ill.: The Free Press.

Aptheker, Herbert (1989). *Abolitionism: A Revolutionary Movement.* Boston: Twayne Publishers.

Ardant, Gabriel (1975). "Financial Policy and Economic Infrastructure of Modern States and Nations," in Charles Tilly, ed., *The Formation of National States in Western Europe.* Princeton: Princeton University Press, pp. 164–242.

Arendt, Hannah (1973). *The Origins of Totalitarianism*. New York: Harcourt, Brace.
Arrighi, Giovanni (1991). "World Income Inequalities and the Future of Socialism," *New Left Review* 189:39–65.
Aya, Rod (1990). *Rethinking Revolutions and Collective Violence. Studies on Concept, Theory and Method*. Amsterdam: Het Spinhuis.
Badie, Bertrand (1976). *Stratégie de la Grève*. Paris: Presses de la Fondation Nationale des Sciences Politiques.
Bailyn, Bernard (1967). *The Ideological Origins of the American Revolution*. Cambridge: Harvard University Press.
Baker, Keith Michael (1990). *Inventing the French Revolution. Essays on French Political Culture in the Eighteenth Century*. Cambridge and New York: Cambridge University Press.
Banfield, Edward (1958). *The Moral Basis of a Backward Society*. Glencoe, Ill.: The Free Press.
Barkan, Steven E. (1984). "Legal Control of the Southern Civil Rights Movement," *American Sociological Review* 49:552–65.
Barnes, Samuel, Max Kaase et al. (1979). *Political Action: Mass Participation in Five Western Democracies*. Beverly Hills: Sage.
Bayley, David H. (1975). "The Police and Political Development in Europe," in Charles Tilly, ed., *The Formation of National States in Western Europe*. Princeton: Princeton University Press, pp. 328–79.
Beissinger, Mark (1993). "Demise of an Empire-State," in Crauford Young, ed., *The Rising Tide of Cultural Pluralism*. Madison: University of Wisconsin Press, pp. 93–115.
Bell, Daniel (1960). *The End of Ideology. On the Exhaustion of Political Ideas in the 1950s*. New York: The Free Press.
Benford, Robert D. (1993). "Frame Disputes Within the Disarmament Movement," *Social Forces* 71:677–701.
Bensel, Richard (1990). *Yankee Leviathan: The Origins of Central State Authority in America, 1859–1877*. Cambridge and New York: Cambridge University Press.
Berejikian, Jeffrey (1992). "Revolutionary Collective Action and the Agent–Structure Problem," *American Political Science Review* 86:649–57.
Bevilacqua, Piero (1980). *Campagne del mezzogriorno tra fascismo e dopoguerra*. Torino: G. Einaudi.
Blackmer, Donald L. M., and Sidney Tarrow, eds. (1975). *Communism in Italy and France*. Princeton: Princeton University Press.
Blake, Donald (1960). "Swedish Trade Unions and the Social Democratic Party: The Formative Years," *Scandinavian Economic History Review* 8:19–44.
Bloch, Marc (1931). *Les caractères originaux de l'histoire rurale française*. Paris: Armand Colin.
Blocker, Jack S., Jr. (1989). *American Temperance Movements: Cycles of Reform*. Boston: Twayne Publishers.
Bonnell, Victoria (1983). *Roots of Rebellion: Workers' Politics and Organizations in St. Petersburg and Moscow, 1900–1914*. Berkeley and Los Angeles: University of California Press.
Brand, Karl-Werner (1990). "Cyclical Aspects of New Social Movements: Waves of Cultural Criticism and Mobilization Cycles of New Middle-class Radicalism," in Russell Dalton and Manfred Kuechler, eds., *Challenging the Political Order*. Oxford and New York: Oxford University Press, pp. 23–42.
Brewer, John (1976). *Party Ideology and Popular Politics at the Accession of George III*. Cambridge and New York: Cambridge University Press.
  (1989). *The Sinews of Power. War, Money and the English State, 1688–1783*. New York: Knopf.

Bridges, Amy (1986). "Becoming American: The Working Classes in the United States Before the Civil War," in Ira Katznelson and Aristide R. Zolberg, eds., *Working Class Formation: Nineteenth Century Patterns in Western Europe and the United States*. Princeton: Princeton University Press, pp. 157–96.

Bridgford, Jeff (1989). "The Events of May: Consequences for Industrial Relations in France," in D. L. Hanley and A. P. Kerr, eds., *May '68: Coming of Age*. London: Macmillan, pp. 100–16.

Bright, Charles C. (1984). "The State in the United States during the Nineteenth Century," in Charles Bright and Susan Harding, eds., *Statemaking and Social Movements: Essays in History and Theory*. Ann Arbor: The University of Michigan Press.

Brockett, Charles D. (1991). "The Structure of Political Opportunities and Peasant Mobilization in Central America," *Comparative Politics* 23:253–74.

Brown, Richard D. (1970). *Revolutionary Politics in Massachusetts: The Boston Committee of Correspondence and the Towns, 1772–1774*. Cambridge: Harvard University Press.

(1989). *Knowledge Is Power: The Diffusion of Information in Early America*. Oxford and New York: Oxford University Press.

Browning, Rufus P., Dale Rogers Marshall, and David H. Tabb (1984). *Protest Is Not Enough. The Struggle of Blacks and Hispanics for Equality in Urban Politics*. Berkeley and Los Angeles: University of California Press.

Buchanan, James M. (1965). "An Economic Theory of Clubs," *Economica* 32:1–14.

Buechler, Steven M. (1986). *The Transformation of the Woman Suffrage Movement: The Case of Illinois, 1850–1920*. New Brunswick, N.J.: Rutgers University Press.

Bunce, Valerie (1991). "Democracy, Stalinism and the Management of Uncertainty", in Gyorgy Szoboszlai, ed., *Democracy and Political Transformation*. Budapest: Hungarian Political Science Association, pp. 138–64.

and Dennis Chong (1990). "The Party's Over: Mass Protest and the End of Communist Rule in Eastern Europe," presented to the annual meeting of the American Political Science Association, San Francisco, Calif.

Burstein, Paul, Rachel L. Einwohner, and Jocelyn A. Hollander (1991). "The Success of Political Movements: A Bargaining Perspective," unpublished paper, Department of Sociology, University of Washington, Seattle.

and William Freudenburg (1978). "Changing Public Policy: The Impact of Public Opinion, Antiwar Demonstrations and War Costs on Senate Voting on Vietnam War Motions," *American Journal of Sociology* 84:99–122.

Bushnell, John (1990). *Moscow Graffiti: Language and Subculture*. Boston: Unwin Hyman.

Button, James W. (1978). *Black Violence: The Political Impact of the 1960s Riots*. Princeton: Princeton University Press.

Calhoun, Craig (1982). *The Question of Class Struggle. Social Foundations of Popular Radicalism during the Industrial Revolution*. Chicago: University of Chicago Press.

(1993). "New Social Movements of the Early Nineteenth Century," *Social Science History* 17:385–427.

Calvino, Italo (1985). *Il barone rampante*. Milan: Garzanti.

Camus, Albert (1956). *The Rebel. An Essay on Man in Revolt*. Translated by Anthony Bower. New York: Vintage.

Canetti, Elias (1963). *Crowds and Power*. Translated by Carol Stewart. New York: Viking.

Capdevielle, Jacques, and René Mouriaux (1988). *Mai 68: L'entre-deux de la modernité*. Paris: Presses de la Fondation Nationale des Sciences Politiques.

Caporaso, James A. (1992). "International Relations Theory and Multilateralism: The Search for Foundations," *International Organization* 46:599–632.

Cardon, Dominique, and Jean-Philippe Huertin (1990). " 'Tenir les rangs.' Les services d'encadrement des manifestations ouvrières (1909–1936)," in Favre, Pierre, ed., *La Manifestation*. Paris: Presses de la Fondation Nationale des Sciences Politiques, pp. 123–55.

Censer, Jack R., and Jeremy D. Popkin, eds. (1987). *Press and Politics in Pre-Revolutionary France*. Berkeley and Los Angeles: University of California Press.

Chalmers, Douglas (1964). *The Social Democratic Party of Germany: From Working-Class Movement to Modern Political Party*. New Haven and London: Yale University Press.

Chamberlin, John (1974). "Provision of Collective Goods as a Function of Group Size," *American Political Science Review* 68:707–16.

Champagne, Patrick (1990). "La manifestation comme action symbolique," in P. Favre, ed., *La Manifestation*. Paris: Presses de la Fondation Nationale des Sciences Politiques, pp. 329–56.

Charlesworth, Andrew (1983). *An Atlas of Rural Protest in Britain, 1548–1900*. Philadelphia: University of Pennsylvania Press.

Chartier, Roger (1987). *The Cultural Uses of Print in Early Modern France*. Princeton: Princeton University Press.

 (1991). *The Cultural Origins of the French Revolution*. Durham, N.C.: Duke University Press.

Chevalier, Louis (1973). *Laboring Classes and Dangerous Classes in Paris during the First Half of the Nineteenth Century*. New York: Howard Fertig.

Chong, Dennis (1991). *Collective Action and the Civil Rights Movement*. Chicago: University of Chicago Press.

Christie, Ian (1982). *Wars and Revolutions: Britain 1760–1815*. Cambridge: Harvard University Press.

Cobban, Alfred (1957). *A History of Modern France*. London: Penguin.

Coase, Ronald H. (1960). "The Problem of Social Cost," *Journal of Law and Economics* 3:1–44.

Cohen, Jean L. (1985). "Strategy or Identity: New Theoretical Paradigms and Contemporary Social Movements," *Social Research* 52:663–716.

Colburn, Forrest D., ed. (1989). *Everyday Forms of Peasant Resistance*. Armonk, N.Y.: M. E. Sharpe.

Cook, Maria (1990). "Organizing Dissent: The Politics of Opposition in the Mexican Teacher's Union," unpublished Ph.D. dissertation, University of California, Berkeley.

Costain, Anne N. (1992). *Inviting Women's Rebellion: A Political Process Interpretation of the Women's Movement*. Baltimore and London: Johns Hopkins University Press.

 and W. Douglas Costain (1987). "Strategy and Tactics of the Women's Movement in the United States: The Role of Political Parties," in Mary Fainsod Katzenstein and Carol McClurg Mueller, eds., *The Women's Movements of the United States and Western Europe: Consciousness, Political Opportunity and Public Policy*. Philadelphia: Temple University Press, pp. 196–214.

Cott, Nancy (1977). *The Bonds of Womanhood*. New Haven and London: Yale University Press.

Countryman, Edward (1981). *A People in Revolution. The American Revolution and Political Society in New York, 1760–1790*. Baltimore and London: Johns Hopkins University Press.

Cross, Whitney R. (1982). *The Burned-Over District. The Social and Intellectual History of Enthusiastic Religion in Western New York, 1800–1850*. Ithaca, N.Y.: Cornell University Press.

Crozier, Michel (1967). *The Bureaucratic Phenomenon*. Chicago: University of Chicago Press.

(1970). *The Stalled Society*. New York: Viking.

d'Anieri, Paul, Claire Ernst, and Elizabeth Kier (1990). "New Social Movements in Historical Perspective," *Comparative Politics* 22:445–58.

Darnton, Robert (1979). *The Business of Enlightenment: A Publishing History of the Encyclopédie, 1775–1800*. Cambridge: Harvard University Press.

(1982). *The Literary Underground of the Old Regime*. Cambridge: Harvard University Press.

(1989). "Philosphy Under the Cloak," in Robert Darnton and Daniel Roche, eds., *Revolution in Print: The Press in France, 1775–1800*. Berkeley and Los Angeles: University of California Press, pp. 27–49.

Davis, John A. (1988). *Conflict and Control: Law and Order in Nineteenth-Century Italy*. Atlantic Highlands, N.J.: Humanities Press International.

Davis, Natalie (1973). "The Rites of Violence: Religious Riot in Sixteenth-Century France," *Past and Present,* 59:51–91.

Dawes, Robyn M., Anthony J. C. Van de Kragt, and John M. Orbell (1988). "Not Me or Thee But We: The Importance of Group Identity in Eliciting Cooperation in Dilemma Situations; Experimental Manipulations," *Acta Psychologica* 68:83–97.

della Porta, Donatella (1988). "Recruitment Processes in Clandestine Political Organizations: Italian Left-Wing Terrorism," in Bert Klandermans, Hanspeter Kriesi, and Sidney Tarrow, eds., *From Structure to Action: Comparing Social Movement Research Across Cultures*. International Social Movement Research, Vol. 1. Greenwich, Conn., pp. 155–69.

(1990). *Organizazzioni politiche clandestine. Il terrorismo di sinistra in Italian durante gli anni Sessanta*. Bologna: Il Mulino.

and Sidney Tarrow (1986). "Unwanted Children: Political Violence and the Cycle of Protest in Italy, 1966–1973," *European Journal of Political Research* 14:607–32.

d'Emilio, John (1992). *Making Trouble. Essays on Gay History, Politics and the University*. New York and London: Routledge.

De Nardo, James (1985). *Power in Numbers. The Political Strategy of Protest and Rebellion*. Princeton: Princeton University Press.

Di Palma, Giuseppe (1990). *To Craft Democracies: An Essay on Democratic Transitions*. Berkeley and Los Angeles: University of California Press.

Dore, Ronald (1986). *Flexibile Rigidities*. Stanford: Stanford University Press.

Drescher, Seymour (1987). *Capitalism and Antislavery: British Mobilization in Comparative Perspective*. Oxford and New York: Oxford University Press.

(1982). "Public Opinion and the Destruction of British Colonial Slavery," in James Walvin, ed., *Slavery and British Society, 1776–1846*. Baton Rouge: Louisiana State University Press, pp. 22–48.

(1991). "British Way, French Way: Opinion Building and Revolution in the Second French Slave Emancipation," *American Historical Review* 96:709–34.

(1994). "Whose Abolition? Popular Pressure and the Ending of the British Slave Trade," *Past and Present*.

Egret, Jean (1977). *The French Prerevolution, 1787–88*. Chicago: University of Chicago Press.

Eisenstein, Elizabeth (1986). "Revolution and the Printed Word," in Roy Porter and Mikulas Teich, eds., *Revolution in History*. Cambridge and New York: Cambridge University Press, pp. 186–205.

204   *References*

Eisinger, Peter K. (1973). "The Conditions of Protest Behavior in American Cities,"
    American Political Science Review 67:11–28.
Esherick, Joseph W., and Jeffrey N. Wasserstrom (1990). "Acting Out Democracy,"
    Journal of Asian Studies 49:835–65.
Evans, Peter B., Dietrich Rueschemeyer, and Theda Skocpol, eds. (1985). *Bringing the
    State Back In*. Cambridge and New York: Cambridge University Press.
Evans, Sara M. (1980). *Personal Politics. The Roots of Women's Liberation in the Civil
    Rights Movement and the New Left*. New York: Vintage.
    and Harry C. Boyte (1992). *Free Spaces. The Sources of Democratic Change in
    America*. Chicago: University of Chicago Press.
Eyerman, Ron, and Andrew Jamison (1991). *Social Movements: A Cognitive Approach*.
    University Park, Pa.: Pennsylvania University Press.
Favre, Pierre, ed. (1990). *La Manifestation*. Paris: Presses de la Fondation Nationale des
    Sciences Politiques.
Fendrich, James M., and Ellis S. Krauss (1978). "Student Activism and Adult Left-
    wing Politics: A Causal Model of Political Socialization for Black, White and
    Japanese Students of the 1960s Generation," in L. Kriesberg, ed., *Research
    in Social Movements, Conflicts and Change*, Vol. 1. Greenwich: JAI, pp. 231–
    55.
Ferree, Myra Marx and Patricia Yancey Martin, eds. (1994). *Feminist Organization:
    Harvest of the New Women's Movement*. Philadelphia: Temple University Press,
    in press.
Fernandez, Roberto M., and Doug McAdam (1989). "Multiorganizational Fields and
    Recruitment to Social Movements," in Bert Klandermans, ed., *Organizing for
    Change. Social Movement Organizations in Europe and the United States*. Interna-
    tional Social Movement Research, Vol. 2. Greenwich, Conn.: JAI, pp. 315–43.
Finer, Samuel E. (1975). "State- and Nation-Building in Europe: The Role of the
    Military," in Charles Tilly, ed., *The Formation of National States in Western
    Europe*. Princeton: Princeton University Press, pp. 84–163.
Fireman, Bruce, and William A. Gamson (1979). "Utilitarian Logic in the Resource
    Mobilization Perspective," in Mayer N. Zald and John D. McCarthy, eds., *The
    Dynamics of Social Movements. Resource Mobilization, Social Control and Tac-
    tics*. Cambridge, Mass.: Winthrop, pp. 8–44.
Fomerand, Jacques (1974). "Policy-Formulation and Change in Gaullist France: The
    1968 Orientation Act of Higher Education," Ph.D. dissertation, City University
    of New York, N.Y.
    (1975). "Policy Formulation and Change in Gaullist France. The 1968 Orientation
    Act of Higher Education," *Comparative Politics* 8:59–89.
Freeman, Jo (1987). "Whom You Know versus Whom Your Represent: Feminist Poli-
    tics in the United States," in Mary Fainsod Katzenstein and Carol McClurg
    Mueller, eds. (1987). *The Women's Movements of the United States and Western
    Europe: Consciousness, Political Opportunity and Public Policy*. Philadelphia:
    Temple University Press, pp. 215–44.
Frohlich, Norman, Joe A. Oppenheimer and Oran Young (1971). *Political Leadership
    and Collective Goods*. Princeton: Princeton University Press.
Fromm, Erich (1969). *Escape From Freedom*. New York: Holt, Rinehart and Winston.
Gamson, William (1988). "Political Discourse and Collective Action," in Bert Klander-
    mans, Hanspeter Kriesi, and Sidney Tarrow, eds., *From Structure to Action:
    Comparing Social Movement Research Across Cultures*. International Social
    Movement Research, Vol. 1. Greenwich, Conn.: JAI, pp. 219–44.
    (1990). *The Strategy of Social Protest*, 2d ed., rev. Belmont, Calif.: Wadsworth.
    (1992). *Talking Politics*. Cambridge and New York: Cambridge University Press.

References 205

Bruce Fireman, and Steven Rytina (1982). *Encounters with Unjust Authority*. Homewood, Ill.: Dorsey Press.

and David Meyer (in preparation). "The Framing of Political Opportunity," in Doug McAdam, John D. McCarthy, and Mayer N. Zald, eds., *Opportunities, Mobilizing Structures and Framing: Comparative Applications of Contemporary Movement Theory*.

Gans, Herbert (1979). *Deciding What's News: A Study of the CBS Evening News, NBC Nightly News, Newsweek and Time*. New York: Pantheon.

Garner, Roberta Ash, and Mayer N. Zald (1985). "The Political Economy of Social Movement Sectors," in Gerald Suttles and Mayer N. Zald, eds., *The Challenge of Social Control. Citizenship and Institution Building in Modern Society. Essays in Honor of Morris Janowitz*. Norwood, N.J.: ABLEX, pp. 119–45.

Garton Ash, Timothy (1984). *The Polish Revolution*. New York: Scribners.

Geary, Roger (1985). *Policing Industrial Disputes: 1893–1895*. Cambridge and New York: Cambridge University Press.

Gelb, Joyce (1987). "Social Movement Success: A Comparative Analysis of Feminism in the United States and the United Kingdom," in Mary Fainsod Katzenstein and Carol McClurg Mueller, eds., *The Women's Movements of the United States and Western Europe: Consciousness, Political Opportunity and Public Policy*. Philadelphia: Temple University Press, pp. 267–89.

Gerhards, Jürgen, and Dieter Rucht (1992). "Mesomobilization: Organizing and Framing in Two Protest Campaigns in West Germany," *American Journal of Sociology* 98:555–96.

Gerlach, Luther P., and Virginia H. Hine (1970). *People, Power, Change: Movements of Social Transformation*. Indianapolis: Bobbs-Merrill.

Gitlin, Todd (1980). *The Whole World Is Watching: Mass Media in the Making & Unmaking of the New Left*. Berkeley and Los Angeles: University of California Press.

(1987). *The Sixties. Years of Hope, Days of Rage*. New York and Toronto: Bantam Books.

Godechot, Jacques (1971). *Les Révolutions de 1848*. Paris: Albin Michel.

ed. (1966). *La Presse Ouvrière, 1819–1850*. Paris: Bibliothèque de la Révolution de 1848.

Goffman, Erving (1974). *Frame Analysis: An Essay on the Organization of Experience*. Cambridge: Harvard University Press.

Goldenberg, Edie W. (1975). *Making the Papers: The Access of Resource-Poor Groups to the Metropolitan Press*. Lexington, Mass.: Heath.

Goodwin, Albert (1979). *The Friends of Liberty. The English Democratic Movement in the Age of the French Revolution*. Cambridge: Harvard University Press.

Goody, Jack, ed. (1968). *Literacy in Traditional Societies*. Cambridge and New York: Cambridge University Press.

Gould, Roger (1991). "Multiple Networks and Mobilization in the Paris Commune, 1871," *American Sociological Review* 56:716–29.

Gouldner, Alvin W. (1975–1976). "Prologue to a Theory of Revolutionary Intellectuals," *Telos* 26:3–36.

Gramsci, Antonio (1971). *Selections from the Prison Notebooks*. Edited and translated by Quintin Hoare and Geoffrey Nowell Smith. New York: International.

Granovetter, Mark (1973). "The Strength of Weak Ties." *American Journal of Sociology* 78:1360–80.

Grew, Raymond (1984). "The Nineteenth-Century European State," in Charles Bright and Susan Harding, eds., *Statemaking and Social Movements: Essays in History and Theory*. Ann Arbor: University of Michigan Press, pp. 83–120.

Griffin, Clifford S. (1960). *Their Brothers' Keepers. Moral Stewardship in the United States, 1800–1865*. New Brunswick, N.J.: Rutgers University Press.

Guérin, Daniel (1970). *Anarchism: From Theory to Practice*. New York and London: Monthly Review Press.

Gurr, Ted R. (1971). *Why Men Rebel*. Princeton: Princeton University Press.

Hamilton, Charles (1986). "Social Policy and the Welfare of Black Americans: From Rights to Resources," *Political Science Quarterly* 101:239–55.

Hardin, Russell (1982) *Collective Action*. Baltimore and London: Johns Hopkins University Press.

Hartz, Louis (1983). *The Liberal Tradition in America. An Interpretation of American Political Thought Since the Revolution*. San Diego: Harcourt, Brace, Jovanovich.

Heberle, Rudolf (1951). *Social Movements: An Introduction to Political Sociology*. New York: Appleton-Century-Crofts.

Hellman, Judith Adler (1987). *Journeys Among Women. Feminism in Five Italian Cities*. Oxford and New York: Oxford University Press.

Hellman, Stephen (1975). "The PCI's Alliance Strategy and the Case of the Middle Classes," in Donald L. M. Blackmer and Sidney Tarrow, eds., *Communism in Italy and France*. Princeton: Princeton University Press, pp. 373–419.

(1987). "Feminism and the Model of Militancy in an Italian Communist Federation," in Mary Fainsod Katzenstein and Carol McClurg Mueller, eds., *The Women's Movements of the United States and Western Europe: Consciousness, Political Opportunity and Public Policy*. Philadelphia: Temple University Press, pp. 132–52.

(1988). *Italian Communism in Transition. The Rise and Fall of the Historic Compromise in Turin, 1975–1980*. Oxford and New York: Oxford University Press.

Hill, Stuart, and Donald Rothchild (1992). "The Impact of Regime on the Diffusion of Political Conflict," in M. Midlarsky, ed., *The Internationalization of Communal Strife*. New York and London: Routledge, pp. 189–206.

Hirschman, Albert (1982). *Shifting Involvements: Private Interest and Public Action*. Princeton: Princeton University Press.

Hobsbawm, Eric J. (1959). *Primitive Rebels: Studies in Archaic Forms of Social Movement in the 19th and 20th Centuries*. Manchester, England: Manchester University Press.

(1962). *The Age of Revolution: 1789–1848*. London: Weidenfeld and Nicolson.

(1964). *Labouring Men: Studies in the History of Labour*. London: Weidenfeld and Nicolson.

(1974). "Peasant Land Occupations," *Past and Present* 62:120–52.

and George Rudé (1975). *Captain Swing*. New York: Norton.

Hoffer, Eric (1951). *The True Believer. Thoughts on the Nature of Mass Movements*. New York: Harper and Row.

Hoffmann, Stanley (1974). "The Ruled: Protest as a National Way of Life," in Hoffmann, *Decline or Renewal: France Since the 1930s*. New York: Viking, pp. 111–44.

Hollis, Patricia (1970). *The Pauper Press. A Study in Working Class Radicalism of the 1830s*. Oxford and New York: Oxford University Press.

Horowitz, Irving Lewis, ed. (1964). *The Anarchists*. New York: Dell.

Hubrecht, Hubert G. (1990). "Le droit français de la manifestation," in P. Favre, ed., *La Manifestation*. Paris: Presses de la Fondation Nationale des Sciences Politiques, pp. 181–206.

Hunt, Lynn (1984). *Politics, Culture, and Class in the French Revolution*. Berkeley and Los Angeles: University of California Press.

(1992). *The Family Romance of the French Revolution*. Berkeley and Los Angeles: University of California Press.
Hunter, James D. (1991). *Culture Wars: The Struggle to Define America*. New York: Basic Books.
Ignazi, Piero (1992). *Dal PCI al PDS*. Bologna: Il Mulino.
Inglehart, Ronald (1977). *The Silent Revolution: Changing Values and Political Styles Among Western Publics*. Princeton: Princeton University Press.
(1990). *Culture Shift in Advanced Industrial Society*. Princeton: Princeton University Press.
Jenkins, J. Craig and Charles Perrow (1977). "Insurgency of the Powerless: Farm Worker Movements (1946–1972)," *American Sociological Review* 42:249–68.
Jenson, Jane, and George Ross (1984). *The View from Inside. A French Communist Cell in Crisis*. Berkeley and Los Angeles: University of California Press.
Johnson, Paul E. (1978). *A Shopkeeper's Millennium. Society and Revivals in Rochester, New York, 1815–1837*. New York: Hill and Wang.
Joll, James (1980). *The Anarchists,* 2d ed. Cambridge: Harvard University Press.
Kafka, Franz (1937). *Parables and Paradoxes*. Dual language edition. Translated by Ernst Kaiser et al. New York: Schoken.
Kaplan, Steven L. (1982). *The Famine Plot Persuasion in Eighteenth Century France*. Transactions of the American Philosophical Society 72, part 3. Philadelphia: The American Philosophical Society.
(1984). *Provisioning Paris: Merchants and Millers in the Grain and Flour Trade During the Eighteenth Century*. Ithaca, N.Y.: Cornell University Press.
(1993). *Adieu 1789*. Paris: Seuil.
Katzenstein, Mary Fainsod (1987). "Comparing the Feminist Movements of the United States and Western Europe: An Overview," in Mary Fainsod Katzenstein and Carol McClurg Mueller, eds., *The Women's Movements of the United States and Western Europe: Consciousness, Political Opportunity and Public Policy*. Philadelphia: Temple University Press, pp. 3–20.
(1990) "Feminism Within American Institutions: Unobtrusive Mobilization in the 1980s," *Signs* 16:27–54.
(1993). "The Spectacle as Political Resistance. Feminist and Gay/Lesbian Politics in the Military," *Minerva: Quarterly Report on Women in the Military* 11:1–16.
and Carol McClurg Mueller, eds. (1987). *The Women's Movements of the United States and Western Europe: Consciousness, Political Opportunity and Public Policy*. Philadelphia: Temple University Press.
Katznelson, Ira (1981). *City Trenches: Urban Politics and the Patterning of Class in the United States*. New York: Pantheon Books.
Kennan, John (1986). "The Economics of Strikes," in Orley Ashenfelter and Richard Layard, eds., *Handbook of Labor Economics*, Vol. 2. Amsterdam: Elsevier Science Publishers B.V., pp. 1091–1137.
Kertzer, David (1980). *Comrades and Christians: Religion and Political Struggle in Communist Italy*. Cambridge and New York: Cambridge University Press.
(1988). *Ritual, Politics and Power*. New Haven and London: Yale University Press.
Kielbowicz, Richard B., and Clifford Scherer (1986). "The Role of the Press in the Dynamics of Social Movements," in L. Kriesberg, ed., *Research in Social Movements, Conflict and Change,* Vol. 8. Greenwich, Conn.: JAI, pp. 71–96.
Kirscheimer, Otto (1957). "The Waning of Opposition in Parliamentary Regimes," *Social Research* 24:127–56.
(1966). "The Transformation of the Western European Party Systems," in Joseph

208 *References*

LaPalombara and Myron Weiner, eds., *Political Parties and Political Development*. Princeton: Princeton University Press, pp. 177–200.

Kitschelt, Herbert (1986). "Political Opportunity Structures and Political Protest: Anti-Nuclear Movements in Four Democracies," *British Journal of Political Science* 16:57–85.

(1991). "Resource Mobilization: A Critique," in Dieter Rucht, ed., *Research on Social Movements. The State of the Art in Western Europe and the USA*. Boulder, Colo.: Westview, pp. 323–47.

Klandermans, Bert (1988). "The Formation and Mobilization of Consensus," in Bert Klandermans, Hanspeter Kriesi, and Sidney Tarrow, eds., *From Structure to Action: Comparing Social Movement Research Across Cultures*. International Social Movement Research, Vol. 1. Greenwich, Conn.: JAI, pp. 173–96.

(1992). "The Social Construction of Protest and Multiorganizational Fields," in Aldon Morris and Carol McClurg Mueller, eds., *Frontiers in Social Movement Theory*. New Haven and London: Yale University Press, pp. 77–103.

ed. (1989). *Organizing for Change: Social Movement Organizations in Europe and the United States*. International Social Movement Research, Vol. 2. Greenwich, Conn. JAI.

H. Kriesi, and S. Tarrow, eds. (1988). *From Structure to Action: Comparing Social Movement Research Across Cultures*. International Social Movement Research, Vol. 1. Greenwich, Conn.: JAI.

and Sidney Tarrow (1988). "Mobilization into Social Movements: Synthesizing European and American Approaches," in Bert Klandermans, Hanspeter Kriesi and Sidney Tarrow, eds., *From Structure to Action: Comparing Social Movement Research Across Cultures*. International Social Movement Research, Vol. 1. Greenwich, Conn.: JAI, pp. 1–38.

Kleidman, Robert (1992). "Organizations and Coalitions in the Cycles of the American Peace Movement," unpublished paper, delivered to the Annual Conference of the American Sociological Association, Pittsburgh, Pa.

(1993). *Organizing for Peace: Neutrality, The Test Ban and the Freeze*. Syracuse: Syracuse University Press.

Klein, Ethel (1987). "The Diffusion of Consciousness in the United States and Western Europe," in Mary Fainsod Katzenstein and Carol McClurg Mueller, eds., *The Women's Movements of the United States and Western Europe: Consciousness, Political Opportunity and Public Policy*. Philadelphia: Temple University Press, pp. 23–43.

Kramnick, Isaac (1990). *Republicanism and Bourgeois Radicalism. Political Ideology in Late Eighteenth-Century England and America*. Ithaca, N.Y.: Cornell University Press.

Knapp, Vincent (1980). *Austrian Social Democracy, 1889–1914*. Washington, D.C.: University Press of America.

Koopmans, Ruud (1993). "The Dynamics of Protest Waves: Germany, 1965 to 1989," *American Sociological Review* 58:637–58.

Kriesi, Hanspeter (1988). "Local Mobilization for the People's Petition of the Dutch Peace Movement," in Bert Klandermans, Hanspeter Kriesi, and Sidney Tarrow, eds., *From Structure to Action: Comparing Social Movement Research Across Cultures*. International Social Movement Research, Vol. 1. Greenwich, Conn.: JAI, pp. 41–81.

(1991). "The Political Opportunity Structure of New Social Movements: Its Impact on Their Mobilization," Occasional Paper No. 91–103, Abteilung: Öffentlichkeit und Sociale Bewegung, Wissenschaftszentrum Berlin.

R. Koopmans, J. W. Duyvendak, and M. G. Giugni (1992). "New Social Movements and Political Opportunities in Western Europe," *European Journal of Political Research* 22:219–44.

Kuklick, Bruce, ed. (1989). *Thomas Paine, Political Writings.* Cambridge and New York: Cambridge University Press.

Kuran, Timur (1991). "Now Out of Never: The Element of Surprise in the East European Revolution of 1989," in Nancy Bermeo, ed., *Liberalization and Democratization: Change in the Soviet Union and Eastern Europe.* Baltimore and London: Johns Hopkins University Press, pp. 7–48.

Laba, Roman (1990). *The Roots of Solidarity. A Political Sociology of Poland's Working Class Democratization.* Princeton: Princeton University Press.

Laitin, David D. (1988). "Political Culture and Political Preferences," *American Political Science Review* 82:589–97.

Lange. Peter, Cynthia Irvin, and Sidney Tarrow (1989). "Phases of Mobilization: Social Movements and the Italian Communist Party Since the 1960s," *British Journal of Political Science* 22:15–42.

LaPalombara, Joseph (1966). "The Decline of Ideology: A Dissent and an Interpretation," *American Political Science Review* 60:5–16.

Le Bon, Gustave (1977). *The Crowd: A Study of the Popular Mind.* New York: Penguin.

Lefebvre, Georges (1967). *The Coming of the French Revolution.* Princeton: Princeton University Press.

Lenin, V. I. (1929). *What Is To Be Done? Burning Questions of Our Movement.* New York: International Publishers.

Levine, Daniel H. (1990). "Popular Groups, Popular Culture, and Popular Religion," *Comparative Studies in Society and History* 32:718–64.

Lichtheim, George (1962). *Marxism: An Historical and Critical Study.* New York: Praeger.

(1970). *A Short History of Socialism.* New York: Praeger.

Lidtke, Vernon (1966). *The Outlawed Party. Social Democracy in Germany, 1878–1890.* Princeton: Princeton University Press.

Lijphart, Arend (1968). *The Politics of Accommodation. Pluralism and Democracy in the Netherlands.* Berkeley and Los Angeles: University of California Press.

Linebaugh, Peter, and Marcus Rediker (1990). "The Many-Headed Hydra: Sailors, Slaves, and the Atlantic Working Class in the Eighteenth Century," *Journal of Historical Sociology* 3:225–52.

Lipset, Seymour Martin (1964). "The Changing Class Structure and Contemporary European Politics," *Daedalus* (winter):271–303.

Lipsky, Michael (1968). "Protest as a Political Resource," *American Political Science Review* 62:1144–58.

and David Olson (1976). "The Processing of Racial Crisis in America," *Politics and Society* 6:79–103.

Lockridge, Kenneth (1974). *Literacy in Colonial New England: An Enquiry into the Social Context of Literacy in the Early Modern West.* New York: Norton.

Lohmann, Susanne (1993). "The Dynamics of Regime Collapse: A Case Study of the Monday Demonstrations in Leipzig, East Germany, 1989–1991," Graduate School of Business Research Paper No. 1225. Stanford University, Stanford, California.

Lowi, Theodore J. (1971). *The Politics of Disorder.* New York: Basic Books.

Lumley, Robert (1990). *States of Emergency: Cultures of Revolt in Italy from 1968 to 1978.* London and New York: Verso.

Lusebrink, Hans-Jürgen (1982). *Kriminalität und Literatur im Frankreich des 18. Jahrhunderts.* München: R. Oldenbourg.

(1983). "L'imaginaire social et ses focalisations en France et en Allemagne à la fin du XVIII siecle," *Revue Roumaine d'Histoire* 22:371–83.

Maguire, Diarmuid (1990). *New Social Movements and Old Political Institutions: The Campaign for Nuclear Disarmament, 1979–1989.* Ph.D. dissertation, Cornell University, Ithaca, N.Y.

Maier, Pauline (1970). "Popular Uprisings and Civil Authority in Eighteenth Century America," *William and Mary Quarterly* 27:3–35.

(1972). *From Resistance to Revolution: Colonial Radicals and the Development of American Opposition to Britain, 1765–1776.* New York: Knopf.

Mandel, Ernest (1980). *Long Waves of Capitalist Development: The Marxist Interpretation.* Cambridge and New York: Cambridge University Press.

Mansbridge, Jane J. (1986). *Why We Lost the ERA.* Chicago: University of Chicago Press.

(1993). "Feminist Identity: Micronegotiation in the Lives of African–American and White Working Class Women", unpublished paper, Department of Political Science, Northwestern University, Evanston, Ill.

(1994). "What Is the Feminist Movement?" in Myra Marx Ferree and Patricia Yancey Martin, eds., *Feminist Organization: Harvest of the New Women's Movement.* Philadelphia: Temple University Press.

Margadant, Ted (1979). *French Peasants in Revolt. The Insurrection of 1851.* Princeton: Princeton University Press.

Markoff, John (1986). "Literacy and Revolt: Some Empirical Notes on 1789 in France," *American Journal of Sociology* 92:323–49.

Marwell, Gerald and Pam Oliver (1993). *The Critical Mass in Collective Action: A Micro-Social Theory.* Cambridge and New York: Cambridge University Press.

Marx, Gary T., and Michael Useem (1971). "Majority Participation in Minority Movements: Civil Rights, Abolition, Untouchability," *Journal of Social Issues* 27:81–104.

Marx, Gary T., and James L. Wood (1975). "Strands of Theory and Research in Collective Behavior," *Annual Review of Sociology,* pp. 363–428.

Marx, Karl (1967). "Towards the Critique of Hegel's Philosophy of Law: Introduction," in Loyd D. Easton and Kurt H. Guddat, eds., *Writings of the Young Marx on Philosophy and Society.* New York: Doubleday, pp. 249–264.

Mathews, Donald G. (1969). "The Second Great Awakening as an Organizing Process, 1780–1830," *American Quarterly* 21:23–43.

McAdam, Doug (1982). *The Political Process and the Development of Black Insurgency.* Chicago: University of Chicago Press.

(1983). "Tactical Innovation and the Pace of Insurgency," *American Sociological Review* 48:735–54.

(1986). "Recruitment to High Risk Activism: The Case of Freedom Summer," *American Journal of Sociology* 92:64–90.

(1988). *Freedom Summer.* Oxford and New York: Oxford University Press.

and Ronnelle Paulsen (1993). "Specifying the Relationship Between Social Ties and Activism," *American Journal of Sociology* 99: in press.

and Dieter Rucht (1993). "The Cross-National Diffusion of Movement Ideas," *Annals of the American Academy of Political and Social Science* 528:56–74.

McCarthy, John D. (1987). "Pro-Life and Pro-Choice Mobilization: Infrastructure Deficits and New Technologies," in Mayer N. Zald and John D. McCarthy, eds., *Social Movements in an Organizational Society.* New Brunswick, N.J.: Transaction, pp. 49–66.

and Mayer N. Zald (1973). "The Trends of Social Movements in America: Professionalization and Resource Mobilization," Monograph. Morristown, N.J.: General Learning Press. Also published in Mayer N. Zald and John D. McCarthy (1987) *Social Movements in an Organizational Society*. New Brunswick, N.J.: Transaction, pp. 337–92.

(1977). "Resource Mobilization and Social Movements: A Partial Theory," *American Journal of Sociology* 82:1212–41. Also published in Mayer N. Zald and John D. McCarthy (1987) *Social Movements in an Organizational Society*. New Brunswick, N.J.: Transaction, pp. 15–48.

David Britt, and Mark Wolfson (1991). "The Institutional Channelling of Social Movements by the State in the United States," in Louis Kriesberg, ed., *Research in Social Movements, Conflict and Change* 13:45–76.

Clark McPhail, and Jackie Smith (1992). "The Tip of the Iceberg: Some Dimensions of Selection Bias in Media Coverage of Demonstrations in Washington, D.C., 1982," unpublished paper delivered to the annual meeting of the American Sociological Association, Pittsburgh, Pa.

and Mark Wolfson (1992). "Consensus Movements, Conflict Movements and the Co-optation of Civic and State Infrastructures," in Aldon Morris and Carol McClurg Mueller, eds., *Frontiers in Social Movement Theory*. New Haven and London: Yale University Press, pp. 273–97.

and Mark Wolfson (1993). " 'You Can Make a Difference': The Role of Agency, Strategy and Structure in Grass-roots Resource Mobilization," unpublished paper.

McPhail, Clark (1991). *The Myth of the Madding Crowd*. New York: Aldine De Gruyter.

Mehta, V. E. D. (1976). *Mahatma Gandhi and His Apostles*. London: Penguin.

Melucci, Alberto (1980). "The New Social Movements: A Theoretical Approach." *Social Science Information* 19:199–226.

(1988). "Getting Involved: Identity and Mobilization in Social Movements," in Bert Klandermans, Hanspeter Kriesi, and Sidney Tarrow, eds., *From Structure to Action: Comparing Social Movement Research Across Cultures*. International Social Movement Research, Vol. 1. Greenwich, Conn.: JAI, pp. 329–48.

(1989). *Nomads of the Present: Social Movements and Individual Needs in Contemporary Society*. Philadelphia: Temple University Press.

Mershon, Carol A. (1990). "Generazioni di leader sindicali in fabbrica. L'eredità dell'autunno caldo," *Polis* 2:277–323.

Meyer, David (1990). *A Winter of Discontent: The Nuclear Freeze and American Politics*. New York: Praeger.

(1993). "Institutionalizing Dissent: The United States Structure of Opportunity and the End of the Nuclear Freeze Movement," *Sociological Forum* 8:157–79.

Meyer, Jean (1966). *La noblesse bretonne au XVIIIe siècle*. 2 vols. Paris: SEVPEN.

Michels, Robert (1962). *Political Parties. A Sociological Study of the Oligarchical Tendencies of Modern Democracy*. New York: Collier Books.

Miller, James (1987). *Democracy Is in the Streets. From Port Huron to the Siege of Chicago*. New York: Simon and Schuster.

Molotch, Harvey (1979). "Media and Movements," in Mayer N. Zald and John D. McCarthy, eds., *Dynamics of Social Movements*. Cambridge, Mass.: Winthrop, pp. 71–93.

Moore, Barrington Jr. (1978). *Injustice: The Social Bases of Obedience and Revolt*. Armonk, N.Y.: M. E. Sharpe.

Morgan, Jane (1987). *Conflict and Order: The Police and Labor Disputes in England and Wales, 1900–1939*. Oxford and New York: Oxford University Press.

Morris, Aldon (1984). *The Origins of the Civil Rights Movement: Black Communities Organizing for Change*. New York: The Free Press.

and Carol McClurg Mueller, eds. (1992). *Frontiers in Social Movement Theory*. New Haven and London: Yale University Press.

Morris, Aldon (1993). "Birmingham Confrontation Reconsidered," *American Sociological Review* 58:621–36.

Morris, R. J. (1983). "Voluntary Societies and British Urban Elites, 1780–1850: An Analysis," *The Historical Journal* 26:95–118.

Mosse, George (1975). *The Nationalization of the Masses: Political Symbolism and Mass Movements in Germany from the Napoleonic Wars Through the Third Reich.* New York: H. Fertig.

Mouriaux, René, et al. (1992). *968. Exploration du Mai français.* 2 vols. Paris: Harmattan.

Mueller, Carol McClurg (1987). "Collective Consciousness, Identity Transformation, and the Rise of Women in Public Office in the United States," in Mary Fainsod Katzenstein and Carol McClurg Mueller, eds., *The Women's Movements of the United States and Western Europe: Consciousness, Political Opportunity and Public Policy,* Philadelphia: Temple University Press, pp. 89–108.

Oberschall, Anthony (1973). *Social Conflict and Social Movements.* Englewood Cliffs, N.J.: Prentice-Hall.

O'Donnell, Guillermo and Philippe Schmitter, (1986). *Transition from Authoritarian Rule: Tentative Conclusions About Uncertain Democracies.* Baltimore and London: Johns Hopkins University Press.

Offe, Claus (1985). "New Social Movements: Challenging the Boundaries of Institutional Politics," *Social Research* 52:817–68.

(1990). "Reflections on the Institutional Self-Transformation of Movement Politics: A Tentative Stage Model," in Russell Dalton and Manfred Kuechler, eds., *Challenging the Political Order.* Oxford and New York: Oxford University Press, pp. 232–50.

Ohlemacher, Thomas (1992). "Social Relays: Micro-Mobilization via the Meso-Level," Discussion Paper FS III 92–104, Wissenschaftszentrum Berlin.

Oliver, Pam (1984). "If You Don't Do It, Nobody Else Will: Active and Token Contributors to Local Collective Action," *American Sociological Review* 49:601–10.

(1989). "Bringing the Crowd Back In: The Nonorganizational Elements of Social Movements," in L. Kriesberg, ed., *Research in Social Movements, Conflict and Change,* Vol. 11. Greenwich, Conn.: JAI, pp. 1–30.

Olson, Mancur (1965). *The Logic of Collective Action.* Cambridge: Harvard University Press.

Open University (1976). *Music and Revolution: Verdi.* London: The Open University.

Ortoleva, Peppino (1988). *Saggio sui movimenti del 1968 in Europa e in America.* Roma: Riuniti.

Ost, David (1990). *Solidarity and the Politics of Anti-Politics: Opposition and Reform in Poland Since 1968.* Philadelphia: Temple University Press.

Ozouf, Mona (1988). *Festivals and the French Revolution.* Translated by Alan Sheridan. Cambridge: Harvard University Press.

Paige, Jeffrey M. (1975). *Agrarian Revolutions. Social Movements and Export Agriculture in the Underdeveloped World.* New York: The Free Press.

Palmer, Robert R. (1959–64). *The Age of the Democratic Revolution. A Political History of Europe and America, 1760–1800.* 2 vols. Princeton: Princeton University Press.

Percheron, Annick (1991). "La mémoire des générations: La guerre d'Algérie – Mai 68," in Olivier Duhamel and Jerôme Jaffré, eds., *SOFRES: L'Etat de l'opinion, 1991.* Paris: Seuil, pp. 39–57.

Perrot, Michelle (1986). "On the Formation of the French Working Class," in Ira Katznelson and Aristide R. Zolberg, eds., *Working Class Formation: Nineteenth*

Century Patterns in Western Europe and the United States. Princeton: Princeton University Press, pp. 71–110.

Pitt-Rivers, Julian (1971). *The People of the Sierra*. 2d ed. Chicago: University of Chicago Press.

Piven, Frances F., and Richard Cloward (1972). *Regulating the Poor*. New York: Vintage Books.

(1979). *Poor People's Movements: Why They Succeed, How They Fail*. New York: Vintage Books.

Plamenatz, John (1954). *German Marxism and Russian Communism*. London and New York: Longmans, Green.

Popkin, Jeremy D. (1989). "Journals: The New Face of News," in Robert Darnton and Daniel Roche, eds., *Revolution in Print: The Press in France, 1775–1800*. Berkeley and Los Angeles: University of California Press, pp. 141–64.

Popkin, Sam (1979). *The Rational Peasant: The Political Economy of Rural Society in Vietnam*. Berkeley and Los Angeles: University of California Press.

Postgate, Raymond (1955). *The Story of a Year: 1848*. London: Cassell.

Price, Roger (1989). *The Revolutions of 1848*. Atlantic Highlands, N.J.: Humanities Press International.

Ramet, Sabrina (1987). *The Soviet Rock Scene*. Washington, D.C.: Kennan Institute for Advanced Russian Studies.

Read, Donald (1964). *The English Provinces, c. 1760–1960: A Study in Influence*. New York: St. Martin's.

Regalia, Ida. (1984). *Eletti e abbandonati*. Bologna: Il Mulino.

Reich, Wilhelm (1970). *The Mass Psychology of Fascism*. New York: Farrar, Straus.

Rochon, Thomas R. (1988). *Mobilizing for Peace. The Antinuclear Movements in Western Europe*. Princeton: Princeton University Press.

Rogers, Kim Lacy (1993). *Righteous Lives. Narratives of the New Orleans Civil Rights Movement*. New York and London: New York University Press.

Rokkan, Stein (1970). *Citizens, Elections, Parties: Approaches to the Comparative Study of the Processes of Development*. Oslo: Universitetsforlaget.

Rosenau, James (1990). *Turbulence in World Politics: A Theory of Change and Continuity*. Princeton: Princeton University Press.

Rosenthal, Naomi B. et al. (1985). "Social Movements and Network Analysis: A Case Study of Nineteenth Century Women's Reform in New York State," *American Journal of Sociology* 90:1022–54.

and Michael Schwartz (1990). "Spontaneity and Democracy in Social Movements," in Bert Klandermans, ed., *Organizing for Change: Social Movement Organizations in Europe and the United States*. International Social Movement Research. Vol. 2. Greenwich, Conn.: JAI, pp. 33–59.

Roth, Guenther (1963). *The Social Democrats in Imperial Germany. A Study on Working-Class Isolation and National Integration*. Totowa, N.J.: Bedminster.

Rotondi, Clementina (1951). *Bibliografia dei periodici toscani, 1847–1852*. Firenze: L. S. Olschki.

Rucht, Dieter (1990). "Campaigns, Skirmishes and Battles: Anti-Nuclear Movements in the USA, France and West Germany," *Industrial Crisis Quarterly* 4:193–222.

(1992). "Studying the Effects of Social Movements: Conceptualization and Problems," unpublished paper presented at the ECPR Joint Meeting, Limerick, Ireland.

(1993). "The Impact of National Contexts on Social Movement Structures: A Cross-Movement and Cross-National Comparison," unpublished paper, Berlin Wissenschaftszentrum.

Rucht, Dieter ed. (1991). *Research on Social Movements. The State of the Art in Western Europe and the USA*. Boulder, Colo.: Westview.

Rule, James (1988). *Theories of Civil Violence*. Berkeley and Los Angeles: University of California Press.

Rupp, Leila J., and Verta A. Taylor (1987). *Survival in the Doldrums. The American Women's Rights Movement, 1945 to the 1960s*. Oxford and New York: Oxford University Press.

Ryerson, Richard A. (1978). *The Revolution Is Now Begun: The Radical Committees of Philadelphia, 1765–1776*. Philadelphia: University of Pennsylvania Press.

Salvati, Michele (1981). "May 1968 and the Hot Autumn of 1969: The Responses of Two Ruling Classes," in Suzanne Berger, ed., *Organizing Interests in Western Europe*. Cambridge and New York: Cambridge University Press, pp. 329–63.

Schama, Simon (1989). *Citizens: A Chronicle of the French Revolution*. New York: Knopf.

Scheler, Max (1972). *Ressentiment*. New York: Schocken.

Schelling, Thomas C. (1960). *The Strategy of Conflict*. Cambridge: Harvard University Press.

(1978). *Micromotives and Macrobehavior*. New York: Norton.

Schennink, Ben (1988). "From Peace Week to Peace Work: Dynamics of the Peace Movement in the Netherlands," in Bert Klandermans, Hanspeter Kriesi and Sidney Tarrow, eds., *From Structure to Action: Comparing Social Movement Research Across Cultures*. International Social Movement Research, Vol. 1. Greenwich: JAI Press, pp. 247–79.

Schlesinger, Arthur M., Jr. (1986). *The Cycles of American History*. Boston: Houghton Mifflin.

Schnapp, Alain, and Pierre Vidal-Naquet (1988). *Journal de la commune étudiante: Textes et documents, novembre 1967–juin 1968*. 2d ed. Paris: Seuil.

Schneider, Jane, and Peter Schneider (1992). "From Peasant Wars to Urban Wars: The Antimafia Movement in Palermo," unpublished paper, Fordham University, New York, N.Y.

Schumaker, Paul D. (1975). "Policy Responsiveness to Protest-Group Demands," *The Journal of Politics*: 37:488–521.

Schwartz, Michael, and Shuva Paul (1992). "Resource Mobilization versus the Mobilization of People," in Aldon Morris and Carol McClurg Mueller, eds., *Frontiers in Social Movement Theory*. New Haven: Yale University Press, pp. 205–23.

Schweitzer, Robert A., and Charles Tilly (1979). "A Study of Contentious Gatherings in Early Nineteenth-Century Great Britain," *Historical Methods* 12:1–4.

Scott, James C. (1986). *Weapons of the Weak: Everyday Forms of Peasant Resistance*. New Haven and London: Yale University Press.

Sewell, William (1980). *Work and Revolution in France. The Language of Labor from the Old Regime to 1848*. Cambridge and New York: Cambridge University Press.

(1986). "Artisans, Factory Workers, and the Formation of the French Working Class, 1789–1848," in Ira Katznelson and Aristide R. Zolberg, eds., *Working Class Formation: Nineteenth Century Patterns in Western Europe and the United States*. Princeton: Princeton University Press, pp. 45–70.

(1990). "Collective Violence and Collective Loyalties in France: Why the French Revolution Made a Difference," *Politics and Society* 18:527–52.

Sharp, Gene (1973). *The Politics of Nonviolent Action*. Boston: Porter Sargent.

Sigmann, Jean (1973). *1848. The Romantic and Democratic Revolutions in Europe*. New York: Harper and Row.

Silver, Beverly (1992a). "Class Struggle and Kondratieff Waves, 1870 to the Present," in Alfred Kleinknecht, Ernest Mandel, and Immanuel Wallerstein, eds.,

New Findings in Long Wave Research. New York: St. Martin's, pp. 279–95.

(1992b). "Labor Unrest and Capital Accumulation on a World Scale." Ph.D. dissertation, State University of New York at Binghamton.

Skocpol, Theda (1979). *States and Social Revolutions: A Comparative Analysis of France, Russia, and China*. Princeton: Princeton University Press.

Snow, David E. et al. (1986). "Frame Alignment Processes, Micromobilization, and Movement Participation," *American Sociological Review* 51:464–81.

and Robert Benford (1988). "Ideology, Frame Resonance, and Participant Mobilization," in Bert Klandermans, Hanspeter Kriesi, and Sidney Tarrow, eds., *From Structure to Action: Comparing Social Movement Research Across Cultures*. International Social Movement Research, Vol. 1. Greenwich: JAI Press, pp. 197–217.

(1992). "Master Frames and Cycles of Protest," in Aldon Morris and Carol McClurg Mueller, eds., *Frontiers in Social Movement Theory*. New Haven and London: Yale University Press, pp. 133–55.

Snyder, David, and Charles Tilly (1972). "Hardship and Collective Violence in France: 1830–1960," *American Sociological Review* 37:520–32.

Soboul, Albert (1964). *The Parisian Sans-culottes and the French Revolution*. Oxford and New York: Oxford University Press.

Soldani, Simonetta (1973). "Contadini, operai e 'popolo' nella rivoluzione del 1848 in Italia," *Studi storici* 14:557–613.

Soskice, David (1978). "Strike Waves and Wage Explosions, 1968–1970: An Economic Interpretation," in Colin Crouch and Alessandro Pizzorno, eds., *The Resurgence of Class Conflict in Western Europe Since 1968*. Vol. 2. New York: Holmes and Meier Publishers, Inc., pp. 221–46.

Soule, Sarah, and Sidney Tarrow (1991). "Acting Collectively, 1847–1849: How the Repertoire of Collective Action Changed and Where It Happened." Paper presented to the annual conference of the Social Science History Association, New Orleans.

Staggenborg, Suzanne (1991). *The Pro-Choice Movement: Organization and Activism in the Abortion Conflict*. Oxford and New York: Oxford University Press.

Staniszkis, Jadwiga (1984). *Poland's Self-Limiting Revolution*. Princeton: Princeton University Press.

Steedly, Homer R., and John W. Foley (1979). "The Success of Protest Groups: Multivariate Analyses," *Social Science Research* 8:1–15.

Stinchcombe, Arthur L. (1987). Review of Charles Tilly, *The Contentious French*, *American Journal of Sociology* 93:1248.

Stone, Lawrence (1969). "Literacy and Education in England, 1640–1900," *Past and Present* No. 42:69–139.

Strang, David, and John W. Meyer (1991). "Institutional Conditions for Diffusion," presented at the Workshop on New Institutional Theory, Ithaca, N.Y.

Swidler, Ann (1986). "Culture in Action: Symbols and Strategies" *American Sociological Review* 51:273–86.

Tamason, Charles (1980). "From Mortuary to Cemetery: Funeral Riots and Funeral Demonstrations in Lille, 1779–1870." *Social Science History* 4:15–31.

Tarde, Gabriel de (1989). *L'opinion et la foule*. Paris: Presses Universitaires de France.

Tarrow, Sidney (1967). *Peasant Communism in Southern Italy*. New Haven and London: Yale University Press.

(1988). "Old Movements in New Cycles of Protest: The Career of an Italian Religious Community," in Bert Klandermans, Hanspeter Kriesi, and Sidney Tarrow, eds., *From Structure to Action: Comparing Social Movements across Cultures*. International Social Movement Research, Vol. 1. Greenwich, Conn.: JAI, pp. 281–304.

(1989a). *Democracy and Disorder. Protest and Politics in Italy, 1965–1975.* Oxford and New York: Oxford University Press.

(1989b). *Struggle, Politics and Reform: Collective Action, Social Movements and Cycles of Protest.* Cornell University, Western Societies Paper no. 21.

(1991). "Kollectives Handeln und Politische Gelegenheitsstruktur in Mobilisierungs-wellen: Theoretische Perspektiven," in *Kölner Zeitschrift für Soziologie und Sozialpsychologie* 43:647–70.

(1992). "Mentalities, Political Cultures and Collective Action Frames: Constructing Meaning Through Action," in Aldon Morris and Carol McClurg Mueller, eds., *Frontiers in Social Movement Research.* New Haven and London: Yale University Press, pp. 174–202.

(1993a). "Modular Collective Action and the Rise of the Social Movement: Why the French Revolution Was Not Enough," *Politics and Society* 21:69–90.

(1993b) "Cycles of Collective Action: Between Moments of Madness and the Repertoire of Contention," *Social Science History* 17:281–307.

(1993c). "Social Protest and Policy Reform: May 1968 and the Loi d'Orientation in France," *Comparative Political Studies* 25:579–607.

Tarrow, Susan (1985). *Exile from the Kingdom. A Political Rereading of Albert Camus.* University, Ala.: University of Alabama Press.

Taylor, Michael, ed. (1988). *Rationality and Revolution.* Cambridge and New York: Cambridge University Press.

Thomas, Daniel (in preparation). "International Norms and Political Change: The Helsinki Process and the Fall of Communism in Eastern Europe, 1975–1990." [Unpublished] Ph.D. dissertation, Cornell University.

Thomis, Malcolm I., and Peter Holt (1977). *Threats of Revolution in Britain, 1789–1848.* Hamden, Conn.: Archon Books.

Thompson, Dorothy (1984). *The Chartists. Popular Politics in the Industrial Revolution.* New York: Pantheon.

Thompson, E. P. (1971). "The Moral Economy of the English Crowd in the Eighteenth Century," *Past and Present* 50:76–136.

Thompson, Michael, Richard Ellis, and Aaron Wildavsky (1990). *Cultural Theory.* Boulder, Colo.: Westview.

Tilly, Charles (1975). "Food Supply and Public Order in Modern Europe," in Charles Tilly, ed., *The Formation of National States in Western Europe.* Princeton: Princeton University Press, pp. 380–455.

(1978). *From Mobilization to Revolution.* Reading, Mass.: Addison-Wesley Publishing Co.

(1982). "Britain Creates the Social Movement," in James Cronin and Jonathan Schneer, eds., *Social Conflict and the Political Order in Modern Britain.* New Brunswick, N.J.: Rutgers University Press, pp. 21–51.

(1983). "Speaking Your Mind Without Elections, Surveys, or Social Movements," *Public Opinion Quarterly* 47:461–78.

(1984). "Social Movements and National Politics," in C. Bright and S. Harding, eds., *Statemaking and Social Movements: Essays in History and Theory.* Ann Arbor: University of Michigan Press, pp. 297–317.

(1984). *Big Structures, Large Processes, Huge Comparisons.* New York: Russell Sage.

(1986). *The Contentious French.* Cambridge: Harvard University Press.

(1990). *Coercion, Capital, and European States, A.D. 990–1990.* Cambridge, Mass. and Oxford: Basil Blackwell.

(1991a). "Prisoners of the State." Working Paper No. 129, the Center for Studies of Social Change, the New School for Social Research, New York.

(1991b). "Selected Papers, 1963–1991, From the Study of Social Change and Collective Action," Working Paper No. 113, the Center for Studies of Social Change, the New School for Social Research, New York.

(1992). "How to Detect, Describe, and Explain Repertoires of Contention," Working Paper No. 150. Center for Studies of Social Change, New School for Social Research, New York, N.Y.

(1993a). "Contentious Repertoires in Britain, 1758–1834," *Social Science History* 17:253–80.

(1993b). *European Revolutions, 1492–1992*. Oxford: Blackwell's.

Louise Tilly, and Richard Tilly, (1975). *The Rebellious Century, 1830–1930*. Cambridge: Harvard University Press.

Tocqueville, Alexis de (1954). *Democracy in America*, 2 vols. New York: Vintage.

(1955). *The Old Regime and the French Revolution*. Translated by Stuart Gilbert. Garden City, N.Y.: Doubleday Anchor.

(1987). *Recollections. The French Revolution of 1848*. New Brunswick, N.J.: Transaction Books.

Touraine, Alain (1988). *Return of the Actor. Social Theory in Postindustrial Society*. Minneapolis: University of Minnesota Press.

Traugott, Marc (1990). "Neighborhoods in Insurrection: The Use of Barricades in the French Revolution of 1848," unpublished paper, University of California, Santa Cruz, California.

(1993). "Barricades as Repertoire: Continuities and Discontinuities in the History of French Contention," *Social Science History* 17:309–23.

Trigilia, Carlo (1986). *Grandi partiti e piccole imprese. Comunisti e democristiani nelle regioni a economia diffusa*. Bologna: Il Mulino.

Tucker, Robert C., ed. (1978). *The Marx-Engels Reader*. 2d ed. New York: Norton.

Tyrrell, Ian R. (1979). *Sobering Up: From Temperance to Prohibition in Antebellum America, 1800–1860*. Westport, Conn.: Greenwood Press.

Valelly, Richard M. (1993). "Party, Coercion and Inclusion: The Two Reconstructions of the South's Electoral Politics," *Politics and Society* 21:37–68.

van Praag Jr., Philip (1992). "The Velvet Revolution: The Role of the Students; Political Opportunities and Informal Networks in an Authoritarian Regime," presented to the First European Conference on Social Movements, Berlin Wissenschaftszentrum.

van Zoonen, Liesbet (1992). " 'A Dance of Death?' New Social Movements and the Media," presented to the First European Conference on Social Movements, Berlin Wissenschaftszentrum.

Vernus, Michel (1989). "A Provincial Perspective," in Robert Darnton and Daniel Roche, eds., *Revolution in Print: The Press in France, 1775–1800*. Berkeley and Los Angeles: University of California Press, pp. 124–38.

Walsh, Richard W. (1959). *Charleston's Sons of Liberty: A Study of the Artisans, 1763–1787*. New York: Columbia University Press.

Walters, Ronald G. (1976). *The Antislavery Appeal: American Abolitionism After 1830*. Baltimore and London: Johns Hopkins University Press.

(1978). *American Reformers, 1815–1860*. New York: Hill and Wang.

Walzer, Michael (1971). *The Revolution of the Saints. A Study in the Origins of Radical Politics*. New York: Atheneum.

Webster, Richard (1960). *The Cross and the Fasces. Christian Democracy and Fascism in Italy*. Stanford: Stanford University Press.

Wejnert, Barbara (1994). "Prerequisites for Diffusion of Collective Protests: Student Movements in the Sixties," in L. Kriesberg, ed., *Research in Social Movements, Conflict and Change*. Vol. 16. Greenwich, Conn.: JAI, in press.

Wilentz, Sean (1984). *Chants Democratic: New York City and the Rise of the American Working Class, 1788–1850.* Oxford and New York: Oxford University Press.

Williamson, Oliver E. (1983). *Markets and Hierarchies: Analysis and Antitrust Implications.* New York: The Free Press.

(1985). *The Economic Institutions of Capitalism.* New York: The Free Press.

Wood, Gordon S. (1991). *The Radicalism of the American Revolution.* New York: Vintage.

Wylie, Laurence (1964). *Village in the Vaucluse.* Cambridge: Harvard University Press.

Zald, Mayer N. (1991). "The Continuing Vitality of Resource Mobilization Theory: Response to Herbert Kitschelt's Critique," in D. Rucht, ed., *Research on Social Movements. The State of the Art in Western Europe and the USA.* Boulder, Colo.: Westview, pp. 348–54.

and Roberta Ash (1966). "Social Movement Organizations: Growth, Decay and Change," *Social Forces* 44:327–41. Also published in Mayer N. Zald and John D. McCarthy, eds., *Social Movements in an Organizational Society.* New Brunswick, N.J.: Transaction Press, 1987, pp. 121–41.

and Michael A. Berger (1978). "Social Movements in Organizations: Coup d'Etat, Bureaucratic Insurgency, and Mass Movement," *American Journal of Sociology* 83:823–61. Also published in Mayer N. Zald and John D. McCarthy, eds., *Social Movements in an Organizational Society.* New Brunswick, N.J.: Transaction Press, 1987, pp. 185–222.

and John D. McCarthy (1980). "Social Movement Industries: Cooperation and Conflict Among Social Movement Organizations," in Louis Kriesberg, ed., *Research in Social Movements, Conflict and Change,* Vol. 3. Greenwich, Conn.: JAI, pp. 1–20. Also published in Mayer N. Zald and John D. McCarthy, eds., *Social Movements in an Organizational Society.* New Brunswick, N.J.: Transaction Books, 1987, pp. 161–80.

and John D. McCarthy, eds. (1979). *The Dynamics of Social Movements.* Cambridge, Mass.: Winthrop, pp. 8–44.

(1987). *Social Movements in an Organizational Society.* New Brunswick, N.J.: Transaction Books.

and Bert Useem (1987). "Movement and Countermovement Interaction: Mobilization, Tactics and State Involvement," in Mayer N. Zald and John D. McCarthy, eds., *Social Movements in an Organizational Society.* New Brunswick, N.J.: Transaction Press, pp. 247–72.

Zolberg, Aristide R. (1972). "Moments of Madness," *Politics and Society* 2:183–207.

(1978). "Belgium" in Raymond Grew, ed., *Crises of Political Development in Europe and the United States.* Princeton: Princeton University Press, pp. 99–138.

(1989). *Escape From Violence: Conflict and the Refugee Crisis in the Developing World.* Oxford and New York: Oxford University Press.

Notes

INTRODUCTION

1. In other words, I cannot agree with Russell Hardin when he writes in his book, *Collective Action*, that "there is no reason to parcel the theory [of collective action] according to the boundaries of substantive problems." Generalizing the explanation of participation would only lead to greater theoretical power if, as Hardin claims, if the resources and problems of coordination of the actors were comparable in all substantive realms (pp. xiii–xiv), a claim that cannot be sustained. Hardin's theoretical contributions provide key hints about how social movements "solve" their problem of collective action; but we will not get very far before we have to turn to economics and sociology, politics and history to find out how these "solutions" work.

2. Charles Tilly writes:

   Authorities and thoughtless historians commonly describe popular contention as disorderly. . . . But the more closely we look at that same contention, the more we discover order. We discover order created by the rooting of collective action in the routines and organization of everyday social life, and by its involvement in a continuous process of signaling, negotiation, and struggle with other parties whose interests the collective action touches. (*The Contentious French*, p. 4)

3. Such a movement is described by political scientist Jane Mansbridge in her article, "What Is the Feminist Movement?" Also see the view of Mary F. Katzenstein, who regards such unobtrusive actions as one among several alternative forms in her "Feminism Within American Institutions: Unobtrusive Mobilization in the 1980s." I will return to these questions in Chapter 7.

4. Some students of social movements take the criterion of common consciousness to an extreme. Rudolf Heberle, for example, thought a movement had to have a well worked out ideology. See his *Social Movements: An Introduction to Political Sociology*. Others, like Alberto Melucci, think that movements purposefully "construct" collective identities. See Melucci's "Getting Involved: Identity and Mobilization in Social Movements."

5. See Scott's *Weapons of the Weak* for the phenomena of subterfuge and foot dragging typical of agrarian communities. The resentment that Scott describes can become the source of positive values, as Max Scheler long ago observed in his classic, *Ressentiment*, and as Scott's vivid ethnographic studies show. But by appropriating for it the term "resistance," Scott runs the risk of obscuring its difference from the forms of sustained interaction with opponents that are found in social movements. Scott only stretches the concept of "resistance": But this has led to conceptual confusion, as in

some of the contributions in Forrest Colburn, et al., *Everyday Forms of Peasant Resistance*, in which the difference between resentment, foot dragging and subterfuge, on the one hand, and sustained social movements, on the other, is obscured.

1: COLLECTIVE ACTION AND SOCIAL MOVEMENTS

1. The material that follows was culled mainly from the *New York Times* and *The Washington Post* on April 26–28, 1993. I am grateful to sociologist Nancy Whittier for additional observations, and to Sung Woo for gathering the material for this section.
2. "Police estimates were 300,000, but that figure was disputed by march organizers, who put the total at a million, a figure supported by the Mayor's office here." *New York Times*, April 26, 1993, p. B8.
3. "Although the marchers came with a broad civil rights agenda, the ban on homosexuals in the military dominated the tone of the day." Ibid., p. 1.
4. All the press sources emphasized this diversity: "Marchers . . . were young and old, black, white, Latino and Asian." *Washington Post*, April 26, 1993, p. 10. "Indeed, many marchers were accompanied by small children and parents." *New York Times*, April 26, 1993, p. B8. There was even a self-designated "Gay parents' group" from Kansas. "Even farmers can be gay," commented the *Times* (ibid.).
5. "Some of them said they feared that some erotic displays and outrageous attire among the marchers . . . could hurt their cause. 'I know some of it is only a joke, but we can't afford that,' " said one marcher quoted by the *Post*, April 26, 1993, p. 10.
6. Many sociologists trace the lineage of the social movement field to the reactions of French theorists to the horrors of the French Revolution and the outrages of the crowd. While writers like Tarde and Le Bon make a conveniently polemical starting point for theorists who reject their ideas about the irrationality of collective action, their work was, in fact, an offshoot of the psychology of the crowd. As will be evident from what follows, in this book, conflicts between challengers and authorities are seen as a normal part of society and not as an aberration. For an account of theorists who focus on civil violence as the antithesis of normal social processes, see James Rule's *Theories of Civil Violence*, ch. 3.
7. Although there are many more elegant (and more obscure) formulations, Marx puts this most succinctly in *The Communist Manifesto:*

    The advance of industry, whose involuntary promoter is the bourgeoisie, replaces the isolation of the labourers, due to competition, by their revolutionary combination, due to association. . . . The real fruit of their battle lies, not in the immediate result, but in the ever-expanding union of the workers. (*The Marx-Engels Reader*, pp. 481, 483)

8. Lenin criticized the theory, then current in some socialist circles, that "the brunt of all the other revolutionary functions (apart from agitation) *must necessarily* fall mainly upon the shoulders of an extremely small intellectual force. It need not 'necessarily' be so. It is because we are backward." *What Is to Be Done?*, p. 123–4.
9. In 1924, Gramci wrote;

    The error of the party has been to have accorded priority in an abstract fashion to the problem of organization, which in practice has simply meant creating an apparatus of functionaries who could be depended on for their orthodoxy towards the official view. (*Selections from the Prison Notebooks*, p. lxii)

10. This was a special danger on the periphery of the working-class party, among the middle class and the peasantry. See Stephen Hellman, "The PCI's Alliance Strategy

and the Case of the Middle Class,'' and Sidney Tarrow, *Peasant Communism in Southern Italy.*

11. The *locus classicus* is, of course, Mancur Olson's *The Logic of Collective Action,* but the tradition of game theory has made a substantial contribution too. In the public choice tradition, the landmark studies were James Buchanan, ''An Economic Theory of Clubs,'' and Norman Frohlich, Joe A. Oppenheimer, and Oran R. Young, *Political Leadership and Collective Goods.* In the game theoretic tradition, the strongest applications have been made by Thomas C. Schelling. See especially his *Strategy of Conflict.* For a stimulating blend of both traditions, see Russell Hardin's *Collective Action.* Also see Dennis Chong's *Collective Action and the Civil Rights Movement,* James De Nardo's *Power in Numbers,* Sam Popkin's *The Rational Peasant* and Michael Taylor, ed., *Rationality and Revolution.*

12. The problem of the size of the group has exercised a great fascination among scholars in both the public choice and game theoretic traditions. See John Chamberlin's ''Provision of Collective Goods as a Function of Group Size,'' Russell Hardin, *Collective Action,* ch. 3, and Gerald Marwell and Pam Oliver's *The Critical Mass in Collective Action: A Micro-Social Theory,* ch. 3, which demonstrates theoretically that the size of the group is not the critical variable that Olson thought it was.

13. Thus, General Motors has enough of an interest in the collective good of American auto production to take on the leadership of all domestic car producers, including those who are too small to take action on their own. If enough members of the group take a free ride, then the leaders' efforts are not only to no avail – their efforts, themselves, will induce free riding.

14. As another economist, Albert Hirschman, wryly pointed out in his *Shifting Involvements,* ''Olson proclaimed the impossibility of collective action for large groups . . . at the precise moment when the Western world was about to be all but engulfed by an unprecedented wave of public movements, marches, protests, strikes and ideologies,'' p. 78.

15. In other words, Olson is not alone in understanding that if everybody ''free rides,'' the collective interest will lose out. See the brief summary of the major critiques from the standpoint of social movement theory in Bert Klandermans, ''New Social Movements and Resource Mobilization: The European and the American Approach Revisited,'' pp. 24–5. Marwell and Oliver's *The Critical Mass* constitutes an elaborate dialogue with Olson's theory, whereas Hardin's *Collective Action* and Chong's *Collective Action and the Civil Rights Movement* formulate variations and alternatives to it.

16. The many contributions of John McCarthy, Mayer Zald and their associates are collected in two readers: Zald and McCarthy, eds., *The Dynamics of Social Movements,* and Zald and McCarthy, eds., *Social Movements in an Organizational Society.* A complementary theoretical effort was made at the same time by Anthony Oberschall, *Social Conflict and Social Movements.*

17. Although they focused mainly on SMOs, McCarthy, Zald and their associates embedded their reasoning in a larger system of social and political relationships. In ''Social Movement Industries,'' Zald and McCarthy saw movement leaders cooperating or competing for popular support with one another in ''movement industries,'' or SMIs. In ''Movement and Countermovement Interaction,'' Zald and Useem believed movements often gave rise to countermovements and became locked into a game of thrust and parry with them. This aggregate of movement organizations and their followers was seen as a ''social movement sector,'' which ebbed and flowed over time, and interacted with the political system, according to Garner and Zald in ''The Political Economy of Social Movement Sectors.'' Unfortunately, this broader sociopolitical aspect of their work was at first downplayed, and much of the critical

reaction to the "resource mobilization" school focused on their use of the unpalatable term "entrepreneurs," which came from the business world, to describe movement leaders.

18. Much of the sociological literature on movements in the 1970s and 1980s constitutes a response to a theory that was never intended to apply to movements – but to interest groups. It is surprising that scholars of movements have not asked more often, if the fundamental elements of the theory applied to their subject. The use of an interest-group-derived theory may help to explain why so many of McCarthy and Zald's SMOs were groups that many would consider not as movements, but as public interest groups. This was the heart of many European scholars' critiques of the theory. Students interested in this debate should see Herbert Kitschelt's "Resource Mobilization Theory: A Critique," and Zald's response, both in Dieter Rucht, ed., *Research on Social Movements.*

19. They do not apply "theoretically" because they do not apply to the logic and resources of social movements, even though one or more of them may apply to particular movement organizations.

20. Some have argued that nonmaterial incentives can be accommodated to Olson's theory. But as Fireman and Gamson argue, expanding the concept of selective incentives to include moral satisfaction reduces the concept to a tautology. "To follow this tautological route is to remove the cutting edge from the selective incentive argument," they write, "as the weight of explanation is carried by the subsequent distinctions among incentives." See their "Utilitarian Logic in the Resource Mobilization Perspective," pp. 19–20.

21. Even when the motives of the subjects of collective action are economic, they may be very different from the calculations of gain and loss that Olson imposed on collective action. Olson conceived of the decision to take collective action as a calculation of the cost incurred in an action, set against the gain to be won from it. But people in conflictual situations often see themselves in a structural situation of *risk* – and not one of gain. The harvest may have failed and rapacious moneylenders are after their land; the economy is in the doldrums and unemployment looms; or, unregulated growth belches out pollution and the environment is threatened: Such situations are more likely to produce a psychology of action than calculations of marginal utility. See Jeffrey Berejikian's article, "Revolutionary Collective Action and the Agent-Structure Problem."

22. As Fireman and Gamson write of an antiwar protest in the 1960s, "When three hundred thousand antiwar demonstrators turned out for a march on Washington during the sixties, they were not hamstrung by the existence of millions of free riders – people who wanted the demonstration to be big and effective but didn't show up" (1979: 16ff.). Although he begins from the postulate that there is "power in numbers," political scientist James De Nardo relaxes this narrow assumption almost immediately. See his *Power in Numbers,* pp. 36ff., where tactics immediately join numbers as indicators of the disruptiveness of a movement.

23. "They are made up of lots of smaller collective units, each acting autonomously in accord with their own internal logic," writes sociologist Pam Oliver, in her "Bringing the Crowd Back In," p. 4. Different parts of a movement interact with one another, with allies and supportive institutions and with opponents and authorities. "All these different kinds of actions affected one another," writes Oliver of the movements of the 1960s, "and it was these *interactions* that created the social movement" (p. 3).

24. *Washington Post,* April 26, 1993, pp. 8–10.

25. The *locus classicus* of transaction cost economics is Ronald Coase's "The Problem

of Social Cost." It is elaborated and extended into institutional economics by Oliver E. Williamson's *Markets and Hierarchies: Analysis and Antitrust Implications;* and in modified form in his *The Economic Institutions of Capitalism,* ch. 1. The integrative thrust of the transaction cost perspective is found in chs. 4 and 5 of *The Economic Institutions.*

26. Needless to say, a movement in formation is unlikely to be able to engage in what Hardin calls "cooperative behavior that involves precise or complex understanding of alternative ends or means to group ends." See his *Collective Action,* p. 182. But this does not mean that such groups cannot cooperate, because knowledge of ways of acting collectively does not need to be specific to particular situations. With sufficient repetition and occasional success, people learn what kinds of collective action they can mount, which ones will succeed and which are likely to trigger the wrath of the forces of order.

27. The concept first appears in Tilly's *From Mobilization to Revolution,* ch. 6; again in his "Acting Collectively without Elections, Surveys or Social Movements," and then in his *The Contentious French,* ch. 1. Chapter 2 will take up the theory in more detail and offer an important modification.

28. As we shall see in later chapters, Agulhon's *The Republic in the Village,* and Margadant's *French Peasants in Revolt,* provide evidence that the social circles of southern French villages were instrumental in the Revolution of 1848 and in the 1851 insurrection that followed.

29. In social dilemma situations, they argue in their article "Not Me or Thee But We" that, "people immediately start discussing what 'we' should do, and spend a great deal of time and effort to persuade others in their own group to cooperate (or defect!), even in situations where these others' behavior is irrelevant to the speaker's own payoffs" (p. 94).

30. Hardin hints at this when he points out that "a convention covering the behavior of a very large class of people, none of whom interacts personally with more than a fraction of the class, can be built up out of smaller subgroup interactions in a large class of situations," *Collective Action,* p. 186.

31. For Marwell and Oliver, it is the heterogeneity of resources that is the key. As they put it:

> If a group is heterogeneous enough that it contains a critical mass who can make large contributions, and if those members are socially connected to one another so that they can act in concert, collective action for jointly supplied collective goods *is* possible and *more* likely in larger groups. (*The Critical Mass,* p. 54)

32. In studying two demonstrations in Berlin in the 1980s, Jurgen Gerhards and Dieter Rucht found that no fewer than 140 groups took part in one, and 133 in the other. See their article, "Mesomobilization: Organizing and Framing in Two Protest Campaigns," Table 1.

33. Some of the main sources are collected in Bert Klandermans, Hanspeter Kriesi, and Sidney Tarrow, eds., *From Structure to Action;* and in Aldon Morris and Carol Mueller, eds., *Frontiers of Social Movement Research.* For an ingenious use of frame analysis to examine the ideas of ordinary American citizens, see William Gamson's *Talking Politics.*

34. As elsewhere in this book, readers will recognize my debt to Charles Tilly, whose difficult but essential book, *From Mobilization to Revolution,* was the origin of much of the thinking represented here.

2: MODULAR COLLECTIVE ACTION

1. An earlier version of parts of this chapter was published as "Modular Collective Action and the Rise of the Social Movement: Why the French Revolution Was Not Enough," in *Politics and Society* 21:69–90.
2. Tilly's contributions to the field of collective action and social movements are so massive as to make them difficult to summarize. For an exhaustive bibliography, see "Selected papers, 1963–1991, From the Study of Social Change and Collective Action," by Charles Tilly. For a brief bibliography and critical analysis, see Sewell, "Collective Violence and Collective Loyalties in France: Why the French Revolution Made a Difference," in *Politics and Society* 18, no. 4 (1990):527–52.
3. The concept was not new to Tilly's work. In his 1978 text, *From Mobilization to Revolution,* p. 151, he wrote:

   At any point in time, the repertoire of collective actions available to a population is surprisingly limited. Surprisingly, given the innumerable ways in which people could, in principle, deploy their resources in pursuit of common ends. Surprisingly, given the many ways real groups have pursued their own common ends at one time or another.

4. In Tilly's more recent article, "Contentious Repertoires in Great Britain," in *Social Science History,* p. 272, he adds the concept of modularity to the national and autonomous sets of popular contention that became predominant during the nineteenth century.
5. Tilly's wording in "Social Movements and National Politics" is:

   A social movement is a sustained series of interactions between power holders and persons successfully claiming to speak on behalf of a constituency lacking formal representation, in the course of which those persons make publicly visible demands for changes in the distribution or exercise of power, and back those demands with public demonstrations of support. (p. 306)

6. "Because similar groups generally have similar repertoires," writes Tilly, "we can speak more loosely of a general repertoire that is available for contention to the population of a time and place." *The Contentious French,* p. 2.
7. The trials, including the one summarized here, have been most thoroughly studied by Hans-Jürgen Lusebrink, in his *Kriminalität und Literatur im Frankreich des 18. Jahrhunderts,* and in his "L'imaginaire social et ses focalisations en France et en Allemagne à la fin du XVIII siècle." The importance of corruption, and especially of popular belief in corruption, may turn out to be a constant in the overthrow of authoritarian regimes, as we saw during the first months of the overthrow of state socialism in Eastern Europe and the former Soviet Union.
8. Lusebrink, "L'imaginaire sociale," pp. 375–6.
9. *Recollections: The French Revolution of 1848,* p. 39. I am grateful to Mauro Calise for underscoring the importance of this passage.
10. Pathbreaking work on the barricades is in progress by Marc Traugott who is investigating their evolution and changing functions. See his article "Barricades as Repertoire: Continuities and Discontinuities Across Nineteenth Century France." I am grateful to Traugott for his helpful comments on an earlier version of this section.
11. In his "Speaking Your Mind Without Elections," Tilly describes the "sacking routine" as common in the eighteenth century, observing that it was frequently used to punish tavern or brothel keepers who cheated their customers, or public officials who had passed the bounds of legitimacy. Its use to punish a venal householder who had abused a servant seems to have been an innovation of the prerevolutionary period. It continues to appear throughout the French Revolution, most dramatically in the Reveillon riots of May 1789. On the latter, see Simon Schama's vivid reconstruction in *Citizens: A Chronicle of the French Revolution,* pp. 326–32.

12. For example, Jacques Godechot, in his inventory of the revolutions of 1848, lists at least nine different claims in which barricades were used in the French revolution of 1848. See Godechot's *Les Révolutions de 1848.* The analysis of how the barricade was used in 1848 is reported in Sarah Soule and Sidney Tarrow, "Acting Collectively, 1847–49: How the Repertoire of Collective Action Changed and Where It Happened."

13. But note that in Tilly's "Food Supply and Public Order in Modern Europe," he writes that "conflicts over the food supply became more widespread and virulent toward the end [of the period 1500–1800], despite the fact that the productivity of agriculture was increasing, the threat of death-dealing famine dwindling" (p. 385).

14. The following paragraphs are based on Tilly's "Food Supply and Public Order in Modern Europe," and on Steven Lawrence Kaplan, *Provisioning Paris.*

15. Natalie Davis, in her "The Rites of Violence," has given us the most vivid evocation of the brutally mimetic qualities of early modern religious conflicts in France.

16. For examples of the reevocation of these historical memories in peasant land seizures in Southern Europe, see Eric Hobsbawm, *Primitive Rebels and Social Bandits;* Julian Pitt-Rivers, *People of the Sierra;* and Sidney Tarrow, *Peasant Communism in Southern Italy.* For similar reenactments in Latin America, see Hobsbawm's "Peasant Land Occupations."

17. Focusing on the protests of agricultural laborers in England, Andrew Charlesworth, in *An Atlas of Rural Protest in Britain,* finds that it was only by the agrarian revolt of 1816 that "men from many different occupations over the whole of a rural area made common cause by each responding to the protests and demonstrations of their fellow workers" (p. 146).

18. Note that the practice existed long before the term "boycott," the colonists using the term "nonimportation." The modern terminology dates only from 1880, when the practice was used against a certain Captain Boycott in the Irish land controversies. It quickly spread across the West, as indicated by the French term *boycotter.*

19. Indeed, it was only to enforce a general boycott that was succeeding elsewhere that a coalition of Boston merchants and publicists employed the older routine of destroying imported tea. See Richard D. Brown, *Revolutionary Politics in Massachusetts.*

20. I am grateful to Seymour Drescher for his comments on an earlier version of the following section. It is based largely on his *Capitalism and Antislavery.* Also see Drescher's articles, "Public Opinion and the Destruction of British Colonial Slavery," and "British Way, French Way: Opinion Building and Revolution in the Second French Slave Emancipation."

21. In fact, when the first great petition against colonial slavery was circulated in 1788, a representative of the Jamaican lobby was incredulous. The abolitionists had neither been injured by slavery, nor would they benefit personally from its abolition: What right had they, he complained, to petition for its abolition. Ibid., pp. 76–7.

22. See Dorothy Thompson, *The Chartists,* ch. 3, on the use of the mass petition by the Chartists. On the unsuccessful Kennington Common demonstration, see Raymond Postgate, *The Story of a Year: 1848,* p. 117.

23. Petitions never gained the success on the continent that they had in Britain – although the British model was crucial in the formation of European antislavery campaigns. The French movement was, at once, more elitist and less effective, and the first use of mass petitions came from a working class newspaper, *L'Union,* in 1844. The method was taken up by more mainstream opinion and a second and a third petition followed in 1846–7. See Drescher's "British Way, French Way," pp. 719–21. "The explicit model for French extraparliamentary mobilization," according to Drescher, "was the 'genius' of British petitioning" (p. 719).

24. The events leading up to the Day of the Tiles, and why it brought together so broad a coalition, are summarized by Schama in *Citizens*, 272–87. The reactions of the provincial aristocrats and parliaments to the edicts are summarized by Jean Egret in *The French Pre-Revolution, 1787–88*, pp. 170–7.
25. See the discussion by Traugott in his "Barricades as Repertoire," pp. 309–23. Also see his "Neighborhoods in Insurrection: The Parisian Quartier in the February Revolution of 1848." It is not clear how much use was made of barricades during the French Revolution. Hobsbawm is the source of the opinion that it was never used at all. See his *The Age of Revolution: 1789–1848*, p. 146.
26. In a letter of 21 April 1848 to his librettist, Piave, quoted in Open University, *Music and Revolution: Verdi*, 1976, p. 42.

3: PRINT, ASSOCIATION, AND THE DIFFUSION OF MOVEMENT

1. Antoine de Baecque analyzes the political pornographic pamphlet from 1787 on, in his "Pamphlets: Libel and Political Mythology" in Darnton and Roche, eds., *Revolution in Print*. Also see the description of "Body Politics" in Schama's *Citizens*, pp. 203–27, and the libels of Marie-Antoinette that he refers to. Schama writes: "It was her [Marie-Antoinette's] transformation in France to the 'Austrian whore' . . . that damaged the legitimacy of the monarchy to an incalculable degree" (p. 205). Lynn Hunt, in her *Family Romance of the French Revolution*, takes the subject up in exhaustive detail.
2. "The Americans," writes historian Gordon Wood in *The Radicalism of the American Revolution*, "did not have to invent republicanism in 1776; they had only to bring it to the surface" (p. 109).
3. I am grateful to Pauline Maier for her comments on an earlier version of the following section. Her book *From Resistance to Revolution* remains the definitive source on the commercial protests of the 1760s and their evolution into the patriot movement. Also see her article, "Popular Uprisings and Civil Authority in Eighteenth Century America" *William and Mary Quarterly* 27:3–35.
4. The breadth of the opposition was symbolized in a report by Governor Bernard. During the last week of October, he reported, "two Gentlemen, called the richest Merchants in this Town, entertained the leaders of the North and South End mobs to 'establish and confirm' an alliance first effected on August 4". Quoted in Maier, *From Resistance to Revolution*, p. 69.
5. The first deliberately constructed example of an association to resist a duty seems to have been the naming of a committee by Philadelphia's merchants in 1764 to oppose the recently revitalized Molasses Act of 1733. See Richard Ryerson, *The Revolution is Now Begun*, Ch. 2.
6. The title of this section is the same as that of the excellent collection edited by Robert Darnton and Daniel Roche on the role of the press in France before and during the revolutionary period. I am also grateful to Benedict Anderson's *Imagined Communities: Reflections on the Origin and Spread of Nationalism*, ch. 3, for the origin of some of the ideas taken up in this section.
7. See the collection edited by Jack Goody, *Literacy in Traditional Societies*, for a good introduction to the subject. Lawrence Stone's "Literacy and Education in England, 1640–1900," Kenneth Lockridge's *Literacy in Colonial New England*, and Roger Chartier's *The Cultural Uses of Print in Early Modern France*, have added to the same debate, respectively, for England, the American colonies and France. Alvin Gouldner, in his "Prologue to a Theory of Revolutionary Intellectuals," goes furthest in linking literacy to rebellion by arguing that modern radicalism is centrally rooted in written modes of discourse.

8. Even the forms of rebellion that appeared in the French Revolution varied with the presence or absence of literacy. For example, in his article "Literacy and Revolt," John Markoff found that rural collective action in different regions varied with the strength or weakness of a primitive indicator of literacy. However, it may not have been literacy itself, but a number of its social structural correlates that produced these cross-regional differences in rural rebellion, as Markoff's analysis indicates.

9. Readers will note the use of the term "invisible" in place of Anderson's "imagined" communities. The distinction is intentional; though Anderson is guided by a stalwart structuralism, his evocative term "imagined" communities could lead unwary readers to the implication that the imagination "made" national communities, and that structures of interest played no role in the process. The coalition of merchants and shippers who launched the stamp boycott in 1765 might not have recognized themselves as "Americans," but might have been surprised to learn that their ties were imagined.

10. Paine's political ideas were not particularly extreme, although he would die an outcast in the country he helped to liberate. He was, as Hobsbawm notes, "the only member of the French Convention who fought openly against the death sentence on Louis XVI." See Hobsbawm's *Labouring Men,* pp. 1–4. For an evocative and penetrating treatment of Paine's importance, see Isaac Kramnick, *Republicanism and Bourgeois Radicalism.*

11. Hobsbawm, *Labouring Men,* p. 2. Paine's language resembled that of the Bible much more than that of the more learned essayists who penned political pamphlets up until his time. For example, he used biblical parallels to convince his Bible-reading public that kingship causes wars and that, for the ancient Hebrews, "it was held sinful to acknowledge any being under that title but the Lord of Hosts." *Common Sense,* Kuklick, ed., pp. 8–9.

12. Bailyn reports that there were thirty-eight American newspapers in 1775, "crowded with columns of arguments and counter-arguments appearing as letters, official documents, extracts of speeches, and sermons." Broadsides appeared everywhere, and even almanacs "carried, in odd corners and occasional columns, a considerable freight of political comment. Above all, there were pamphlets." See his *Ideological Origins of the American Revolution,* pp. 1–2.

13. The same was soon true back in Britain; when the reaction began against the French Revolution in 1792, repressing Paine's *Rights of Man,* Part II, and his *Address to the Addressers,* was one of the first tasks that the magistrates set themselves. See Albert Goodwin's *The Friends of Liberty,* ch. 8.

14. See Elizabeth Eisenstein's "Revolution and the Printed Word," p. 195. For a history of book production and reading between the sixteenth and eighteenth centuries in France, see Roger Chartier's *The Cultural Uses of Print in Early Modern France.* Robert Darnton's work is required reading for understanding the importance of prohibited books and pamphlets leading up to the French Revolution. See his *The Business of Enlightenment* and *The Literary Underground of the Old Regime.*

15. Quoted in Darnton's "Philosophy under the Cloak," in his and Daniel Roche's *Revolution in Print,* p. 31. Note that the term "philosophical works" was a code name for a wide range of censored subjects ranging from pure philosophy through political tracts to more or less pure pornography.

16. Most of these vehicles were radical in political coloration, although a few were Christian. At first sold unstamped and distributed mainly hand-to-hand in London, they quickly spread to the provinces. See Patricia Hollis, *The Pauper Press,* for estimates of their circulation. For a comparative treatment of the working class press in the early nineteenth century, see Jacques Godechot, ed., *La Presse Ouvrière.*

17. The 1848 figure for Paris is from Godechot, *Les Révolutions de 1848.* For the

developments of a working class press in Germany and Italy in 1848, see Godechot, et al., *La Presse Ouvrière*. On the explosion of new journals in Florence, see Clementina Rotondi, *Bibliografia dei periodici toscani, 1847–1852*.

18. The major published sources, in addition to Maier's *From Resistance to Revolution*, are Richard Ryerson, *The Revolution Is Now Begun* for Philadelphia, Edward Countryman, *A People in Revolution* for New York, Richard D. Brown, *Revolutionary Politics in Massachusetts* for Boston and its hinterland and Richard W. Walsh, *Charleston's Sons of Liberty* for the South Carolina city.

19. As Richard D. Brown, in his *Knowledge Is Power*, writes:

> The diffusion of information regarding the Battles of Lexington and Concord was at once contagious, spreading spontaneously from person-to-person and place-to-place, and pre-arranged and channeled through patriot networks. As a result, word of the bloody conflict moved with a rapidity, social penetration, and territorial reach never before witnessed in colonial America. (p. 247)

20. For example, Johnson shows how the sabbatarian movement in Rochester was organized by an organization of Protestant laymen from several local churches. See his *Shopkeeper's Millenium*, p. 109.

21. For some typical patterns of diffusion, see Donald G. Mathews, "The Second Great Awakening as an Organizing Process, 1780–1830." On the role of religion in producing movements for civic morality, see Clifford S. Griffin, *Their Brother's Keeper*, Ian R. Tyrrell, *Sobering Up* and Ronald G. Walters, *American Reformers, 1815–1830*. The relationship between religion and antislavery is dealt with by Walters' *The Antislavery Appeal*. A study which emphasizes class, gender and political – as well as the religious – origins of abolitionism is Herbert Aptheker's *Abolitionism: A Revolutionary Movement*.

22. For example, Hobsbawm and Rudé report a number of cases in which networks of Swing agitators were organized along family lines. See *Captain Swing*, pp. 205–6.

23. See Eisenstein's "Revolution and the Printed Word," p. 197. Also see Darnton's *The Literary Underground of the Old Regime* and Jack R. Censer and Jeremy Popkin, eds., *Press and Politics in Pre-Revolutionary France*.

24. Georges Lefebvre, *The Coming of the French Revolution*, p. 54. At the same time, an amnesty was granted to booksellers and merchants who had been arrested for distributing tracts critical of the government, as Eisenstein points out in her "Revolution and the Printed Word," p. 199.

25. Craig Calhoun calls these movements "populist," arguing that "they were . . . deeply rooted in many cases in traditional communities of both craft and locality. They acted on this social basis, not on the wider one of class; they thought in these terms, not in the rationalistic ones of class exploitation." See his *The Question of Class Conflict*, p. xi.

26. As two contemporary sociologists, Gerald Marwell and Pam Oliver, put it, heterogeneity produces collective action as a result of the *interdependence* between better-endowed individuals and their less well endowed followers. See their *The Critical Mass*, ch. 4. For a historical example that supports their theory, see Chapter 8 of this study.

4: STATES AND SOCIAL MOVEMENTS

1. Some of the material in this chapter was first presented at the conference on European/American Perspectives on Social Movements, held at the Catholic University in Washington D.C., on August 13–15, 1992. I am grateful to Craig Jenkins and Doug McAdam for comments on that paper.

2. This is not to say that national state building only began in the nineteenth century, but that consolidation implying the creation of national citizenship dates from that period. For example, even in France, arguably the most centralized Old Regime state, rule was indirect until after the Revolution, and the concept of citizenship dates only from the decades just before the Revolution. On the imbrication between state consolidation and citizenship in France, see Simon Schama's *Citizens*, Part One. On the general relation between state consolidation and citizenship, see Charles Tilly, *Coercion, Capital, and European States*, ch. 4.

3. For exceptions, see Tilly's *The Contentious French* and *Coercion, Capital, and European States*. The crossnational persuasion is best reflected in the social movement field in Herbert Kitschelt's article, "Political Opportunity Structure and Political Protest."

4. Alexis de Tocqueville, *Recollections*, pp. 61–8. Tocqueville's most literal interpreter is Michel Crozier, who adumbrates the strong thesis of centralization and disorder into the language of modern organizational sociology. See Crozier's *The Bureaucratic Phenomenon*, especially ch. 8. Also see Stanley Hoffmann's essay, "The Ruled," pp. 111–44, on how state centralization and civil society atomization have produced a characteristic French style of protest behavior.

5. Samuel Finer reports that, whereas the number of French troops used against Spain in 1635 was 155,000, Napoleon mustered 700,000 for the Russian campaign in 1812. And whereas the Prussians assembled 160,000 men for the Seven Years' War, as many as 300,000 were recruited in 1814. For England, the numbers were always smaller, but growth was proportional: from the 75,000 troops assembled in 1712 to the 250,000 called up at the peak of the Napoleonic campaigns. See Finer's "State- and Nation-Building in Europe: The Role of the Military," p. 101.

6. Finer notes that "as late as the third quarter of the eighteenth century, from one-half to one-third of the troops of any state would have been foreigners. See his "State- and Nation-Building," pp. 101–2.

7. In fact, the early use of the term "public" refers not to spontaneous movements of opinion, but to the extra-parliamentary followings of parliamentary groups. Donald Read (1964: 288) dates one of the first uses of the term to Burke during the Wilkes crisis, who wrote to Rockingham; "If we mean to get *redress*, we must strengthen the hands of the minority within Doors by the accession of the publick opinion." According to Brewer's *Party Ideology and Popular Politics at the Accession of George III*, p. 13, when Rockingham used the term "the Publick," he appears to have meant the parliamentary classes.

8. The provincial administrator was Bertier de Sauvigny, whose unpublished manuscript from the Bibliothèque National, "Observations sur le commerce des grains" is quoted by Steven Lawrence Kaplan in his *Provisioning Paris*, p. 23.

9. Primary responsibility for assuring the capital's food supply was divided among a number of agencies and inspectors. National power was vested in the *lieutenance générale de police*, which maintained a large staff for this purpose. But it contested the "police" of food with the Parlement of Paris, with its Procurator General and with the *prévôt des marchands* on behalf of the municipality, in a continuing tug-of-war that reflected as much the struggle of state-builders to gain ascendancy against defenders of local privilege, as it did the fear of famine. See Kaplan's *Provisioning Paris*, pp. 36–7, for the architecture of food regulation in Paris.

10. According to Gabriel Ardant, in his essay "Financial Policy and Economic Infrastructure of Modern States and Nations," pp. 202–3, between 1736 and 1738, English domestic revenues, on average, came from: land, 17.5%; windows, annuities and functions, 2.4%; customs, 24.6%; excise, 52.8%; and stamps, 2.6%.

11. For example, New York's expenses were met from an import duty, an excise on

various commodities and a license fee paid by hawkers and peddlers. As in England, land was taxed only in times of war, leaving large landholders bearing a slim portion of the colonies' expenses, with cities like New York and Albany bearing disproportionate amounts of the tax. See Edward Countryman's *A People in Revolution,* p. 83, for New York's revenue structure.

12. For example, in New York, writes Countryman,

> the Sugar Act, the Stamp Act, and the Townshend Acts all threatened the assembly's control over provincial finance. The revamping of the customs service introduced an alien bureaucracy, and the stationing of British troops was intended to give that bureaucracy the strength to enforce its will. (*A People in Revolution,* p. 85)

13. Of the many preliminary reports of Tilly's Great Britain Study, the most directly related to the findings summarized here are his "Britain Creates the Social Movement," "Speaking Your Mind Without Elections, Surveys, or Social Movements," "How to Detect, Describe, and Explain Repertoires of Contention" and "Contentious Repertoires in Britain, 1758–1834." The methodology of the study is briefly presented in Robert A. Schweitzer and Charles Tilly, "A Study of Contentious Gatherings in Early Nineteenth-Century Great Britain."

14. The sequence is actually more complicated, but no less interesting. Peel, who had served the government in Ireland before becoming Prime Minister, created the predecessors of the bobbies there under the far more trying circumstances of colonial government. Like the Indian civil service whose lessons were later transferred to Britain, the colonies were an experimenting ground for later metropolitan innovations in state-building.

15. On this development, see Roger Geary, *Policing Industrial Disputes, 1893–1895* and Jane Morgan, *Conflict and Order: The Police and Labor Disputes in England and Wales.*

16. On the connection between periods of prolonged political turbulence and social violence, see David Bayley's "The Police and Political Development in Europe" pp. 356 ff). Bayley cautions that "if domestic turmoil did play a role in the formation of the 'new police,' it did so in a way that must surprise and confound most social historians" (p. 357).

5: SEIZING AND MAKING OPPORTUNITIES

1. Parts of this chapter were first published in different form in an earlier monograph, *Struggle, Politics and Reform,* ch. 2, and in a more recent version in an article, "Kollectives Handeln und Politische Gelegenheitsstruktur in Mobilisierungswellen: Theoretische Perspektiven" in the *Kölner Zeitschrift fur Soziologie und Sozialpsychologie.*

2. The idea that people in crowds were dangerous may have grown out of Europe's early encounter with revolution and industrialization, as Louis Chevalier argues in his *Laboring Classes and Dangerous Classes in Paris,* part 2, ch. 1. The classical sources are Gabriel Tarde, *L'opinion et la foule,* and Gustave Le Bon, *The Crowd.* For a more social scientific approach to crowds, see Elias Canetti, *Crowds and Power.* For a sympathetic and systematic approach to the "deprivation" hypothesis, but one which specifies it as "relative" deprivation, see Ted Gurr's *Why Men Rebel.* For a less sympathetic view, see Rod Aya's *Rethinking Revolutions and Collective Violence.* James Rule provides an elegant exegesis and criticism of collective behavior theory in his *Theories of Civil Violence,* ch. 3.

3. The "end of ideology" school was most notably represented in the work of Daniel

Bell, in *The End of Ideology,* by Otto Kirchheimer, in "The Waning of Opposition in Parliamentary Regimes," and by S. M. Lipset in "The Changing Class Structure in Contemporary European Politics." It is one of the ironies of intellectual history that much of this work was popularized just as the West was about to explode in a new cycle of collective action. But there were dissenters: A 1966 essay that has kept its timeliness is Joseph LaPalombara's "The Decline of Ideology: A Dissent and an Interpretation."

4. The most repeated proposition of this insight is the work of Ronald Inglehart: first in his *The Silent Revolution,* and then in a series of articles culminating in *Culture Shift in Advanced Industrial Society.* But the work of Samuel Barnes, Max Kaase and their collaborators, in *Political Action,* is equally important and makes a more direct connection between individual attributes and orientations to collective action.

5. The most accessible source for the contributions of this school are the essays published in *Social Research* in 1985, especially those of Jean Cohen and Claus Offe. Also see Alberto Melucci's seminal article, "The New Social Movements: A Theoretical Approach." A comparative survey and a basic bibliography of sources up to 1988 will be found in Klandermans' and Tarrow's essay, "Mobilization into Social Movements: Synthesizing European and American Approaches." For skeptical assessments of the more global claims of the new social movement school, see Craig Calhoun's "New Social Movements of the Nineteenth Century," and Tarrow, *Struggle, Politics and Reform,* ch. 4.

6. The bifurcation was not a simple geographic one, as much as a derivation from European or American models. For example, European scholars like Bert Klandermans began from a social–psychological perspective that was much closer to resource mobilization, whereas American authors like Frances Piven and Richard Cloward and Charles Tilly showed a "European-like" preference for structural models.

7. Readers who have followed international debates on the relations between American and European approaches will recognize the approach taken here as the one put forward in Bert Klandermans' and my essay, "Mobilization into Social Movements: Synthesizing European and American Approaches."

8. But note that Roberta Ash Garner and Mayer Zald broadened their resource mobilization approach in the 1980s to include explicitly political variables. See their "The Political Economy of Social Movement Sectors." Conversely, Herbert Kitschelt shifted from a "new social movement" perspective to examine institutional variables and compare four different countries in his "Political Opportunity Structures and Political Protest." In a more recent essay, "Reflections on the Institutional Self-Transformation of Movement Politics: A Tentative Stage Model," new social movement theorist Claus Offe stepped back from proclaiming the absolute newness of the new movements to a more dynamic approach that resembles the traditional idea that movements follow a "career" – from emergence to institutionalization.

9. For an analysis of the period of institutionalization and decline of the new social movements in four European countries, see Hanspeter Kriesi, "The Political Opportunity Structure of New Social Movements," Kriesi, Koopmans, Duyvendak and Giugni, "New Social Movements and Political Opportunities in Western Europe," and Koopmans' "The Dynamics of Protest Waves."

10. There is a long and somewhat technical literature on the relations between economic conditions and strikes. The most thorough summary and assessment is found in John Kennan's "The Economics of Strikes," in Orley Ashenfelter and Richard Layard, eds., *Handbook of Labor Economics.*

11. The most synthetic interpretation of the economic sources of the wage explosions of

the late 1960s is David Soskice, "Strike Waves and Wage Explosions, 1968–1970: An Economic Interpretation," in Crouch and Pizzorno, eds., *The Resurgence of Class Conflict in Western Europe Since 1968,* vol. 2.

12. Silver's measure is a three-year moving average of the "index of acuteness" that she calculates from the newspaper data that she analyzed as part of the research of the World Labor Research Working Group at the Fernand Braudel Center at SUNY, Binghamton. This represents the number of mentions of labor unrest worldwide per year. For details of the scale, see Appendix E of her "Labor Unrest and Capital Accumulation."

13. The ultimate – but not always recognized – source of political opportunity theory was Charles Tilly's *From Mobilization to Revolution,* ch. 4. Also see his and David Snyder's article "Hardship and Collective Violence" above. Explicit building blocks in the United States were Doug McAdam, *The Political Process and the Development of Black Insurgency,* Anne Costain, *Inviting Women's Rebellion,* Suzanne Staggenborg, *The Pro-Choice Movement,* and David Meyer, *A Winter of Discontent: The Nuclear Freeze and American Politics.* For Western Europe, see Hanspeter Kriesi, "The Political Opportunity Structure of New Social Movements: Its Impact on Their Mobilization," Kriesi, et al., "New Social Movements and Political Opportunities in Western Europe," and Dieter Rucht, "The Impact of National Contexts on Social Movement Structures," and Sidney Tarrow, *Democracy and Disorder.* Explicitly comparative use of the concept was made by Charles Brockett, "The Structure of Political Opportunities and Peasant Mobilization in Central America," by Mary Katzenstein and Carol Mueller in their edited volume, *The Women's Movements of the United States and Western Europe;* by Herbert Kitschelt in his "Political Opportunity Structures and Political Protest."

14. Other researchers, working along similar lines, emphasize somewhat different elements of opportunity. See McAdam, *Political Process and the Development of Black Insurgency,* ch. 3, Kriesi, "The Political Opportunity Structure of the New Social Movements," and Rucht, "The Impact of National Contexts on Social Movement Structures: A Cross-Movement and Cross-National Comparison."

15. The whole revolutionary decade was punctuated by a series of *journées* each time a faction of the leadership needed popular support against one of its enemies. The image of the revolutionary decade as a rolling series of opening and closing opportunities, as first one group and then another tried to take advantage of popular rebellion, is most simply conveyed in Alfred Cobban's *History of Modern France,* vol. 1, and most exquisitely portrayed by Simon Schama in his *Citizens.*

16. Eisinger's claim was based on more than a Tocquevillian hunch. Operationalizing opportunity structure in American cities through the differences in the formal and informal political structures of local government, he studied the behavior of urban protest groups in a sample of fifty-three cities during the turbulent 1960s. He found that the level of activism of these groups was highest not where access was either open or closed, but at intermediate levels of political opportunity.

17. Realignment was also relevant to variations in the local implementation and impact of federal programs for minority hiring in different California cities, as Rufus Browning and his collaborators point out in their *Protest Is Not Enough,* p. 252. I am grateful to Jeremy Hein for pointing me to this finding.

18. In their essay, "The Framing of Political Opportunity," William Gamson and David Meyer distinguish "stable" from "volatile" opportunities. Hanspeter Kriesi, in his "Political Opportunity Structure," focuses on the party system as a stable element of opportunity. Herbert Kitschelt, in "Political Opportunities and Political Protest," analyzes national differences in state structure. Eisinger, in "The Conditions of

Protest Behavior,'' and and Meyer, in ''Institutionalizing Dissent,'' focus on elements of the American system that structure collective action.

19. The major published source is Peter Evans, Dietrich Reuschmeyer and Theda Skocpol, eds., *Bringing the State Back In*. Though its link to the statist literature is unacknowledged, Kitschelt's ''Political Opportunity Structures and Political Protest'' is a fundamentally statist analysis of the impact of different state configurations on the environmental movement. Also see Richard Vallely's work on the two American reconstructions, ''Party, Coercion and Inclusion,'' which compares American state structures and party systems over time.

20. For example, Herbert Kitschelt traces differences in the environmental movements of France, Germany, Sweden and the United States to such institutional differences in state structure. See his article, ''Political Opportunity Structure and the Political Process.''

21. On the French educational reform, see the summary in Chapter 10 of this study; for a comparison of France's strong economic policy response to the events of May, compared to Italy's ineffective one, see Michele Salvati, ''May 1968 and the Hot Autumn of 1969: The Response of Two Ruling Classes.''

22. Even within ''strong parties,'' we find such a difference. The resistence of the French Communist Party to the legitimacy of women's issues is an example of the first outcome as shown in Jane Jenson and George Ross, *The View from Inside*, while the permeability of the Italian communists to feminism is an example of the second in Stephen Hellman's ''Feminism and the Model of Militancy in Italy.''

23. See Open University, *Music and Revolution: Verdi*. On rock music as an expression of dissent in the Soviet Union before 1989, see Sabrina Ramet's *The Soviet Rock Scene*. Rock began to play a similar role in authoritarian Indonesia during the 1980s.

24. This was not dissimilar to the situation of the Communist parties of Western Europe, which had, for all intents and purposes, accepted the rules of the game of parliamentary politics long before the power of international communism began to unravel. For studies of French and Italian communism that produced evidence of this as early as the 1960s, see the research collected in Blackmer and Tarrow, eds., *Communism in Italy and France*.

25. See his ''Towards the Critique of Hegel's Philosophy of Law: Introduction,'' in Easton and Guddat, *Writings of the Young Marx on Religion and Philosophy*, pp. 262–3.

26. On the suppression of the English radical movement after 1793, see Albert Goodwin's *The Friends of Liberty*, chs. 9–12. On the effect of the Combination laws on the antislavery movement, see Seymour Drescher's ''Public Opinion and the Destruction of British Slavery,'' p. 26.

27. Susanne Lohmann points to the extraordinary proportion of the East German population that appeared to be spying on one another for the *STASI*. See her ''The Dynamics of Regime Collapse,'' for estimates of the number of full-time *STASI* employees and part-time informers.

28. See the ongoing research on American demonstration permits by John McCarthy and his collaborators, initially reported in McCarthy, Britt and Wolfson's ''The Institutional Channelling of Social Movements by the State in the United States,'' and in McCarthy, McPhail and Smith's ''The Tip of the Iceberg.''

29. This sequence of Pro-Choice and Pro-Life movements, and their dynamic interaction, deserves a concerted study. For interesting insights, see both Suzanne Staggenborg's *The Pro-Choice Movement*, especially part three, and Jane Mansbridge's *Why We Lost the ERA*.

6: ACTING COLLECTIVELY

1. On the Mölln firebombing, see "Es brennt Heil Hitler," in *Dei Tageszeitung*, Nov. 24, 1992, p. 3.
2. On the Berlin demonstration, see "Ein Radikalenerlass gegen Rechts?, in *Dei Tageszeitung*, December 7, 1992, p. 4.
3. Scott would be quick to agree that such practices are not limited to the countries of the Third World or to subsistence peasants. Anybody who has lived in a village in Southern Italy has experienced similarly poisoned relations and knows the gimmicks that peasants use to trick landlords or middlemen.
4. "I rebel," concludes Camus, "therefore *we* exist." From *The Rebel*, p. 22. The Janus-faced nature of rebellion, for Camus, is, in Susan Tarrow's words, in *Exile From the Kingdom*, "that people developed solidarity with their fellows, but it could not change the structures that cause injustice" (p. 148). The importance of preexisting solidarities in recruitment to activism has been demonstrated by Doug McAdam's book on *Freedom Summer*.
5. However, protracted violence and stalemate can eventually lead to the formation of an antiviolent center – as in the anti-Mafia movement in Sicily. See Jane and Peter Schneider's "From Peasant Wars to Urban Wars: The Antimafia Movement in Palermo."
6. For a more detailed analysis of the strategy of internalization and its mixed outcomes, see Chapter 8 of this study.
7. As late as the 1872 French census, writes Ronald Aminzade, though artisans in both handicraft and industrial production "constituted only 21.9% of the labor force and 29.5% of the working class, handicraft artisans alone accounted for 72% of the strikes during the years from 1830 to 1879" (pp. 77–8).
8. An early example: The English weavers who convened at Spitalfields in 1765 marched to London by three different routes to petition for relief against the importation of French silk. See Gene Sharp's *The Politics of Nonviolent Action*, p. 152, for this and other early examples.
9. Pierre Favre, in *La Manifestation*, defines the demonstration as "a collective movement organized in a public space with the goal of producing a political outcome through the peaceful expression of an opinion or a demand" (p. 5 [Author's trans.]). But note that it was not until later in the nineteenth century that French dictionaries recognized the *manifestation* as a simple noun – long after the practice had become general. Favre distinguishes the demonstration from the assembly, which was static; the procession, which was organized for religious ends; unorganized movements (*attroupements*); and the riot, which used urban space as a battlefield. For this discussion, see Favre's introduction to *La Manifestation*, pp. 14–17.
10. After the 1960s, the District of Columbia police began to offer seminars to organizers on how to mount and control participants in their demonstrations. The permit system used by the National Park Service in Washington is another form of social regulation. On the social control of demonstrations, see John D. McCarthy, David W. Britt, and Mark Wolfson's "The Institutional Channeling of Social Movements by the State in the United States."
11. In her current research, Mansbridge is finding evidence that phrases from the earlier women's movement, such as "male chauvinist," are turning up among the poor white and African American women she has interviewed in Chicago. Mansbridge is cautious in assigning a political valence to the use of such symbols in private life, but her evidence shows that these women employ them in "naming" unwelcome actions from their partners in terms broader than those usually ascribed to nasty

behavior. I am grateful to Professor Mansbridge for allowing me to consult her unpublished paper, "Feminist Identity: Micronegotiation in the Lives of African-American and White Working Class Women."

12. With some stretching of the concept, Gene Sharp, in *The Politics of Nonviolent Action*, finds it as far back as the Roman plebeians who, rather than attack the consuls, withdrew from Rome to a hill later called "the Sacred Mount" (p. 75). He also finds examples of it in the American Revolution, in Hungarian resistance against Austrian rule in the nineteenth century and in the general strike and shutdown of governmental functions that defeated the Kapp putsch in Weimar Germany (pp. 76–80).

13. On the role of "theorization" in the diffusion of innovation, see David Strang and John Meyer's essay, "Institutional Conditions for Diffusion."

14. See Chapter 7, where this argument will be elaborated further.

15. At a town near Amritsar, troops under General Dyer fired on participants in a "hartal" called by Gandhi to protest the extension of the wartime British ban on demonstrations. See V. E. D. Mehta's *Mahatma Gandhi and His Apostles*, pp. 140–1, for this incident, which appeared at the opening of David Attenborough's film, "Gandhi."

16. Here, a movement that rejected much of the cultural and ideological baggage of the New Left adopted the tactic of blocking the entrances of abortion clinics and resisting nonviolently as its militants were being carried off by the police. Its effectiveness was demonstrated by the increasing unwillingness of American doctors or hospitals to perform abortions during the 1980s, and by the shame and guilt induced in women who were forced to go through with unwanted pregnancies. It was only with the murder of a doctor in Florida in 1993 that the states and the federal government began to take more determined action against Operation Rescue. The antiabortion movement still awaits a definitive study. It is dealt with sensitively by Suzanne Staggenborg in her *The Pro-Choice Movement*, Part 3. Some organizational and tactical aspects are analyzed by John McCarthy in his article, "Pro-Life and Pro-Choice Mobilization." The role of Phyllis Schlafly's organization in defeating the American Equal Rights Amendment is intelligently treated by Mansbridge in her *Why We Lost the ERA*.

17. The data in Table 6.1 are calculated from a total population of daily articles reporting on national and local collective action events from Milan's *Corriere della Sera*. In the table, each form of action is expressed as a proportion of the total number of forms of action observed. The following working definitions were employed for the three aggregate types: *conventional* – strikes, marches, public meetings, assemblies, petitions, audiences, leafletting and legal actions; *disruptive* – occupations, obstructions, forced entries, direct actions; *violent* – violent attacks on people or property, clashes with other protestors or police, rampages and random violence.

   For a more detailed discussion of the data and the study, see my *Democracy and Disorder*, ch. 3 and Appendixes A and B.

18. Such was the case for the "armed demonstrations" used by the French Montagnards during the 1851 insurrection against Louis Napoleon's coup d'état. "In taking arms against the government," writes historian Ted Margadant, "they appeared to engage in an intrinsically violent form of collective action. . . . But as an instrument of military force," he continues, "it was hopelessly outclassed by the French army." Henceforth, "the predominant form of collective action in rural confrontations with the state would become the *unarmed* demonstration". See Margadant's *French Peasants in Revolt*, p. 267.

19. The practice of occupying school buildings in Italy in the 1960s was a good

example. It was only when the police, pushed by the authorities, began to roust demonstrators from the schools that the movement – unleashed onto the streets – became violent. For this history, see Tarrow, *Democracy and Disorder,* ch. 6.

20. The inversion dated from July 14, 1789, when the head of the governor of the Bastille was sawn off and carried around Paris by the crowd that filled the streets. "This display of punitive sacrifice," writes Simon Schama, "constituted a kind of revolutionary sacrament." See his *Citizens,* pp. 405–6 for this incident, which set a precedent that was followed after the murder of other Parisian officials.

21. From Franz Kafka, *Parables and Paradoxes,* pp. 92–3.

22. Thus, William Sewell writes in "Collective Violence and Collective Loyalties" that, before the French Revolution, challengers who organized along corporate or communal lines made competitive or reactive challenges to others, while those who organize along associational lines since then tend to make proactive claims. Similarly, sociologist Jeffrey Paige has argued in *Agrarian Revolutions* that different kinds of peasant agriculture produce different forms of collective action. In the same way, students of "new" social movements like the peace, environmental and women's movements have argued that these movements have an affinity for confrontational forms of action.

23. The same was true of the American Civil Rights movement. Doug McAdam determined from a detailed analysis of the movement's actions that each time it approached a crisis in participation or opposition, it raised the threshold of collective action to a new level – always innovating around the margins of the same nonviolent repertoire, but using its tools selectively and creatively to outguess opponents and increase participation. See his article, "Tactical Innovation and the Pace of Insurgency." But for a contrasting view, see Aldon Morris' "Birmingham Confrontation Reconsidered," pp. 621–3.

7: FRAMING COLLECTIVE ACTION

1. I am grateful to Ron Aminzade, Ben Anderson, David Blatt, Stuart Blumin, John Borneman, Lynn Hunt, Mary Katzenstein, David Kertzer, Roman Laba, David Laitin, George Mosse, David Snow, Dan Thomas and Aaron Wildavsky for comments on an earlier version of this chapter. An earlier version was published in *Sisyphus,* under the title "Costumes of Revolt: the Symbolic Politics of Social Movements."

2. Archives Nationales, III Isère 9, Correspondence, 1791–1853, "Adresse du Commissaire du pouvoir exécutif près l'administration centrale du départment de l'Isère. Quoted by Lynn Hunt in her *Politics, Culture, and Class in the French Revolution,* p. 52.

3. In addition to Hunt's work, the most thorough treatment of the festivals of the French Revolution is Mona Ozouf's *Festivals and the French Revolution.* But their importance for the future of mass politics was first signaled by George Mosse whose 1975 book, *The Nationalization of the Masses,* is curiously little cited by "new" cultural historians of France.

4. The cockade and the phrygian cap; the fierce, yet graceful figure of Marianne; the festival of reason designed to stamp out religion: These attempts by the new elite to create a revolutionary myth had gotten out of hand. By the mid-1790s, it was thought to be time to slow things down, and the Directory was quietly allowing religion to return and transforming the enthusiastic republican festivals of the early revolutionary years into stiff ceremonials. "The festivals," writes their premier historian, Mona Ozouf, in *Festivals and the French Revolution,* "became a camou-

flage, a facade plastered onto a gloomy reality that it was their mission to conceal'', (p. 11).

5. So did Mussolini in our century when he remarked that "each revolution created new political forms, new myths and cults; it was necessary now to use old traditions and to adapt them to a new purpose." See George Mosse's *The Nationalization of the Masses*, p. 1.

6. Recent versions of the constructivist perspective are Ron Eyerman and Andrew Jamison's *Social Movements: A Cognitive Approach*, William Gamson's *Talking Politics*, and Bert Klandermans's, "The Social Construction of Protest," in addition to the work by David Snow and his collaborators. Eyerman and Jamison go further than most when, after claiming they wish to transcend partial understandings of social movements (p. 2), they define movements as "forms of cognitive praxis" (pp. 3–4)! For a longer review of this constructivist literature, see my "Mentalities, Political Cultures and Collective Action Frames."

7. For example, when analyzed by region, the data collected by Almond and Verba for Southern Italy showed that most southern Italians shared a culture of apathy, cynicism and lack of involvement in politics. Almond and Verba's findings were correct for the passive attitudes that southern Italians hold towards government. But periodically since 1848, they have risen up in *jacqueries,* strikes, land occupations, organized rebellions and social movements – most recently when Sicilians mounted an anti-Mafia campaign as shown in Schneider and Schneider's "From Peasant Wars to Urban Wars." The symbols of revolt in many of these episodes were remarkably similar – but they differed sharply from the culture of alienation that pervades southern Italian public life and were tapped in *The Civic Culture*. For the classical study of the culture of alienation in Southern Italy, see Edward Banfield, *The Moral Basis of a Backward Society*. For a regional reanalysis of the Italian *Civil Culture* data, see Sidney Tarrow, *Peasant Communism in Southern Italy*, ch. 4.

8. For their most important theoretical contributions, see Snow, Rochford, Worden and Benford, "Frame Alignment Processes," Snow and Benford, "Ideology, Frame Resonance, and Participant Mobilization" and "Master Frames and Cycles of Protest." For the application of the concept to a specific movement, see Robert Benford's "Frame Disputes Within the Disarmament Movement."

9. In their 1986 article, Snow and his collaborators describe four alignment processes through which movements formulate their messages in relation to the existing culture of politics. The first three make only incremental innovations in symbolism. Through "frame bridging," "frame amplification," and "frame extension," movements link existing cultural frames to a particular issue or problem, clarifiy and invigorate a frame that bears on a particular issue, and expand the boundaries of a movement's primary framework to encompass broader interests or points of view (pp. 467–76). The most ambitious strategy, "frame transformation," is important to movements that seek substantial social change. It refers to the redefinition of "activities, events, and biographies that are already meaningful from the standpoint of some primary framework, such that they are now seen by the participants to be quite something else" (p. 474).

10. On this period of Italian communist strategy, see Stephen Hellman's *Italian Communism in Transition*, chs. 5 and 6.

11. I am grateful to Sarah Soule for her help in assembling the materials on which the discussion of media framing is based.

12. Translated by Bob Lumley and quoted in his *States of Emergency*, p. 223.

13. For example, the May Events in France were dutifully reported on government radio, informing people in different parts of the country about marches, strikes and

factory occupations. During the Cold War, BBC and Radio Free Europe played an important role in diffusing information to Eastern Europe, especially after dissidents in those countries learned how to get press releases out to these media sources.
14. This was evident in the Civil Rights movements when, after the first demonstrations in the South, the news media reported only the largest ones or on those that led to violence according to Herbert Gans in *Deciding What's News* p. 169.
15. It is significant that, in August 1980, at the Lenin shipyard gate, above the wooden cross, the portraits of the Pope, a picture of the Black Madonna of Czestochowa and the crowned White Eagle of Poland, there flew a banner saying "Workers of all factories, unite!" Laba, *Roots of Solidarity*, p. 130.

8: MOBILIZING STRUCTURES

1. For a comparison of Hobsbawm's and Piven and Cloward's approaches, see the introduction to my *Struggle, Politics and Reform.* Also see Hobsbawm's interesting review of Piven and Cloward's work, "The Left and the Crisis of Organization," and the response of Piven and Cloward to their critics in the preface to the 1979 edition of *Poor People's Movements.*
2. The section that follows is much in debt to the work of Ted Margadant, whose *French Peasants in Revolt. The Insurrection of 1851* is a model of theoretically informed social and political history.
3. See the brief review of the literature on the insurrection in Margadant, pp. xxvii–xxii. The quote is from p. 39 of his *French Peasants in Revolt.*
4. The insurgents attacking Béziers proclaimed: "In the name of the French People! The President of the Republic has violated the Constitution, so the People reclaim their rights," in *French Peasants,* p. 5.
5. This sketch oversimplifies a complex and interesting development from movement to party. For the best treatments in English, see Vernon Lidtke, *The Outlawed Party,* especially ch. 7, Guenther Roth, *The Social Democrats in Imperial Germany,* especially ch. 10, and Douglas Chalmers, *The Social Democratic Party of Germany,* ch. 1, on the main periods of party formation.
6. On the formation of the SAP, see Donald Blake, "Swedish Trade Unions and the Social Democratic Party: The Formative Years." On the Austrian party and its relation to the German model, see Vincent Knapp, *Austrian Social Democracy, 1889–1914,* ch. 1. On the influence of German Marxism on the development of Russian Social Democracy, see John Plamenatz, *German Marxism and Russian Communism,* pp. 317–29.
7. Otto Kirschheimer, in his landmark 1966 article, "The Transformation of the Western European Party Systems," refers to these as "denominational mass parties," in contrast to the "class-mass parties" developed by the Socialists.
8. Arend Lijphart's study of Dutch *verzuiling,* in his *The Politics of Accommodation,* stresses the accommodation among these pillars, but earlier students were more inclined to emphasize their potential for stalemate and conflict.
9. Basic materials on this poorly understood movement will be found in Daniel Guérin, *Anarchism: From Theory to Practice,* Irving Louis Horowitz, ed., *The Anarchists,* and James Joll, *The Anarchists.* A succinct doctrinal analysis of anarchism and a comparison with marxism and syndicalism is found in George Lichtheim's *Marxism: An Historical and Critical Study,* pp. 222–33.
10. The conflicts within the Civil Rights movement that led to its black power offshoot have not yet found an adequate historical account. On the evolution and splits within the New Left that produced the Weather Underground, see James Miller's *Democracy Is in the Streets,* ch. 12.

11. For the best account of this progression, see Donatella della Porta's "Recruitment Processes in Clandestine Political Organizations" and her definitive study of left-wing terrorism in Italy, *Organizazzioni politiche clandestine*.
12. See his article "Multiple Networks and Mobilization in the Paris Commune, 1871."
13. For example, during antiapartheid protests in the United States, student groups circulated the "Divestment Disk" – a computer disk with membership lists and strategies being used on different campuses. I am grateful to Sarah Soule for this information.
14. The research agenda of the "resource mobilization" school has done the most to explicate this type of professional movement organization. See the essays in Zald and McCarthy, *Dynamics of Social Movements,* and their collaborators' articles collected in *Social Movements in an Organizational Society*.
15. For example, the Dutch Committee Against Cruise Missiles brought together at least ten major peace organizations, in addition to the largest trade union federations and the leading left wing parties in a series of national peace demonstrations. See Rochon, *Mobilizing for Peace,* pp. 79–80, and Schennink, "From Peace Week to Peace Work." In France, twenty-four major peace organizations combined in 1981 to form the Committee for Nuclear Disarmament according to Rochon's *Mobilizing for Peace,* p. 79. In the United States, each major wave of peace protest led to coalitions and joint campaigns. Robert Kleidman's analysis of three successive American peace campaigns shows that "when formal SMO's closely controlled campaigns, activism tended to be less grassroots-based, and briefer, than when they allowed campaigns to develop independent organizations." See his "Organizations and Coalitions in the Cycles of the American Peace Movement," and his book, *Organizing for Peace: Neutrality, the Test-Ban and the Freeze*.
16. The theoretical argument about the importance of intra-organizational insurgency in the birth of new movements is introduced in Mayer Zald and Michael Berger's "Social Movements in Organizations." On base communities in Latin America, see Daniel H. Levine, "Popular Groups, Popular Culture, and Popular Religion," pp. 721–6. In Italy, see Tarrow, "Old Movements in New Cycles of Protest: The Career of an Italian Religious Community." On the role of nuns in the American Catholic Church, see Mary F. Katzenstein, "Feminism Within American Institutions: Unobtrusive Mobilization in the 1980s."
17. Fernandez and McAdam write that, in such movements, individuals are drawn into the movement "by virtue of their involvement in organizations that serve as the associational network out of which a new movement emerges." See their "Multiorganizational Fields," p. 317. In a recent reanalysis of these data, McAdam and Paulsen conclude: "It is a strong subjective identification with a particular identity, reinforced by organizational or individual ties, that is especially likely to encourage participation." See their "Specifying the Relationship Between Social Ties and Activism."
18. Ben Schennink, in his "From Peace Week to Peace Work," pp. 259ff., details how the Dutch Interdenominational Council (IKV) used a network of religious and political organizations to recruit supporters and gain financial support.
19. Thomas Ohlemacher summarizes the defining characteristics of social relays in his "Social Relays" in four points:

> First, they connect previously unconnected networks, acting as brokers or transmitters of contacts between strangers or groups of strangers. Second, they form the immediate environment, the organizational background, or the institutional grounding of several face-to-face networks. Third, some of the networks in this environment generate new networks, "loading" pre-existing contacts in a new way. Fourth, social relays spread the mobilization to networks outside themselves. (p. 7)

20. By decentralization, Gerlach and Hine mean the lack of a single leadership and the absence of a concept of card-carrying membership. See *People, Power and Change,* pp. 34 ff. By segmentation, they mean that the movement "is composed of a great variety of localized groups or cells which are essentially independent, but which can combine to form larger configurations or divide to form smaller units" (p. 41). And by reticulation, they refer to a weblike structure "in which the cells, or nodes, are tied together, not through any central point, but rather through intersecting sets of personal relationships and other intergroup linkages" (p. 55).

9: CYCLES OF PROTEST

1. The outline below reflects experience in Western Europe and the United States since the 1960s and was developed in the context of research on Italy, perhaps not a typical case. It will be for empirical investigation to determine whether and in what ways the picture resembles waves of collective action in other systems and other periods of history. For a comparison of the West German experience, see Koopmans' "The Dynamics of Protest Waves."
2. The following section summarizes parts of the analysis in Soule and Tarrow, "Acting Collectively, 1847–1849: How the Repertoire of Collective Action Changed and Where It Happened," presented in 1991 to the Annual Conference of the Social Science History Association, New Orleans. I am grateful to Sarah Soule for her collaboration in analyzing the data on which this section is based, and for her helpful comments on a draft of this chapter.
3. For a survey of the main "background causes" of the revolutions in the various European countries, see Roger Price, *The Revolutions of 1848,* and the excellent basic bibliography he provides.
4. Generally speaking, religious cleavages were dominant in Switzerland, ethnic and nationalist ones in the Hapsburg Empire outside of Austria, and issues of political representation in France and Germany. Although the national question came to dominate the Italian *quarantotto,* it began with agitations for liberal reform in Rome and the Kingdom of the Two Sicilies, and only as it moved northward to areas controlled by the Hapsburgs, did it take on a nationalist coloration. In France and Germany, although food riots occurred in the early stages of the conflagration, the major axes of conflict were over representative institutions and workers' rights.
5. From Jacques Godechot's rich compendium, *Les Révolutions de 1848.* No information is provided by Godechot for Scandinavia (except for the brief war between Denmark and Prussia over Schleswig-Holstein); none for Greece and Portugal; and none for the European parts of the Ottoman Empire. For a more detailed analysis of his data and of some of the problems that they present see Soule and Tarrow, "Acting Collectively."
6. Based on an unpublished manuscript kindly provided to the author by Aristide Zolberg, and eventually published in shorter form in his "Belgium," in Raymond Grew, ed., *Crises of Political Development.*
7. This was especially true in Calabria, where, on the eve of the 1848 events, the government was so alarmed that it established a commission to compensate peasants who had been deprived of customary rights. On this episode, see John Davis, *Conflict and Control: Law and Order in Nineteenth Century Italy,* pp. 47–9.
8. But the rest of the Hapsburg Empire was much less serene. On the agitations in the empire, particularly in Bohemia and Hungary, see Price's *The Revolutions of 1848,* pp. 28–9.
9. Here we must be cautious, since Godechot's term *manifestation* may lack the specificity of the form of collective action that we now call by that term; what Pierre

Favre, in *La Manifestation,* defines as "a collective movement organized in public space with the goal of producing a political outcome by the peaceful expression of an opinion or a demand" (p. 15 [Author's translation]).

10. For a useful case study of the factory occupation at the key Renault plant at Boulogne-Billancourt, see Bernard Badie's *Strategie de la grève,* ch. 3.

11. On the French "events," the most detached recent treatment is by Jacques Capdevielle and René Mouriaux, *May 68: L'entre-deux de la modernité.* For a recent compendium of reflections, see Mouriaux, et al., *1968: Exploration du Mai français.* On the Italian *sessantotto,* see Peppino Ortoleva, *Saggio sui movimenti del 1968 in Europa e in America* and Sidney Tarrow, *Democracy and Disorder,* ch. 6. For the United States, the most pungent reflections on this period are found in Todd Gitlin's *The Sixties,* and James Miller's *Democracy Is in the Streets.*

12. For almost instant – and highly politicized – responses to the phenomenon of Solidarity, both reflecting something of the "privileged witness" syndrome, see Timothy Garton Ash's *The Polish Revolution,* Jadwiga Staniszkis' *Poland's Self-Limiting Revolution.* For the most reflective analyses in English, see Roman Laba's *The Roots of Solidarity,* and David Ost's *Solidarity and the Politics of Anti-Politics.*

10: STRUGGLING TO REFORM

1. When we add nonpolicy goals like personal transformation and movement stabilization to the list, the possible dimensions of success become even larger and it is clear why Marx and Wood had to conclude that "the systematic study of social movement consequences is much less developed than that of the prior conditions that give rise to movements." See their "Strands of Theory and Research in Collective Behavior," p. 405.

2. I am indebted to Doug McAdam for many of the insights in this section, as well as for his helpful comments on an earlier version of this chapter.

3. These comparisons are summarized from Lange, Irvin and Tarrow, "Mobilization, Social Movements and Party Recruitment," Table 3. The percentages include all those who reported having had any activity in any social movement, regardless of their other routes of entry into the party. For the original analysis of these data, see Accornero et al., *L'identità comunista,* 1983.

4. Tarrow, *Democracy and Disorder,* ch. 11. This observation is based on too few cases to present statistically, but occupational marginality was true of most of the former leaders interviewed.

5. The first part of the subtitle is the same as one of McAdam's, in *Freedom Summer,* pp. 213–19, but it was too good a title not to appropriate!

6. This was the experience of both Doug McAdam in researching *Freedom Summer,* and my own in gathering information on Italian extraparliamentary groups for *Democracy and Disorder.*

7. The following section summarizes my article, "Social Protest and Policy Reform: May 1968 and the Loi d'Orientation in France."

8. Faure's reform proposed to replace the broad old university faculties with specialized departments; it broke up the massive University of Paris into twelve different "campuses"; and it provided the machinery for all the universities to elect governing councils including the students, and create their own internal statutes. Jacques F. Fomerand's thesis, "Policy-Formulation and Change in Gaullist France: The 1968 Orientation Act of Higher Education," is the best existing analysis of the policy process surrounding the Orientation Act and its policy outcomes. Also see his article, "Policy Formulation and Change in Gaullist France. The 1968 Orientation Act of Higher Education."

9. This section is a synthesis of what I have learned about the American women's movement from the following sources: Anne Costain, *Inviting Women's Rebellion*, Sara Evans, *Personal Politics*, the essays in Mary Katzenstein and Carol Mueller, eds., *The Women's Movements of the United States and Western Europe*, Jane Mansbridge's *Why We Lost the ERA*, and Suzanne Staggenborg's *The Pro-Choice Movement* and from working next door to my friend and colleague Mary Katzenstein.

10. The expression *"chien-lit,"* used by General de Gaulle to denigrate the students, means both a masquerade and a disorder.

11. Organization has been the weak point of studies of the women's movement, with more feminist scholars focusing on consciousness than on the interesting structure of the movement – perhaps reflecting its emphasis on discourse and collective identity. However, studies that analyze organization, and especially informal movement networks, are beginning to multiply. For example, see Anne Costain's *Inviting Women's Rebellion*, ch. 3, Myra Marx Ferree and Patricia Yancey Martin, eds., *Feminist Organization: Harvest of the New Women's Movement*, Mary Katzenstein's "Feminism within American Institutions," Jane Mansbridge's *Why We Lost the ERA*, chs. 12–13 and Suzanne Staggenborg's *The Pro-Choice Movement*.

12. The following section draws on my "Cycles of Collective Action: Between Moments of Madness and the Repertoire of Contention," *Social Science History*, pp. 281–307.

11: A MOVEMENT SOCIETY

1. "No hint of subsequent radicalization, no echo of social conflict, no shadow of the Terror could mar this season of commemoration," observed historians Keith Baker and Steven Kaplan of the Bicentennial in their preface to Roger Chartier's *The Cultural Origins of the French Revolution*, p. xii. Even as they celebrated it, the French in 1989 were interring their Revolution. See Kaplan's *Adieu 1789*, which reads the Bicentennial as a celebratory rite for the funeral of the Revolution.

2. In a 1991 paper, Charles Tilly provocatively writes; "As Europeans unconsciously subvert the state in the very act of affirming its desirability, comparative-historical sociologists are unwittingly peripheralizing the state while declaring its centrality." See his "Prisoners of the State," p. 1.

3. The most articulate advocates of this global view of industrial conflict are Giovanni Arrighi, and Beverly Silver. See the former's "World Income Inequalities and the Future of Socialism," and the latter's "Class Struggle and Kondratieff Waves, 1870 to the Present," as well as her "Labor Unrest and Capital Accumulation on a World Scale."

4. See the account of the links between Afghan-trained Islamic militants and the attackers of the World Trade Center in the *New York Times*, August 11, 1993.

5. Aristide Zolberg, "Moments of Madness," p. 206.

Index

Kennedy administration, 87, 98, 130
King, Martin Luther, Jr., 20, 113
Knights of Labor, 147

labor
  Knights of (*see* Knights of Labor)
  organized, 176
Labour Party in Britain, 139
Lafayette, Marquis Marie-Joseph de, 88
land revolt, 38
latifundia, 87
Latin America, 104
Le Chapelier law, 56, 63
Lenin shipyard, 167
  1979 demonstration at, 132
Lenin, Vladimir, 10
  and collective action, 11–12
  and political opportunity structure, 12
liberals, 57
liberty trees, 40, 49
Lisbon, 45
literacy, 47–8
  spread of, 47, 51
Loi d'Orientation (*see* Orientation Law of 1968), 179
London corresponding society, 58
Lotta Continua, 176
Louis Napoleon, 57, 59, 137
Loyal Nine, The, 50

Madrid, 45
mairies, 138
Malaysia, 93
Manchester antislavery petition, 42
manifestation (*see* demonstration)
Manila, 121
March on Washington, April 1993, 9–10, 16, 18, 26
Marcos, Ferdinand, 109
Marx, Karl, 9–10, 59
  and collective action, 10–13
marxist theories, 6, 60
mass media (*see* media, television), 126
master frames, master framing, 131
May 1968 (*see* events of May 1968)
Mazzini, Giuseppe, 158, 196
McGovern, George, 176
media
  and consensus formation, 129
  and framing, 126–7
  and "making news," 119, 129
  and movement organization, 127–9
mesomobilization, 145
Messina, 45, 161
Mexican Teacher's Movement, 148
Mickiewicz, Adam, 166

Midland Association of Ironmasters, 55
migration, 196
Milan, 45, 162
Mississippi (*see* Freedom Summer)
mobilization
  action (*see* action mobilization)
  consensus (*see* consensus mobilization), 123–9
  unobtrusive, 181
mobilizing structures, 21, 135–50
mock trial, 40
modular repertoire, 6, 43, 73
  of collective action, 19, 31, 39–45, 73, 114
modularity, 33
  of association, 55–6
Montagnards, 57, 138
Moses, Bob, 173
movement entrepreneurs, 7, 15, 122
movement society, 187–97, 198
movements (*see* social movements)
Mussolini, Benito, 87

NAACP (*see* National Association for the Advancement of Colored People)
Najy, Imre, 193
Naples, 161
Napoleon Bonaparte, 57, 59, 137
narodniki, 140
National Association for the Advancement of Colored People (NAACP), 133
National Gay and Lesbian Task Force, 18
National Organization for Women (NOW), 183
national states, 46, 65, 191–3
National Welfare Rights Organization (NWRO), 114
National Women's Political Caucus (NWPC), 183
Nationalism, 11
  long-distance, 196–7
nationalist conflicts, 198
Naziskins, 100, 197
Nelson, Jack, 173
Netherlands, 139, 159
networks
  interclass, 60
  movement, 54–7
New Deal, 84, 156
New Left
  in Europe, 141–2
  in the United States, 23, 112–13, 141–2, 174
newspapers
  subversive power of, 53–4
Newport
  effigy burnings in, 49
  1919–21 strike wave, 46

250 Index

society, 186
subculture, 176
transaction cost problems of, 16, 26–7, 192–3
transnational, 160, 192–5
social networks
transnational, 197
social transaction costs, 22
solidarity, 5, 11, 102, 189
Solidarnosc (Solidarity in Poland), 90, 119, 123, 131–2, 168, 193
Société Typographique de Neuchâtel, 52
Society of West India Merchants, 55
songs, 10, 119
Sons of Liberty, 50, 58
Soviet Union
collapse of, 165, 186
speak-out, 116
Sri Lanka, 104
stalinism, 82
Stamp Act, 45, 49–51, 58, 71
stamp duties (*see* Stamp Act)
state
in France, 191–3
in the United States, 191–3
strength, 89
weakness, 91, 104
state-building
and collective action, 62–3, 65–72
state socialism
collapse of, 167, 188
states
and collective action, 64
and opportunities, 89–90
centralized, 90, 191
national, 46, 62, 191–3
strikes, 2, 19, 84, 106, 114
and other forms of collective action, 192
in Poland, 90
sit-down, 156
student movements
in China, 121
in Europe, 168
in France, 175–9, 181
in the United States, 166–7
long-term effects of activism in, 176
sliding May in Italy, 166–7
Student Non-Violent Coordinating Committee (SNCC), 141, 173
Student Press and Information Center, 86
Sudan, the, 146
suffrage (*see* women's suffrage movement), 42, 66, 158, 161, 185
suffragettes (*see* women's suffrage movement)
Sugar Act of 1764, 40
Switzerland, 160, 172
symbols, 119, 181

TV (*see* television), 126
tax revolts, 48, 61
taxes, 70–2
television, 126, 143–5
and the anti-nuclear movement, 143
and the Civil Rights movement, 143
implications of, for movement organization, 143
and the student movement, 143
global, 194
terrorism
Italian, 111
Third Estate, 86, 88
Third World, 101, 148, 196
Thomas, Clarence, 180
Three Mile Island, 126
Tienanmen Square, 121
Tilly, Charles, 2, 6, 31–3, 36–7, 72, 103, 153, 196
and repertoire of contention, 19, 31
Tocqueville, Alexis de, 34, 44, 158
and state-building, 62–5
Townshend Acts of 1767, 49
traditional repertoire, 35–9, 45
transaction costs (*see* social transaction costs)
Williamson's theory of, 16–17
transnational movements (*see* social movements, transnational)

underground railroad, 101
unions
collective good of, 14
United Farm Workers, 88
United States, 27
urban insurrection, 19
in France, 42–4

Vendée Rebellion, 73
Venice, 162
Verdi, Giuseppe, 45, 93
Vienna, 45
Congress of, 162
Vietnam War, 73, 91, 167
protests against, 91, 141, 144, 166
violence, 2–3, 103–4, 181, 186, 195
as type of collective action, 103
attraction of, 105
interethnic, 164
threat of, 104
vanguard, 142
Virginia Merchants, 55
Voting Rights Act of 1965, 87

Wałęsa, Lech, 131–2
wars
and social movements, 67–8

WEAL (*see* Women's Equity Action League)
Weather Underground, 141, 177
Whigs, 57
Wilkes, John, 53
workers' movement, 139
working class
    American, 74–5
Women's Equity Action League (WEAL), 183
women's movement
    free spaces in, 183
    in France, 183

in Italy, 149, 183
in the United States, 87, 94, 116, 174, 180–4
naming in the, 182
women's suffrage movement, 42, 66, 142, 185
Wyvill, Christopher, 68

Yorkshire, 68
Yorkshire Association, 55, 68
Young Poland movement, 132